Advances in Mental Health and Addiction

Series Editor

Masood Zangeneh, Richmond Hill, Canada

Over the past several decades we have witnessed dramatic shifts in prevailing approaches to mental health and addiction. Significant scientific achievements have led to novel treatment options that impacted the experiences of individuals with mental disorders. In recent years, new perspectives have begun to influence the way we address mental health and substance dependencies, resulting in a greater emphasis on mental health promotion and prevention strategies. Despite these progressions, mental health care systems too often remain stagnant, fragmented, and peripheral.

Tracey Bone
Editor

Deaf Mental Health

From Theory to Practice

Springer

Editor
Tracey Bone
Faculty of Social Work
University of Manitoba
Winnipeg, MB, Canada

ISSN 2570-3390 ISSN 2570-3404 (electronic)
Advances in Mental Health and Addiction
ISBN 978-3-032-06273-4 ISBN 978-3-032-06274-1 (eBook)
https://doi.org/10.1007/978-3-032-06274-1

This Springer imprint is published by the registered company Springer Nature Switzerland AG
The registered company address is: Gewerbestrasse 11, 6330 Cham, Switzerland

Foreword

The Canadian Association of the Deaf (CAD) is honored to introduce this vital collection of work edited by Dr. Tracey Bone, which brings together the latest research and insights on mental health in Deaf communities. This book represents a significant step forward in understanding the unique challenges faced by Deaf, Hard of Hearing, and DeafBlind individuals, while also celebrating the resilience and expertise within these communities.

The diversity of contributors in this collection is remarkable, encompassing professionals from various disciplines, including social work, psychology, public health, and forensic evaluations. What makes this work particularly powerful is the inclusion of Deaf authors and researchers, whose lived experiences and professional expertise provide invaluable perspectives. Their contributions ensure that the voices of Deaf individuals are not only heard but are central to shaping the future of mental health care.

We are especially proud to notice the work of Deaf and CODA authors and researchers, in this compilation. Their involvement underscores the importance of centering Deaf voices in research and practice. The diversity of perspectives, including those of Deaf professionals, hearing allies, and individuals with lived experience, demonstrates the power of collaboration in driving meaningful change.

This book is more than a collection of research—it is a call to action, and a timely one indeed. It highlights the need for accessible, inclusive, and culturally sensitive mental health services for Deaf individuals and the maturing and evolving academic research by its diversity of topic and inclusiveness of researchers with lived experience.

The CAD commends Dr. Tracey Bone and all contributors for their dedication to this critical work. We hope this book serves as a resource, inspiration, and catalyst for continued progress in mental health care for Deaf communities in Canada and beyond. Together, we can build a future where mental health services are equitable and empowering for all.

Sincerely,

Canadian Association of the Deaf
Ottawa, ON, Canada
https://cad-asc.ca

Shawna Joynt
Richard Belzile

Preface

"Why is it taking him so long to put the puzzle pieces together!" (*Participant, Bone, 2013*)

The above statement was made by a participant in my doctoral research study exploring Deaf depression narratives (Bone, 2013). This participant shared how exhausting and frustrating it was attempting to secure health care for the "darkness" that permeated her life. She reported she met with her long-time family physician several times, each time hoping to finally receive information that would help her understand how she was feeling, and how to manage the impact this "darkness" was having on her life. She is a native American Sign Language (ASL) users. She had requested an ASL English interpreter for every appointment with her physician, but the physician refused, citing cost. Instead, he attempted to communicate with her through gestures and written notes. As ASL is a visual language with a syntax and grammar different from spoken English, the notes shared between the two created additional confusion, ultimately delaying the diagnosis of Major Depressive Disorder, and, by extension, an appropriate intervention plan.

A second participant described his experiences this way, he said, *"I had one garbage can that was full, now I have two... but I have no way to empty them... I need someone to listen to me,"* (Participant, Bone, 2013). This participant had similar experiences within the health/mental health system. He explained how his inability to communicate clearly with his hearing family members and medical professionals reinforced his feelings of hopelessness and worthlessness, contributing to his feelings of isolation, and suicidal thoughts. He knew he needed mental health support, but as none of the mental health professionals he met were familiar with Deaf culture, or American Sign Language, he had no way to share his feelings or learn coping strategies. These two mental health narratives are but two of the factors that ultimately contributed to my interest in a book on this topic.

This book, Deaf Mental Health: From Theory to Practice, is written for two primary groups. The first is post-secondary students in social work, psychology, medicine, and other allied health professions, as well as criminal justice for reasons that will become clear in the chapters that follow. The second is clinicians including social workers, clinical psychologists, psychiatrists, family doctors, and other professional disciplines, including those working in community-based non-profits who have little to no previous experience working with d/Deaf or hard of hearing children or adults. The aim is to provide content that will enhance the readers' understanding of the heterogeneity of the Deaf, hard of hearing, and Deafblind communities; factors that may contribute to mental health challenges within these communities, and; more importantly, strategies for working effectively in and with the members of these communities.

Terminology

Before I introduce the various chapters, I feel it necessary to lay the foundation regarding terminology. You will see a variety of terms used to describe those who are the focus of this text. In past writing, it was common convention to distinguish those who are members of the Deaf community and American Sign Language native language users with a capital "D"—Deaf, from those who live with hearing loss, even if profound but not part of the Deaf community, as deaf (small "d"). This has changed over the years. While some do still follow this more common convention in their writing, others do not. In brief, there is no longer a common method through which to describe the Deaf or Hard of Hearing communities with the terms and use of the various terms evolving. For that reason, I invited each chapter author(s) to clarify the terminology they use within their own chapters. It is important for those intending to or working with Deaf or Hard of Hearing clients that you ask your client/individual how they identify or what term they prefer to use. It is also important to acknowledge that each person's identity preference may change throughout their lifetime and may or may not align with others in the same community; it remains important to ask.

Chapters

This edited collection provides an opportunity to enhance one's understanding about a little known and underrepresented community, from professionals working in or related to Deaf mental health, and those with lived experience as members of the Deaf community. Part I of *Deaf Mental Health: From Theory to Practice* provides the reader with theoretical and foundational information on which to begin to or better understand the Deaf, Hard of Hearing, and DeafBlind communities. Part II provides enhanced understanding of some of the challenges the larger Deaf community experiences in specialized areas. Part III provides concrete examples of what a Deaf-centric approach to service provision looks like from the voices of service providers themselves. The text concludes with a revised version of a Deaf Mental Health Strategy I first proposed in 2014. Each chapter author or authors were invited to enhance their content through the inclusion of a hypothetical case example, and many chose to do so.

Part 1—Introduction: Setting the Stage for Understanding

This introductory section begins with Chapter 1, "The Benefits and Challenges of Specialized Mental Health Practice in the Deaf Community" by Day and Gile. The chapter sets the foundation for the text by providing a historical review of Deaf mental health care, including the impact of the medical-pathological view of the Deaf community historically, and currently. It moves to discussing a more recent shift to a cultural view of the Deaf community which incorporates cultural sensitivity, respect, and acknowledgment of the unique cultural and linguistic experiences of Deaf individuals.

Chapter 2, "The Role of Early Language Experience in Deaf and Hard of Hearing (DHH) Children: Implications for Mental Health" by Ofori-Sanzo, explores the importance of early language access for communication and positive mental health, and the impact language deprivation has on many deaf children born into hearing families. Chapter 3, "Understanding and Teaching Theory of Mind in DHH Children" by Chovaz and Tesfamariam, continues to explore the impact that limited access to communication has for deaf and hard of hearing children. This chapter introduces the social-cognitive skill, Theory of Mind (ToM), that commonly emerges between the ages of three and five. The chapter reports on the development of ToM family modules that support the development of ToM in DHH children.

Chapter 4, "The Biopsychosocial Assessment of the Patient who is Deaf or Hard of Hearing" by Mathos and Macioce, discusses various protective and risk factors professionals should consider when conducting biopsychosocial assessments with Deaf or Hard of Hearing individuals. It includes a discussion on the impact stereotypes, biases, and lack of cultural awareness may have on the assessment process with members of the Deaf and Hard of Hearing communities, and strategies to counteract this.

Part II—Specialized/Unique Circumstances

Chapter 5, "The Practice of Forensic Psychology and the Deaf Community: Key Issues for Clinical Practice and the Legal System" by Feldman, Silvasi, Schwenke, and Shir, explores best practices in conducting forensic assessments, competency evaluations, and competency restoration of legally involved deaf and hard of hearing defendants.

In Chapter 6, "Mental Health and Deaf LGBTQ Adults," Wagner and Miller discuss the research, practice, and anecdotal findings to increase readers' knowledge and understanding of psychological health risks and protective factors among

Deaf and Hard of Hearing (DHH) LGBTQ adults. They offer clinical approaches to treatment, highlighted through various case examples.

In Chapter 7, Kordus and Somdal explore lateral violence as a concept, and the factors that influence the perpetuation of lateral traumas in the Deaf community. "Lateral Violence within the Deaf Community" challenges readers to move beyond the opinion that lateral violence in this minority community results from an internal flaw, focusing instead on the role systemic oppression plays.

Chapter 8 focuses on a unique sub-set of the larger Deaf community, namely those who identify as Deafblind. In "Why are the Complexities of Deafblind Identity Relevant to Mental Health?", Simcock and Wittich encourage students and professionals to acknowledge the heterogeneity within the deafblind community and accept that, just as there are different ways of being deaf/Deaf, there are different ways of "being deafblind." The authors discuss adaptability as an essential skill for those working with this community.

In Chapter 9, Guthmann, Schafer, Gannon, and Ikegami focus on the issue of alcohol and substance abuse within the Deaf and hard of hearing communities. The chapter, "Alcohol and Substance Use Among Deaf and hard of Hearing Individuals: Addressing the Unique Needs" begins with an introduction to initial attempts and associated challenges providing substance abuse treatment for Deaf and hard of hearing individuals, moving to factors fundamental to enhance successful intervention.

Chapter 10. In "Lived Experiences" Wanis and Zemach share their personal narratives experiencing the intersection of Deafness and mental health. As professionals, and ASL native language users, their narratives provide a glimpse into their experiences with some of the issues discussed in preceding chapters. They move beyond their challenges however and invite the reader to "Be the Change."

Part III—A Deaf-centric Approach to Practice and Why It Matters

Chapter 11, "Supporting Recovery and Community Integration of Deaf and Hard of Hearing Adults with Serious Mental Illness" by Crowe, explores the complexities and challenges in supporting recovery and community integration, though, as importantly, the opportunities when incorporating a rehabilitation and recovery model with this population.

Chapter 12, titled "New Directions D.R.E.A.M. Program: Staff reflections on effective engagement," is based on interviews conducted by Tracey A. Bone, with three staff in the D.R.E.A.M. program. Montney and Newhook share their experiences as Deaf native ASL users working with individuals with intellectual disabilities who are Deaf, Hard of Hearing or use non-verbal forms of communication. They and Claeys share what they feel professionals need to know to work effectively with this heterogeneous population with whom they work.

Chapter 13, titled "Working in the field of Deaf mental health: What Clinicians Need to Know" by Kaluba, Schmidt, Morgan, Likely, and Dawthorne, introduces essential concepts to incorporate when providing psychotherapy to d/Deaf, Deafblind, and deafened clients. They provide a discussion on an important foundational communication concept, the difference in the conversational structure of spoken English (triangle) versus that of ASL (diamond). They discuss various traditional therapeutic approaches that have been proven helpful when working in the field of Deaf mental health. They introduce fourth-wave approaches including compassion-focused virtual therapy, and trauma-informed treatments that are specifically aligned with social constructionist, strengths-based perspectives on Deafness that support personal growth and agency.

The concluding chapter 14 "A Deaf Mental Health Strategy" (DMHS) builds on a Deaf Mental Health Strategy I first conceptualized and presented in 2014 at a two-day Professional Development Conference I, alongside members of the (Deaf) Mental Health Committee coordinated in Winnipeg, Manitoba. At that time, I drew on knowledge acquired through my academic research and my collaborative work in and with the Deaf community. This revised strategy builds on additional experiences and conversations since 2014. It is a vision that incorporates broad goals for enhancing Canada's (2012) Mental Health Strategy and mental health strategies elsewhere around the world towards a culturally and linguistically appropriate public health approach to mental health care for members of the Deaf, Hard of Hearing and Deafblind communities in Canada.

Winnipeg, MB, Canada Tracey A. Bone

Contents

About the Editor and Contributors

About the Editor

Tracey A. Bone BSW, MSW, PhD., RSW, is an Associate Professor in the Faculty of Social Work at the University of Manitoba, Canada. She teaches undergraduate and graduate courses in mental health, research, and criminal justice social work. Prior to academia she worked in adult corrections. Much of Dr. Bone's career was spent working in and with members of the Deaf and Hard of Hearing (DHH) communities as well as with hearing adults who have experienced coping, mental health, and other challenges. Her research and publications focus on critical and intersectional social work, the mental health experience of DHH adults, the impact of art on mental health recovery, and social work pedagogy. She has given many presentations related to her research nationally and internationally.

About the Contributors

Richard Belzile LL.B, Law—Human Rights, Executive Director, Canadian Association of the Deaf.

Cathy Chovaz C.Psych. is a Full Professor of psychology at King's University College at Western University in London, Ontario, Canada. Dr. Chovaz is Canada's first Deaf clinical psychologist and is the Director of the Centre of Deaf Education and Accessibility Forum (CDEAF). She teaches courses in clinical psychology and her area of expertise is mental health and deafness. She is recognized as an international expert, has published two textbooks, journal articles, and given many national and international presentations. Additionally, Dr. Chovaz maintains a private consultation practice. She most recently published a fiction novel No, No, Bad Dog based on her many years of clinical practice with Deaf and hard of hearing children and their families (No No Bad Dog).

Richard Claeys Coordinator, Diversity, Respect, Empowerment, Achievement and More (D.R.E.A.M.) Program, a specialized Adult Day program for individuals with intellectual disabilities who are Deaf or hard of hearing at New Directions—For Children, Youth, Adults, and Families, in Winnipeg, Canada.

Teresa Crowe PhD, LCSWC, is a Professor of social work in the Master of Social Work Program at Gallaudet University, USA. She is a clinical social worker working with Deaf and Hard-of-Hearing (DHH) adults with chronic mental illness. Her research and publications focus on mental health issues in the DHH community, such as intimate partner violence, mental health service utilization, trauma, resilience, substance use, and adverse childhood experiences.

Lori Day Ph.D., is a licensed psychologist and Professor in the Department of Psychology at Gallaudet University. As a core faculty member in the Clinical Psychology Program, she is engaged in training the next generation of psychologists to support the behavioral health of deaf people. As the Director of the Deaf and Hard of Hearing Child Resilience Center, Lori is leading a team of professionals to address disparities in mental health services and deaf and hard of hearing youth by adapting and translating child behavioral and trauma measures, supporting the development of a measure of language experience, adapting evidence-based treatments, and providing training and ongoing consultation for clinicians.

Michael Dawthorne (BA, CHE) works as Director of Programs and Services Operations at Canadian Hearing Services.

David M. Feldman PhD, is a Licensed Psychologist and Professor of Psychology at Nova Southeastern University. There he serves as Coordinator of the Clinical Forensic Psychology Concentration and directs the Sexual Abuse and Forensic Research (SAFR) lab. Dr. Feldman specializes in offenders who are Deaf and hard-of-hearing. He has been called on as an expert witness and consultant. Dr. Feldman's research has appeared in numerous publications, and he has presented at a variety professional, academic, and community venues on forensic evaluations, competency, sexual offending, treatment, and the Deaf community. He currently serves on the board of the Florida Association for the Treatment of Sexual Abuse (FATSA) and the Broward County Advisory Board for Individuals with Disabilities.

Christine Gannon combined her personal experience as the daughter of deaf parents with her professional work. She has provided health education to the Deaf community since 1995 and is currently an associate professor and program director in the public health program at Gallaudet University. She completed her dissertation on deaf and hard of hearing students' alcohol use. She has degrees in sociology, human sexuality education, chemical dependency rehabilitation, and health education and promotion.

Kristine D. Gile is a Licensed Clinical Professional Counselor with over 20 years of experience providing mental health therapy to Deaf, hearing, and hard-of-hearing individuals with diverse mental health needs. She holds a Bachelor's degree in Deaf Education from the University of Tulsa and a Master's degree in Counseling Psychology from Lewis and Clark College. Kristine specializes in working with youth and families affected by trauma, utilizing evidence-based therapeutic approaches to foster healing and resilience. Currently, Kristine serves as both a clinician and supervisor at My Deaf Therapy, offering clinical supervision and direct therapeutic services. She also works as a consultant with the Deaf and Hard of Hearing Child Resilience Center, where she contributes her expertise to support the well-being of this unique community.

Deb Guthmann is a National Consultant in the Deaf community with over 40 years' experience in substance use disorders (SUD), mental health, education, medical and legal settings. Dr. Guthmann is the founding director of the Minnesota Substance Use Dependency Program for Deaf and Hard of Hearing Individuals and has been involved with the ASL translation and validation of substance use, mental health, and career interest screeners. Dr. Guthmann provides training nationally, is an adjunct faculty member, and has publications focused on substance use, criminal justice, and ethics within the deaf community.

Makoto Ikegami is a licensed clinical social worker who specializes in mental health and addiction for the Deaf and hard-of-hearing community. He owns Deaf Multicultural Counseling, LLC, and is the President of ADARA. He has over 15 years of experience improving mental health accessibility and culturally competent care.

Shawna Joynt President, Board of Directors, Canadian Association of the Deaf.

Megan Kaluba is a social work clinician and manager in the field of Deaf mental health (Canadian Hearing Services) and has previously worked with the police, in children's mental health, child protective services, settlement services, groups for homicide and suicide survivors, and with adults with eating disorders.

M. Natasha Kordus Ph.D. earned her doctorate from the Clinical Psychology program at Gallaudet University in Washington DC. She has worked at the School for the Deaf in Fremont, St. John's Mental Health Program for the Deaf and Hard of Hearing in Santa Monica and at the California School for the Deaf in Riverside. Dr. Kordus has also worked as an Adjunct Professor for the DeafTEC program at the Rochester Institute of Technology and Western Oregon University teaching classes on classroom and therapeutic interventions. At present, Dr. Kordus is the Supervisor of Assessment and Training at Collaborative Psychology Group private practice in Riverside. She also conducts assessments full time. She specializes in diagnosis, trauma, LGBTQ, anxiety, and depression.

Tim Likely is a registered social worker performing the controlled act of psychotherapy with Canadian Hearing Services. As a hearing counselor learning ASL as a second language, all his appointments with deaf clients include the use of interpreters.

Jennifer Macioce LCSW ICGC-1 worked in community mental health for 30 years before leaving to work solely in a private practice she started in 2012. She taught Mental Health First Aid for 10 years and supported the first 2 trainers in the United States who were Deaf. She has been a member of the Allegheny County Behavioral Task Force for Persons who are Deaf, Deaf Blind, or Hard of hearing since its inception (2004) and serves on a committee for HealthBridges (www.HealthBridges.info). She has been volunteering for Sage's Army (www.SagesArmy.com) for over 7 years cofacilitating a grief group for people who have lost someone to addiction. She helped start a Substance Addiction Ministry (SAM) at her church in which she remains active.

Kimberly Mathos Dr. Mathos is an Assistant Professor of Psychiatry at the University of Pittsburgh Medical Center. She is employed at a variety of community and academic sites where people who are Deaf, Hard of Hearing or Blind receive services. She developed a task force designed to improve mental health service development and access for people with sensory differences in Pittsburgh, Pennsylvania. She enjoys a mix of teaching, community-based research, and clinical care. In 2009 she was awarded the National Alliance of Mental Illness Exemplary Psychiatrist Award for her innovative practice ideas for recovery and rehabilitation initiatives with people with complex mental health needs who also have sensory disabilities. In 2015, she was the Disability Inclusion Champion at the University of Pittsburgh Medical Center.

Cara Miller is an Associate Professor of Psychology at Gallaudet University, and a core faculty member in the Clinical Psychology Ph.D. program. Her clinical, research, and teaching interests encompass the areas of trauma, grief, and bereavement; human–animal interaction; and gender and sexuality. Previously the Coordinator of the Gallaudet University LGBTQA Resource Center, she has previously conducted research on Deaf and hard of hearing LGBTQ populations with the Center for Deaf Health Equity.

Aaron J. Montney Direct Support Worker at Diversity, Respect, Empowerment, Achievement and More (D.R.E.A.M.) Program, a specialized Adult Day program for individuals with intellectual disabilities who are Deaf or hard of hearing at New Directions—For Children, Youth, Adults, and Families, in Winnipeg, Canada.

Michal Morgan is a registered psychotherapist with the College of Registered Psychotherapists of Ontario (CRPO). She completed a graduate program from Gallaudet University in Washington, D.C. and currently works at Canadian Hearing

Services. She uses expressive and receptive English and ASL to communicate. I have some high frequency hearing loss and tinnitus, but I identify as "hearing."

Elaine Newhook Direct Support Worker, Diversity, Respect, Empowerment, Achievement and More (D.R.E.A.M.) Program, a specialized Adult Day program for individuals with intellectual disabilities who are Deaf or hard of hearing at New Directions—For Children, Youth, Adults, and Families, in Winnipeg, Canada.

Kimberly Ofori-Sanzo is a speech-language pathologist (SLP) who has experience working at a school for the deaf, as well as presenting and publishing on topics related to language acquisition and language deprivation. She earned her B.A. in Psychology and in Communication Sciences and Disorders from the University of Vermont in 2010, her M.S. in Speech-Language Pathology from Gallaudet University in 2012, and her Doctor of Speech-Language Pathology (SLPD) in 2022. She is a board-certified specialist in child language (BCS-CL) through the American Board of Child Language and Language Disorders and serves as a board member on the American Board of Deaf and Hard of Hearing Specialists (ABDHHS).

Margalit Roitman is a hearing student in the Clinical Psychology PhD program at Gallaudet University. She graduated from Pennsylvania State University with a Bachelor of Science in Human Development & Family Studies with minors in Child Maltreatment & Advocacy Studies and Deafness & Hearing Studies. Her current research interests focus on adverse childhood experiences in the Deaf and Hard of Hearing population.

Kent Schafer has an educational background in psychology and special education, giving him expertise in addiction and mental health. He has provided administrative oversight in schools and hospitals and is currently at the Alabama Institute for Deaf and Blind, overseeing regional services for deaf and/or blind individuals from birth to geriatrics in rural western Alabama. In addition to his work, Schafer is an active guest lecturer and author, holding various leadership roles advancing mental health awareness and access to education for sign language users.

William Schmidt is from a 2nd generation Deaf family. He attended a mainstream school with a deaf program, Deaf school, and Gallaudet University. He is a mental health counselor for the Deaf community (Canadian Hearing Services) where he provides support and feedback to help them adjust to their needs.

Tomina J. Schwenke PhD, ABPP, is a licensed and board-certified psychologist with a post-doctoral juris master's degree from Emory School of Law. She's a nationally certified sign language interpreter (CI/CT) with a specialized certificate in mental health interpreting (QMHI). She is an Assistant Professor at the Emory School of Medicine, where she serves as the forensic psychology director for the Emory Psychiatry and Law Service and holds the clinical distinction of Senior Psychologist within the Emory Brain Health Clinic. She provides forensic evaluations and conducts therapy to a variety of patients, including those who are deaf, hard-of-hearing, and deaf-blind.

Tali M. Shir B.S., is a Clinical Psychology PsyD candidate at Nova Southeastern University (NSU) in Davie, Florida. She received her Bachelor of Science from the University of Central Florida with a major in Psychology, a minor in Crime Law and Deviance, and two certificates in Behavioral Forensics and Criminal Profiling. Her primary interests include forensic evaluations and the treatment of sexual abusers with an emphasis in Deaf and hard-of-hearing populations. Currently, she serves as the President of the NSU American Sign Language and Deaf Culture Club. Moreover, she was an events chair for the NSU Forensic Advocates for Rehabilitation and Reintegration Club. She is also a member of the Sexual Abuse & Forensic Research (SAFR) lab at NSU.

Paul M. Silvasi Ph.D., is a licensed psychologist based in Utah, who is employed as a forensic evaluator at Utah State Hospital. Dr. Silvasi is a Deaf individual with native fluency in ASL, and a graduate from Gallaudet University, where he received specialized training in the provision of clinical services with Deaf, Hard of Hearing, and DeafBlind (DHHDB) individuals. His primary research interest relates to the interactions between DHHDB individuals and the legal system, which began during his undergraduate studies at Rochester Institute of Technology. Clinically, he is passionate about developing best practices when conducting forensic evaluations with DHHDB individuals, and how forensic treatment approaches can be best adapted to meet the needs of this population.

Peter Simcock Peter is Associate Professor of Social Work at Birmingham City University, UK, where he leads the Certificate and Diploma in Professional Studies (Deafblind Studies) programs and conducts research in deafblindness and dual sensory loss. Prior to working in academia, Peter was a specialist social worker for d/Deaf and deafblind people. He is Chair of the Deafblind International Acquired Deafblindness Network, and an Ambassador for Deafblind UK. Peter is widely published in the field of social work and deafblindness.

Amanda G. Somdal DSW, LCSW, LICSW-S, is a licensed clinical social worker supervisor in California and Alabama. She holds a Doctorate in Social Work from the University of Tennessee, Knoxville, and is the Director of the Office of Deaf Services at the Alabama Department of Mental Health. With over 30 years of experience serving the Deaf community, Dr. Somdal specializes in therapy for Deaf survivors of sexual assault, Deaf batterers, LGBTQIA+ community, and Deaf mental health-related issues. She has served on several boards, including the Advocacy Council for Abused Deaf Children and the National Human Trafficking and Disabilities Working Group. Dr. Somdal regularly presents workshops on topics such as deaf mental health, self-harm, domestic violence, Deaf culture, and mental health interpreting.

Emnette Tesfamariam an alumnus of King's University College at Western University in London, Ontario, holds an Honours Bachelor of Arts with a Specialization in Psychology and a Major in English. Her senior thesis "*Theory of Mind and Deafness: Developing a Non-Verbal Assessment Tool*" focused on improving accessibility and cultural sensitivity in Theory of Mind assessments for deaf and hard of hearing children. She presented her thesis at the 2024 CPA National Convention and published in the *Western Undergraduate Psychology Journal* (Tesfamariam & Chovaz, 2024). Currently, Emnette is engaged in furthering this work through clinical research and resource development.

Kathryn Wagner is an associate professor of psychology at Gallaudet University, where she teaches in the Clinical Psychology PhD program. She conducts qualitative research exploring the lived experiences of deaf and hard of hearing LGBTQ individuals, as well as academic parents raising young children. Dr. Wagner earned her PhD in clinical psychology from Duquesne University.

Rosemary Wanis is a Certified Deaf Interpreter living in Central California. She was born Deaf to hearing parents in Egypt. They were the first of the family to immigrate to the US in 1975 and have brought most of the family over since that time. Rosemary is an adjunct faculty at two colleges teaching Deaf Studies and Interpreting. She is also a national trainer with the Deaf Interpreter Curriculum through NCIEC and a meta-facilitator with the Center for Atypical Language Interpreting. She is a momma, daughter, immigrant, teacher, interpreter, researcher, presenter, author, upstander, and human. She has a BA in psychology, Master of Social Work, Master of Public Administration from Gallaudet, and Doctorate in Educational Leadership from California State University, Fresno.

Walter Wittich is an Associate Professor at the School of Optometry at the University of Montreal, Quebec, Canada. He conducts research in dual sensory loss and acquired deafblindness, with a particular focus on the rehabilitation of older adults with combined hearing and sight loss and is widely published in the field. Walter is the inaugural Chair of the Deafblind International Research Network and Co-Chair of the Visual Impairment and Rehabilitation axis of the Quebec Vision Health Research Network. He is a Fellow of the American Academy of Optometry and is Quebec's first Certified Low Vision Therapist.

Rachel Zemach Rachel Zemach is a Deaf author and former teacher. Her book "The Butterfly Cage; Joy Heartache and Corruption. Teaching While Deaf in a California Public School" was released in 2023. It describes her career, personal identity shift, and the trajectories of individual students, as well as the stunning dysfunction in mainstream Deaf education. Her book is an attempt to trigger a national dialogue on the topic, and its foreword is written by Dr. Paddy Ladd. Zemach lives in Northern California.

Part I
Introduction: Setting the Stage for Understanding

Chapter 1
The Benefits and Challenges of Specialized Mental Health Practice in the Deaf Community

Kristine D. Gile and Lori A. Day

What Is Deaf Mental Health Care?

History

Mental health care has undergone significant transformation over the centuries, evolving from the era of psychiatric hospitals to outpatient care. However, mental health services for deaf[1] individuals were virtually non-existent until more recent times. Without specialized services, deaf individuals were hospitalized with the general population, which amplified their isolation and language barriers. This situation led to what has been described as "antitherapeutic custodial isolation," exacerbating symptoms, contributing to overmedication, misdiagnoses, and lengthened hospital stay in comparison to their hearing counterparts (Vernon, 2006, p. 817).

The emergence of specialized mental health care for deaf and hard-of-hearing people began in the 1960s during the deinstitutionalization movement. This movement marked a pivotal shift in mental health care, emphasizing the transition of patients from large, often overcrowded psychiatric hospitals to community-based treatment settings. Factors driving this shift included the advent of more effective antipsychotic medications, the recognition of the high costs and inhumane conditions in asylums, and a broader shift toward individual rights and autonomy

[1] Throughout this chapter, 'deaf' will be used to be inclusive of all deaf, hard of hearing, DeafBlind, and DeafDisabled individuals. Instances when referring to specific subgroups of individuals will be clarified (e.g., hard-of-hearing, culturally Deaf, and DeafBlind).

K. D. Gile (✉)
My Deaf Therapy, Rockville, MD, USA

L. A. Day
Department of Psychology, Gallaudet University, Washington, DC, USA

T. Bone (ed.), *Deaf Mental Health*, Advances in Mental Health and Addiction,
https://doi.org/10.1007/978-3-032-06274-1_1

(Koyanagi & Bazelon, 2007). As deinstitutionalization progressed, it became increasingly evident that deaf people required specialized services to address their unique needs.

Despite the progress made through deinstitutionalization, the needs of marginalized groups, including deaf individuals, were not adequately addressed. Deaf individuals faced unique challenges in accessing mental health care during this period. The lack of communication access and cultural sensitivity, coupled with the historical stigmatization of deaf individuals, often led to cultural differences and communication barriers being misinterpreted as symptoms of mental illness. Many psychiatric facilities lacked qualified interpreters or trained staff capable of communicating effectively with deaf patients. Consequently, deaf individuals often received inadequate psychotherapy and an undue emphasis on behavioral modification (Rayson, 1987). Moreover, a limited number of psychiatrists and clinicians possess proficiency in sign language or are adequately equipped with cultural competence regarding the deaf community. While professionals may undergo training focused on understanding deaf individuals, they often lack the necessary self-reflection and cultural awareness to enhance their own cultural competence in working with this population (Glickman, 2012; Vernon & Leigh, 2007). Studies have shown that these factors contributed to misunderstandings, misdiagnoses, and ineffective treatments (Basilier, 1964; Vernon & Miller, 2005).

Since the deinstitutionalization process, deaf individuals and their families have identified significant inequities in mental health services, including disparities in the treatment of care, medication, access to services, and communication. These inequities culminated in several civil lawsuits, which highlighted the systemic barriers faced by the deaf community in accessing equitable mental health care. Notable cases include *Doe v. Wilzack*, 1986; *Tugg v. Towey*, 1994; *Bailey v. Sawyer*, 2001; and *Janet Devinney and the USA v. Maine Medical Center*, 1998. Key legislation was enacted in the United States, beginning with the Americans with Disabilities Act of 1990, and amended in 2008, which prohibits the discrimination of people with disabilities and mandates effective communication in healthcare settings. And, between 1997 and 2005, universal newborn hearing screening (UNHS) legislation was enacted, which significantly expanded access to hearing screenings for newborns. This legislation increased healthcare access, enabling earlier identification and better communication, and leading to more accurate medical and mental health diagnoses for deaf individuals (Kushalnagar et al., 2019).

The above context has driven the establishment of a deaf mental health care specialization that shifts from a medical-pathological model to a cultural model of the Deaf community that is sensitive to the unique cultural and linguistic experiences of deaf individuals (Glickman, 1996; Pollard, 1996). Pollard (1996) advocated for recognizing deaf culture and language as central to effective treatment and discussed how language deprivation, communication barriers, and societal marginalization contribute to the unique mental health challenges faced by deaf individuals, necessitating specialized therapeutic approaches. A major point in the emerging psychology of deafness is the importance of training mental health professionals to work effectively with deaf clients (Pollard, 1996).

Glickman (1996) argued that traditional psychotherapy models, designed for hearing clients, often overlooked the specific needs and experiences of deaf clients, such as communication barriers, cultural identity, and the psychological effects of social marginalization. He emphasized the need for therapists to recognize deaf culture as distinct, with its own language and social norms. Culturally affirmative psychotherapy, therefore, involves respecting deaf identity, using accessible communication methods, and addressing the psychological impact of experiences like language deprivation and discrimination (Glickman, 1996). Ultimately, Glickman's framework encouraged clinicians to move beyond simply accommodating deaf clients to actively affirming and valuing their cultural identity, leading to more effective and empowering therapeutic outcomes.

Benefits and Challenges

Specialized mental health services are crucial for delivering equitable and culturally competent care to deaf individuals. These services aim to address treatment disparities by meeting the unique needs of the deaf community, with success hinging on cultural competency, accessibility, effective communication, accurate assessments, professional development, and the integration of evolving research. An understanding of both the benefits and challenges of these services is vital for enhancing care quality and improving outcomes. Mental health services for deaf individuals require a heightened focus on accessibility, health literacy, and cultural awareness. Beyond addressing hearing loss, effective care must consider the individual's broader sociocultural context, including ethnic, religious, and community-specific influences.

Excellence in deaf mental health care demands ongoing research, adaptive therapeutic strategies, and continual updates to training and language skills. Providers must remain attentive to their own competencies, available resources, and the accessibility of their services, ensuring that each deaf client receives a personalized, culturally responsive treatment plan. By prioritizing cultural sensitivity, effective communication, and accessible assessments, mental health professionals can significantly improve outcomes for deaf clients. Recognizing and respecting the unique cultural and communication needs of the deaf community is essential for delivering truly inclusive care.

Cultural Sensitivity and Respect

When working with deaf individuals, the importance of cultural awareness often becomes especially evident. This includes an understanding that members of the Deaf community are viewed as cultural and linguistic minorities, and not as people with a disability (Glickman, 2012). Deaf individuals may possess unique cultural backgrounds and communication preferences that differ significantly from hearing individuals (Glickman, 1996).

Culturally affirmative therapy is an approach that is guided by sociocultural awareness, incorporates culturally appropriate methods, and aims to empower clients and their community (Glickman, 1996). The framework outlines three primary dimensions for culturally affirmative services: self-awareness, knowledge, and the development of specialized skills (Glickman, 1996, 2012). These elements enable providers to deliver treatment that is culturally sensitive and inclusive, recognizing and addressing the complexities that cultural differences bring to the therapeutic relationship. While it is often referred to as a "therapy," it is actually a set of principles and strategies that can be integrated within the broad spectrum of existing psychotherapies.

The importance of cultural competence is readily agreed upon in the mental health professions, as evidenced by the incorporation of guidance on cultural competence across professional codes of ethics (e.g., American Counseling Association, 2014; American Psychological Association, 2017; National Association of Social Workers, 2017). For example, the National Association of Social Workers (NASW) Code of Ethics posits that social workers must not only recognize the diverse cultural backgrounds of their clients but must actively seek knowledge and apply this understanding to ensure effective service delivery (NASW, 2017). Mental health providers are encouraged to reflect on their own cultural biases and privileges in order to provide culturally sensitive care. This professional framework aligns with the goals of culturally affirmative therapy, reinforcing the need for cultural awareness in social work and therapy alike.

While many deaf individuals' mental health needs mirror those of hearing individuals in many respects, the barriers they face can be more significant due to communication and cultural differences. Deaf individuals tend to experience higher satisfaction with therapy when their specific cultural needs are identified and addressed (Shafaat et al., 2024). As such, therapists must learn to adapt their practice to ensure they are meeting the unique needs of deaf clients, which includes offering services tailored to their cultural context.

Despite the overwhelming support for culturally sensitive services, challenges remain in training providers to effectively serve culturally diverse populations, including deaf individuals. Effective cultural sensitivity with deaf individuals requires therapists to recognize the unique social, emotional, and psychological impacts of hearing loss, including challenges related to language access, cultural isolation, and societal stigma (Shafaat et al., 2024). Providers often struggle to deliver effective therapy if cultural differences are misunderstood as limitations rather than recognized as cultural nuances. These misunderstandings can disrupt trust and rapport, ultimately compromising therapeutic outcomes (Morere et al., 2019). Misunderstandings regarding Deaf cultural norms can further complicate the therapeutic process, as behaviors perceived as polite or acceptable in Deaf culture may be interpreted as rude or inappropriate by hearing providers, and vice versa. Thus, providers must engage in culturally sensitive practice, employing non-judgmental care and individualized approaches to address language barriers and cultural isolation, which are common challenges for deaf individuals (Morisod et al., 2022).

Accessibility and Health Literacy

Accessibility and health literacy are critical components of effective mental health services for deaf individuals. For deaf individuals, communication barriers—particularly the reliance on spoken language in traditional mental health settings—create significant challenges in accessing appropriate care. Deaf individuals often report feelings of fear, mistrust, and dissatisfaction with healthcare providers, stemming from limited access to effective communication and a lack of understanding of deaf individuals' unique needs (Steinberg et al., 2006).

Mental health literacy refers to the "knowledge and beliefs about mental disorders which aid their recognition, management, or prevention" (Jorm et al., 1997, p. 182). Deaf individuals often face significant health literacy barriers compared to their hearing peers, contributing to poorer mental and physical health outcomes (Morisod et al., 2022). Traditional methods of health communication, such as print media, radio, and television, are often inaccessible to deaf people. In particular, printed materials, newspaper articles, and live captions are generally less effective for deaf individuals, who may also miss out on ambient information, like overhearing conversations or listening to podcasts, that hearing people easily access (Barnett, 1999). In clinical settings, the reliance on written questionnaires or verbal communication during assessments and intake procedures can exacerbate these barriers, complicating access to care.

The efforts to reduce health literacy disparities for deaf individuals is a long-term commitment to research, evaluation, and the development of accessible materials. While advancements in technology—such as automatic captioning and video-hosting platforms -have improved access to information, significant gaps remain. The majority of health materials available in the United States are in English, with a noticeable lack of resources in non-English languages, particularly ASL (Pollard et al., 2009). The translation process from English to ASL is complex, involving more than direct translation; it often necessitates adjustments to account for linguistic and cultural differences (Pollard et al., 2009). To truly improve accessibility, it is not enough to simply translate information; it must also be culturally and linguistically appropriate to ensure effective communication with deaf individuals.

A variety of initiatives have been launched to enhance accessibility and mental health literacy within the Deaf community. In Rochester, NY, the Deaf Wellness Center focuses on creating accessible health education materials specifically tailored for Deaf individuals. The Deaf Yes Center for Empowerment and Recovery in Worcester, MA offers training on trauma, mental health, and addiction, equipping members of the Deaf community with vital knowledge and support. Similarly, the Deaf and Hard of Hearing Child Resilience Center (DHHCRC) in Washington,

D.C. has developed resources and trainings aimed at improving access to trauma-informed mental health information geared for deaf and hard-of- hearing youth. Deaf Unity serves as an advocacy organization dedicated to mental health accessibility, offering resources to help Deaf individuals find Deaf-friendly therapists and access inclusive mental health services. Deaf AA provides an Alcoholics Anonymous (AA) resource designed specifically for Deaf individuals, featuring ASL-accessible meetings, support groups, and recovery resources. Focusing on educational and workforce settings, the National Deaf Center on Postsecondary Outcomes addresses the mental health and well-being of Deaf students and professionals. Through resources on self-advocacy, accessibility, and mental health support, the center empowers Deaf individuals to thrive in academic and professional environments. Collectively, these initiatives illustrate significant progress toward culturally and linguistically appropriate mental health resources for the Deaf community. While these efforts are bridging gaps in accessibility and awareness, continued work remains essential to achieving full equity in mental health care.

Communication

Communication access in mental healthcare is essential, as it plays a pivotal role in shaping both treatment outcomes and the quality of client engagement. When working with deaf individuals, it is crucial to consider both cultural and communicative factors, ensuring engagement occurs through their preferred mode of communication. Deaf individuals communicate through visual, auditory, or tactile modes. Visual communication includes ASL, cued speech, speech reading (lip reading), and gestures. Auditory communication relies on residual hearing, spoken language, and assistive devices like hearing aids or cochlear implants. For individuals who are deafblind, tactile communication involves touch-based methods to convey information through the hands or body (National Deaf Center on Postsecondary Outcomes, 2025). It is equally important to avoid assuming that any type of communication—whether ASL or another form—applies universally to all deaf individuals. Effective communication is best achieved when it is tailored to everyone's unique language preferences and cultural and linguistic background, promoting more meaningful and respectful interactions (National Deaf Center on Postsecondary Outcomes, 2025).

Deaf clients often encounter substantial barriers in mental health settings when they lack proper access to communication. These challenges are further impacted by factors such as socioeconomic status, educational opportunities, and literacy levels (Barnett, 1999). Individuals who have experienced language deprivation are particularly vulnerable to misdiagnosis. The absence of fluent communication may manifest in behaviors that are perceived as more severe or indicative of illness than they truly are (Glickman, 2012). For example, a deaf client using gestures may appear disorganized or confused when, in fact, they are attempting to communicate with the tools they have available. In turn, an untrained clinician may pathologize such behaviors, such as attributing the communication style to a thought disorder or cognitive impairment. Such misinterpretations of symptoms can result in inappropriate or ineffective treatment plans.

Services in One's Preferred Language

Providing mental health services in a deaf individual's preferred language, whether a signed and/or spoken language, is essential for effective communication in therapeutic settings. Many deaf individuals express a strong preference for therapy in their preferred language, as it allows for clearer, more authentic self-expression (Barnett, 2002). When this preference is respected, it can not only enhance the quality of the therapeutic experience but also strengthen the therapeutic alliance, fostering greater engagement, understanding, and rapport (Steinberg et al., 2006). Effective communication contributes to improved treatment outcomes and increased compliance with treatment plans.

However, providing services in a preferred language can present significant challenges, particularly in smaller or rural communities or when seeking specialized services where qualified professionals may be limited. Deaf individuals in these instances may seek services from hearing professionals outside of their community who use interpreters or adaptive equipment to facilitate communication. While these alternatives may offer some access to services, access and cultural sensitivity are likely reduced, as hearing providers may lack understanding of the specific linguistic and cultural needs of deaf individuals. This lack of cultural competence contributes to feelings of mistrust, particularly when communication barriers lead to misinterpretations or misunderstandings (Steinberg et al., 2006). Additionally, rural communities often face challenges such as limited access to trained interpreters and healthcare providers, which exacerbates the barriers to effective communication (Mead, 2019). Concerns about confidentiality are also prevalent, as the deaf community is typically close-knit, and sharing sensitive information with an interpreter or a hearing provider may feel like a breach of privacy, particularly in instances when clients are likely to encounter providers in everyday community settings (Cabral et al., 2013).

Interpreters

In situations where qualified providers who communicate directly with deaf clients are unavailable, interpreters are often an important accommodation. In these instances, effective communication includes accurate interpretation. However, an interpreter's role extends beyond mere translation; interpreters are essential for conveying not only words but also the thoughts, feelings, and intentions of deaf individuals. This is especially important in mental health settings, where nuanced understanding is key to accurate diagnosis and effective treatment planning. For this reason, it is crucial that interpreters working in mental health contexts possess specialized training that equips them with the skills to handle complex psychological concepts accurately and sensitively.

Qualified interpreters enhance the therapeutic process by fostering mutual understanding and trust, facilitating effective communication during diagnosis and treatment planning, and promoting a culturally sensitive, patient-centered approach. However, simply having an interpreter present does not guarantee equitable care. Effective communication also depends on the interpreter's expertise, cultural sensitivity, and familiarity with mental health terminology. Deaf individuals may have diverse communication preferences, including various dialects or modes of sign language that differ from mainstream ASL. Mental health providers and interpreters must recognize these differences to prevent misunderstandings and miscommunications.

Deaf individuals may experience language dysfluency, which complicates the accurate diagnosis and treatment of mental health conditions. Language dysfluency can result from various factors, including neurological conditions, language deprivation, aphasia, or psychotic disorders (Crump & Glickman, 2011). In such cases, traditional ASL-English interpreting methods may not suffice. Specialized strategies—like the use of simplified language, visual aids, gestures, or the involvement of Certified Deaf Interpreters (CDIs)—may be required to bridge communication gaps. Interpreters must balance faithful interpretation with the need to clarify meaning, ensuring clinicians accurately understand the client's language abilities without altering their communication patterns. Best practices emphasize a team-based approach where interpreters and mental health providers collaborate to accommodate language dysfluency in assessments and treatment planning.

A shortage of qualified interpreters remains a significant barrier to effective mental health care for deaf individuals. In their absence, deaf individuals sometimes resort to alternative communication methods, such as speechreading, written notes, or involving family members to facilitate communication. However, these strategies are inadequate for conveying complex emotional or psychological information, leading to miscommunication and inaccuracies in care (Steinberg et al., 2006). A common misconception about speechreading is that it enables deaf individuals to fully understand speech. Speechreading provides only partial access to speech, capturing approximately 30–40% of spoken words and is further hindered by speech speed, lip shape, word formation, and background noise. This method demands high levels of contextual inference from Deaf individuals, often resulting in cognitive fatigue and communication breakdowns.

Interpreters also face challenges when facilitating discussions on sensitive topics that can occur during mental health treatment (Morisod et al., 2022). Certain topics can be particularly difficult for deaf individuals to discuss due to cultural stigma or discomfort, which may prevent the sharing of crucial personal information that impacts mental health treatment. In such scenarios, it is critical for interpreters to exercise cultural sensitivity and professionalism, fostering an environment where clients feel safe to share important aspects of their identity and experiences.

Assessment

Despite the wide range of mental health assessment tools available, very few have been specifically developed or culturally and linguistically adapted to meet the needs of the diverse deaf population. Effective mental health treatment begins with a thorough assessment to identify relevant areas for intervention. However, there remains a significant gap in tools specifically designed for or empirically validated with deaf individuals.

It is essential to recognize that assessments tailored for deaf individuals must be adapted to account for the community's diversity. For instance, tools designed for individuals who primarily use ASL may not be appropriate for those who rely on oral communication. Moreover, the use of interpreters during assessments can introduce variability that may compromise the accuracy of responses (Morere et al., 2019). Therefore, it is critical to develop and utilize tools that are sensitive to these linguistic and cultural differences, ensuring a comprehensive and accurate understanding of each individual's needs.

Notable efforts in this area include (Reesman et al., 2014) which provided a summary of intellectual assessment measures with regard to specific guidance on accommodations, score interpretation, subtest selection, and other test-specific considerations for deaf children. Another example is the Deaf-C, a structured interview that has been developed to consider the unique ecological factors that are relevant for deaf children (Whitaker & Morere, 2024). These tools represent critical steps toward equitable assessment practices, but more research and development are needed.

Many standardized assessments include normative data to compare an individual's performance against a broader population. However, deaf individuals are often excluded from these normative groups, and when they are included, the sample size is often small and poorly described in terms of key language and access variables. This lack of representative data makes it difficult to draw accurate conclusions about the abilities and needs of deaf individuals. To address this gap, there is a pressing need for empirically validated assessments that reflect diverse linguistic and cultural experiences. The scarcity of comprehensive and culturally relevant assessment tools remains a barrier to equitable mental health care for Deaf individuals, underscoring the need for continued research, development, and adaptation of assessment practices in the field.

Professional Development

The importance of providing clinicians with in-depth training in working with deaf individuals cannot be overstated. Effective therapeutic strategies for deaf individuals must be adapted to account for linguistic differences and cultural nuances. Clinicians should integrate deaf-friendly approaches, including skills-based learning, visual aids, interactive role-playing, and the use of visual metaphors into treatment processes (Leigh et al., 2004). Moreover, training should not be limited to an introduction to Deaf culture, but rather an ongoing learning process that fosters reflection and the application of inclusive practices for the diverse deaf population. Continuous engagement with the deaf community allows clinicians to stay informed about the needs, preferences, and cultural context of deaf clients, ensuring treatment approaches are both relevant and effective.

However, basic training alone is not enough to overcome the challenges faced in clinical interactions with deaf individuals. Limited exposure to Deaf culture and communication can lead to biases that negatively impact therapeutic relationships. Leigh et al. (2004) highlight that inadequate training often perpetuates misconceptions and reinforces stereotypes about deaf individuals. This can lead clinicians to adopt inappropriate treatment approaches and view deafness solely as a disability to be "fixed," disregarding its cultural and identity-related aspects. Therefore, specialized training must not only introduce Deaf culture but also deepen clinicians' understanding of the linguistic and social realities of deaf individuals.

Despite the benefits of specialized training, several challenges persist. The lack of formal training around visual communication access can further complicate the clinician's ability to effectively engage with deaf individuals, making it difficult to determine whether communication is effective. Additionally, many training programs fail to provide a comprehensive understanding of Deaf culture, resulting in cultural conflicts between clinicians and their deaf clients. Consequently, healthcare providers are left to navigate these challenges without the proper tools or knowledge to adapt their approaches in a culturally sensitive manner.

The gap in training around effective care for deaf individuals has significant consequences. Mead (2019) discusses how healthcare providers frequently lack training on adapting evidence-based therapies to meet the cultural and linguistic needs of deaf individuals. While foundational therapeutic models are often emphasized in training, there is limited research or guidance on how to culturally adapt these models for deaf clients. This leaves clinicians to navigate the complexities of Deaf culture and communication without proper support, often leading to less effective treatment and reduced quality of care. Prioritizing specialized training that includes Deaf culture, effective communication strategies, and inclusive practices can enhance clinicians' ability to engage with the deaf clients. Training that is culturally sensitive, linguistically appropriate, and delivered by experienced trainers can improve understanding and support more equitable care for deaf individuals.

Professional Training for Deaf Providers

While the number of deaf clinicians in the United States is increasing, the availability of deaf providers is still inadequate to meet the clinical needs of the deaf population (Brice et al., 2013; Wilkins et al., 2022). Furthermore, barriers still exist in the training pipeline for deaf individuals to enter the mental health workforce as well as to participate in advanced training once they are in the workforce (Schooler et al.,

2021). In a qualitative study of clinicians who use play therapy with deaf clients, access was a major theme that was raised by clinicians (Dowtin & Day, 2019). A disparity in access to peer supervision and consultation between deaf and hearing clinicians was highlighted. In one particularly salient example, a deaf clinician shared how they watched their hearing students advance to receive more credentials while they struggled to find enough training or supervisors to obtain the same credentials (Dowtin & Day, 2019).

Deaf providers often encounter substantial barriers during professional training, particularly when materials are not presented in their preferred language, forcing reliance on interpreters. While necessary, the presence of an interpreter to facilitate communication during training can inadvertently introduce complexities that disrupt effective learning for the deaf provider in training. Now, the deaf provider must navigate multiple, often simultaneous, sources of information—including the interpreter, written materials, and visual content—while also contending with temporal delays between the original spoken message and its interpreted delivery. Additionally, many trainers are not equipped to address the unique linguistic and cultural needs of deaf individuals, leaving deaf providers with the additional need to independently adapt training materials on their own to meet their clients' needs. This challenge is further compounded by internalized stigmatization, which may lead some to perceive deaf and hard-of-hearing clinicians as less knowledgeable than their hearing counterparts (Cabral et al., 2013; Tomaszewski et al., 2025) Unlike hearing trainees who can passively receive information, deaf providers must actively engage their heightened visual and cognitive faculties to absorb and process content, increasing cognitive load and leading to physical exhaustion. Even after training sessions are completed, gaps remain, as most programs fail to account for the linguistic and cultural considerations necessary for effective practice with deaf clients.

Professional organizations such as the American Deafness and Rehabilitation Association (ADARA) play a critical role in supporting the professional development of deaf providers. By facilitating national networking and collaboration, ADARA enables providers to exchange specialized knowledge, research, and strategies. This collaboration strengthens the collective ability of clinicians to address the specific needs of the deaf population. Further, training programs such as the Deaf and Hard of Hearing Child Resilience Center (DHHCRC) have made a significant improvement in the accessibility and effectiveness of professional development for deaf providers. These programs, which include training in ASL and culturally adapted materials, offer an accessible learning experience by allowing deaf providers to receive instruction in their preferred language. Moreover, the inclusion of real-time discussions among peers further supports learning by providing opportunities for clinicians to share experiences and insights regarding the adaptation of therapeutic techniques.

Evolving Areas of Research

The shift toward evidence-based mental health therapy began in the twentieth century, and today, evidence-based therapy is the standard of care. Despite the plethora of evidence-based therapy models available for a myriad of referral reasons, there are still no evidence-based therapies that have been formally validated to meet the needs of deaf clients (Anderson et al., 2021; Anderson & Craig, 2018). However, that landscape is shifting. Pioneering work at the Deaf Wellness Center in Rochester, New York, and by Neil Glickman and colleagues at the State Hospital Deaf Unit in Westborough, Massachusetts, and PAHrtners Deaf Services in Glenside, Pennsylvania, has led to the identification of principles to guide attempts to modify therapy approaches for deaf clients (Glickman, 1996; Pollard, 1996). These principles generally include adaptation for language, attention to fund of information deficits, use of storytelling and visual metaphors, teaching through examples, use of role play, use of technology, and peer-to-peer education (Anderson & Craig, 2018; Glickman, 2012; Pollard et al., 2009). And now, following groundbreaking work being done at DeafYES by Anderson and colleagues, the first psychotherapy clinical trial is underway.

Dialectical Behavior Therapy

The Deaf Wellness Center has adapted dialectical behavior therapy (DBT) for deaf individuals. The modifications focused on improving accessibility, cultural relevance, and effectiveness. Standard DBT relies heavily on written materials and spoken language, making it difficult for many Deaf clients who use American Sign Language (ASL) and may have lower English literacy levels. To address this, therapists adapted DBT by simplifying written materials, using visual aids, and developing ASL-translated resources, including videos featuring Deaf actors using culturally relevant examples (Pollard & Dimeff, 2006, 2008). Additionally, DBT group therapy was modified to account for the visual nature of ASL, requiring longer sessions to allow for dialogue, storytelling, and concept explanation. Common English mnemonics used in DBT (e.g., "DEAR MAN") were restructured into ASL-friendly versions. Since standard mindfulness exercises often rely on auditory cues, Deaf-friendly alternatives were developed, focusing on visual and tactile mindfulness techniques. Telephone coaching, a key DBT component, was adapted to use video calls or text-based options, as traditional phone calls are not accessible for many Deaf clients. Confidentiality was another critical concern due to the small and close-knit nature of Deaf communities, requiring additional guidance on maintaining privacy in group settings (O'Hearn & Pollard Jr, 2008). Overall, these adaptations aimed to increase the effectiveness and inclusivity of DBT for Deaf individuals, ensuring that treatment was both linguistically and culturally appropriate.

A preliminary investigation of DBT was conducted in Australia for Australian Deaf mental health consumers. The pilot project team adapted DBT materials to fit the needs of the Deaf population and incorporated participant feedback during the pilot. The results showed that participants reported improvements in interpersonal skills and emotional regulation, and the therapy was generally well-received. The DBT adaptations for Deaf individuals were beneficial, and future research should focus on developing culturally valid measures and comparing various adapted therapeutic methods.

Pre-therapy and Cognitive Behavior Therapy

Glickman's (2008) book, *Cognitive-Behavioral Therapy for Deaf and Hearing Persons with Language and Learning Challenges*, explores adapting traditional Cognitive-Behavioral Therapy (CBT) for individuals with language, learning, and cognitive barriers, particularly focusing on Deaf and hard-of-hearing populations. The book emphasizes the importance of understanding the linguistic, cultural, and educational experiences of Deaf individuals, who often face communication challenges and limited access to information. Glickman presents practical strategies for modifying CBT techniques, including simplifying language, using visual aids, and incorporating culturally relevant examples. He also highlights the role of therapists' cultural competence in improving client engagement and treatment outcomes. The book offers a comprehensive framework for clinicians working with clients who have unique language and cognitive needs, promoting more inclusive and effective mental health care.

Glickman's (2016) manual, *Preparing Deaf and Hearing Persons with Language and Learning Challenges for CBT: A Pre-Therapy Workbook*, provides a structured, accessible guide designed to help individuals with language, learning, and cognitive barriers prepare for CBT. The workbook offers exercises and activities that introduce foundational CBT concepts in simplified, visual, and concrete formats, making them accessible to Deaf clients and others with limited language skills. It focuses on building basic skills such as identifying emotions, understanding thoughts and behaviors, and developing self-awareness before formal therapy begins. The book also serves as a resource for therapists, offering strategies to bridge communication gaps and promote better engagement in CBT for clients with unique linguistic and learning needs.

Trauma and Substance Use Disorders

Anderson and colleagues have developed Signs of Safety, which is a deaf-accessible counseling toolkit to support symptoms related to trauma and addiction, given the increased rate of these issues in the deaf population (e.g., Anderson et al., 2018;

Anderson & Leigh, 2011; Black & Glickman, 2006; Schild & Dalenberg, 2012) Signs of Safety was developed to be used with Seeking Safety, a manualized intervention that follows a cognitive behavioral therapy model and prioritizes clients' safety (Najavits, 2002). It is a toolkit that includes a therapist companion guide and deaf-accessible client materials (Anderson & Craig, 2018). It is designed to be accessible to a wide range of deaf people, including those who are culturally deaf, hard of hearing, late-deafened, and deafblind (Anderson & Craig, 2018).

During the initial development process, a multidisciplinary team of Deaf and hearing researchers, clinicians, filmmakers, and Deaf people in recovery developed the Signs of Safety toolkit, including ASL teaching stories, inspirational quotations performed by a Deaf poet, visual handouts, and a supplemental counselor guide (Anderson et al., 2021). Next, a pilot study ($N = 15$) evaluated the feasibility, acceptability, and clinical outcomes for Seeking Safety supplemented by the Signs of Safety toolkit, showing clinically significant reductions in PTSD symptoms and alcohol use. However, drug use frequency remained unchanged, likely influenced by the mid-study legalization of recreational marijuana (Anderson et al., 2021). Based on participant feedback, the next steps involved redesigning and refilming the Signs of Safety toolkit to enhance clarity, representation, and cultural relevance.

A randomized controlled trial was then conducted between 2019 and 2022 (Anderson et al., 2025). The study highlighted five key lessons: the need to expand the study reach to a nationwide sample, the importance of formally assessing ASL fluency prior to enrolling in the study to ensure an appropriate fit for the language level requirements and best participant-therapist match, ethical concerns around waitlist control groups, challenges in video fidelity monitoring for ASL-based therapy, and the necessity of ASL-accessible outcome assessments. These findings informed the design of the first full-scale psychotherapy clinical trial for Deaf individuals in the United States, set to take place from 2024 to 2028 (Anderson et al., 2025). This project marks a crucial step toward developing the first evidence-based psychotherapy validated for Deaf ASL users, addressing long-standing behavioral health disparities in this underserved population.

Parent–Child Relationships

Research regarding treatments that have been adapted for use with Deaf children is scant. One evidence-based intervention, Parent–Child Interaction Therapy (PCIT), has been adapted for use with a wide range of Deaf families, including those who communicate via ASL and spoken language (Costa et al., 2019; Day et al., 2018). PCIT is a parent-training program that supports parents/caregivers in building secure relationships with their children and effectively utilizing developmentally appropriate discipline (McNeil et al., 2010). It has also been used effectively with hearing children as a family-based language intervention (Allen & Marshall, 2010; Bagner et al., 2016; Falkus et al., 2016; Garcia et al., 2015; Tempel et al., 2009), further supporting the possible utility for families with DHH children. Initial evidence suggests that it can be a helpful intervention for Deaf children and their parents (e.g., Barrett, 2020; Costa et al., 2019; Previ, 2018); however, this data is preliminary because these studies are limited to case studies, studies with small sample sizes, and/or a lack of a control sample.

Costa et al. (2019) conducted a study of parents of children with hearing loss who use spoken language ($N = 18$) and found significant improvements in parenting skills and reductions in child disruptive behavior. Additionally, a subset of this sample ($N = 6$) was compared to a matched control group of children with hearing loss who did not participate in PCIT services to assess language. Children who received PCIT produced significantly longer utterances at both the morpheme and word levels than children who did not participate in PCIT.

Four single-case studies explored the use of Parent–Child Interaction Therapy (PCIT) with families that included at least one deaf member. Shinn's (2013) case study included a deaf mother and her hard-of-hearing child, who used ASL, who worked with a hearing therapist who utilized an interpreter. Over the course of treatment, the mother improved her use of PCIT skills, and the son's behavior problems decreased (Shinn, 2013). This study emphasized the importance of including interpreters as consistent team members, though the use of Signed Exact English as the language for treatment was a limitation and likely impacts the generalizability of the results. Armstrong et al. (2014) adapted PCIT for a deaf mother and hearing child by using a consistent interpreting team and a video communication app for remote coaching. The parents' skills improved and were sustained at post-treatment, and the child's behavior improved and was also sustained post-treatment. Weinstein et al.'s (2015) case included a hearing parent and a deaf child who received the first of two phases of PCIT treatment in spoken English. At the end of the first phase, the parent demonstrated mastery of the positive attention skills, and the child's disruptive behaviors decreased to non-clinical levels. Finally, Previ (2015) worked with a deaf parent and hearing child using ASL directly, eliminating the need for interpreters. Significant behavioral improvements following treatment were indicated by reduced scores on the Eyberg Child Behavior Inventory (ECBI).

Previ (2018) examined the reliability and validity of the observational instruments that assess parent–child interaction quality, the Dyadic Parent–Child Interaction Coding System (DPICS-IV), for use with ASL via a retrospective analysis of data of clients who completed PCIT treatment ($N = 8$). Therapists' coding reliability improved over time. Parent skills also improved across treatment, further supporting the system's validity for use in ASL, though the need for an ASL-specific addendum was identified due to linguistic differences from English. Mercado (2022) explored child language outcomes during PCIT in a sample of 19 caregiver-child dyads who participated in a minimum of one PCIT coaching session and found no significant changes in the quality of child utterances. This outcome may be due to the small sample size, varying amount of coaching received, and varying baseline language skills. Nonetheless, the study provided qualitative information about the types of signs commonly used in dyadic interactions and further supported the ASL addendum of the DPICS. Barrett (2020) investigated how ASL's syntactic rhetorical questions affect DPICS-IV coding, noting that while no adjustments to the coding system were deemed necessary, clinicians should consider the unique role of rhetorical questions in ASL during treatment discussions with parents.

Deaf in the Criminal Justice System

Martin et al. (2021) summarized the current state of research available on deaf people in the US criminal justice system, current practices, and relevant issues for deaf people within the justice system, as well as legal aspects. Important gaps in data regarding the number of Deaf individuals in the criminal justice system, communication access at different stages of the legal process, qualified advocates to work with Deaf people, and the lack of prevention, assessment, and treatment for Deaf individuals to prevent recidivism were identified. Future directions are identified in terms of accessibility needs, data collection and research, training for personnel within the criminal justice system, disrupting the school-to-prison pipeline, and advocacy (Martin et al., 2021).

Trauma Processing

There is promising adaptation work happening with several child-focused trauma-processing psychotherapeutic interventions. Beginning at the Walden School in Framingham, Massachusetts (United States), clinicians started adapting and implementing Sensory Motor Arousal Regulation Treatment (SMART; Warner et al., 2020) with their clients. This work is now being led by the Deaf and Hard of Hearing Child Resilience Center in Washington, DC (United States) where ASL-based training materials have been created, and clinicians serving deaf clients have been trained. Additionally, the Deaf and Hard of Hearing Child Resilience Center in Washington, DC (United States) is currently adapting and implementing Trauma-Focused Cognitive Behavior Therapy (TF-CBT) with deaf youth (Mannarino et al., 2014). Published guidance for each of these interventions with deaf children is forthcoming.

Call to Action

Each of these interventions has a growing body of evidence to support its effectiveness with Deaf clients for a range of presenting problems. However, significantly more work is needed in terms of the dissemination of these interventions broadly to clinicians, collecting data on their effectiveness, and including a broader range of interventions.

The field of mental health and deaf people is slowly making gains in knowledge, research, and resources. Yet, this progress still lags behind the general population. When considering the historical mistreatment of deaf individuals, combined with the continued lack of research to support effective assessment and intervention with deaf children, it is easy to see why many deaf individuals struggle to obtain appropriate mental health services. This current lack serves to perpetuate the ongoing disparity of mental health support for deaf children. This systemic failure does not end in childhood. Deaf adults often bear the long-term consequences of early misdiagnosis, underdiagnosis, or lack of culturally and linguistically appropriate intervention. Many deaf individuals grow up without access to mental health care that affirms their language and identity, leaving trauma, language deprivation, and untreated mental health conditions to persist into adulthood. To break this cycle, the field must prioritize sustained investment in research, training, and policy that centers deaf individuals across the lifespan, ensuring that accessible, affirming, and evidence-based mental health care becomes the norm, not the exception.

References

Allen, J., & Marshall, C. R. (2010). Parent–child interaction therapy (PCIT) in school-aged children with specific language impairment. *International Journal of Language & Communication Disorders, 101018023331052*. https://doi.org/10.3109/13682822.2010.517600

American Counseling Association. (2014). *American Counseling Association Code of Ethics*. https://www.counseling.org/knowledge-center/ethics

American Psychological Association. (2017). *American Psychological Association Code of Ethics*. https://www.apa.org/ethics/code

Americans with Disabilities Act Amendments Act of 2008, Pub. L. No. 110-325, 122 Stat. 3558 (2008). https://www.ada.gov/pubs/adastatute08.htm

Americans with Disabilities Act of 1990, No. 42 U.S.C. § 12101 et seq (1990). https://www.ada.gov/pubs/adastatute08.htm

Anderson, M. L., & Craig, K. S. W. (2018). Developing therapy approaches for deaf clients impacted by language deprivation. In *Language deprivation and deaf mental health* (pp. 83–100). Routledge.

Anderson, M. L., & Leigh, I. W. (2011). Intimate partner violence against deaf female college students. *Violence Against Women, 17*(7), 822–834.

Anderson, M. L., Chang, B.-H., & Kini, N. (2018). Alcohol and drug use among deaf and hard-of-hearing individuals: A secondary analysis of NHANES 2013–2014. *Substance Abuse, 39*(3), 390–397.

Anderson, M. L., Glickman, N. S., Wolf Craig, K. S., Sortwell Crane, A. K., Wilkins, A. M., & Najavits, L. M. (2021). Developing Signs of Safety: A Deaf-accessible counselling toolkit for trauma and addiction. *Clinical Psychology & Psychotherapy, 28*(6), 1562–1573.

Anderson, M. L., Wilkins, A. M., Hostovsky, S., Pici-D'Ottavio, E., Aldalur, A., McGinnis, F., & Meza, K. (2025). Psychotherapy research in the deaf community: Pilot clinical trial lessons learned. *Journal of Deaf Studies and Deaf Education*, enaf007.

Armstrong, K., David, A., & Goldberg, K. (2014). Parent–child interaction therapy with deaf parents and their hearing child: A case study. *Sage Journals, 13*(2), 115–127.

Bagner, D. M., Garcia, D., & Hill, R. (2016). Direct and indirect effects of behavioral parent training on infant language production. *Behavior Therapy, 47*(2), 184–197. https://doi.org/10.1016/j.beth.2015.11.001

Bailey v. Sawyer, No. No. 99-A-1321-N (2001).
Barnett, S. (1999). Clinical and cultural issues in caring for deaf people. *Family Medicine, 31*(1), 17–22.
Barnett, S. (2002). Cross-cultural communication with patients who use American sign language. *Family Medicine, 34*(5), 376–382.
Barrett, G. E. (2020). *An exploration of questions as they apply to signing and Oral deaf children participating in the baseline session of parent-child interaction therapy (PCIT)*. Gallaudet University.
Basilier, T. (1964). SURDOPHRENIA: The psychic consequences of congenital or early acquired deafness. Some theoretical and clinical considerations. *Acta Psychiatrica Scandinavica, 39*(S180), 363–372.
Black, P. A., & Glickman, N. S. (2006). Demographics, psychiatric diagnoses, and other characteristics of north American deaf and hard-of-hearing inpatients. *Journal of Deaf Studies and Deaf Education, 11*(3), 303–321.
Brice, P. J., Leigh, I. W., Sheridan, M., & Smith, K. (2013). Training of mental health professionals: Yesterday, today, and tomorrow. In *Deaf mental health care* (pp. 316–340). Routledge.
Cabral, L., Muhr, K., & Savageau, J. (2013). Perspectives of people who are deaf and hard of hearing on mental health, recovery, and peer support. *Community Mental Health Journal, 49*(6), 649–657. https://doi.org/10.1007/s10597-012-9569-z
Costa, E. A., Day, L., Caverly, C., Mellon, N., Ouellette, M., & Wilson Ottley, S. (2019). Parent–child interaction therapy as a behavior and spoken language intervention for young children with hearing loss. *Language, Speech, and Hearing Services in Schools, 50*(1), 34–52. https://doi.org/10.1044/2018_LSHSS-18-0054
Crump, C., & Glickman, N. (2011). Mental health interpreting with language dysfluent deaf clients. *Journal of Interpretation, 21*(1), 3.
Day, L. A., Costa, E. A., Previ, D., & Caverly, C. (2018). Adapting parent–child interaction therapy for deaf families that communicate via American sign language: A formal adaptation approach. *Cognitive and Behavioral Practice, 25*(1), 7–21. https://doi.org/10.1016/j.cbpra.2017.01.008
Doe v. Wilzack, 517 A.2d 758 (Md. 1986).
Dowtin, L. L., & Day, L. A. (2019). Signs and barriers: Play therapy training experiences of deaf and hearing clinicians. *International Journal of Play Therapy, 28*(4), 195–206. https://doi.org/10.1037/pla0000105
Falkus, G., Tilley, C., Thomas, C., Hockey, H., Kennedy, A., Arnold, T., Thorburn, B., Jones, K., Patel, B., Pimenta, C., et al. (2016). Assessing the effectiveness of parent–child interaction therapy with language delayed children: A clinical investigation. *Child Language Teaching and Therapy, 32*(1), 7–17.
Garcia, D., Bagner, D. M., Pruden, S. M., & Nichols-Lopez, K. (2015). Language production in children with and at risk for delay: Mediating role of parenting skills. *Journal of Clinical Child & Adolescent Psychology, 44*(5), 814–825. https://doi.org/10.1080/15374416.2014.900718
Glickman, N. S. (1996). What is culturally affirmative psychotherapy? In N. S. Glickman & M. A. Harvey (Eds.), *Culturally affirmative psychotherapy with deaf persons*. Taylor & Francis Group.
Glickman, N. (2008). *Cognitive-behavioral therapy for deaf and hearing persons with language and learning challenges*. Routledge.
Glickman, N. S. (2012). In N. S. Glickman (Ed.), *Deaf mental health care*. Taylor & Francis Group.
Glickman, N. S. (2016). Preparing deaf and hearing persons with language and learning challenges for CBT: A pretherapyworkbook. Routledge.
Janet Devinney and the USA v. Maine Medical Center, No. No. 97-276-P-C (1998).
Jorm, A. F., Korten, A. E., Jacomb, P. A., Christensen, H., Rodgers, B., & Pollitt, P. (1997). "Mental health literacy": A survey of the public's ability to recognise mental disorders and their beliefs about the effectiveness of treatment. *Medical Journal of Australia, 166*(4), 182–186.

Koyanagi, C., & Bazelon, D. (2007). *Learning From History: Deinstitutionalization of People with Mental Illness as Precursor to Long-Term Care Reform*. Kaiser Commission on Medicaid and the Uninsured. https://www.kff.org/wp-content/uploads/2013/01/7684.pdf

Kushalnagar, P., Reesman, J., Holcomb, T., & Ryan, C. (2019). Prevalence of anxiety or depression diagnosis in deaf adults. *The Journal of Deaf Studies and Deaf Education, 24*(4), 378–385.

Leigh, I. W., Powers, L., Vash, C., & Nettles, R. (2004). Survey of psychological services to clients with disabilities: The need for awareness. *Rehabilitation Psychology, 49*(1), 48.

Mannarino, A. P., Cohen, J. A., & Deblinger, E. (2014). Trauma-focused cognitive-behavioral therapy. In *Evidence-based approaches for the treatment of maltreated children: Considering Core components and treatment effectiveness* (pp. 165–185). Springer.

Martin, G. A., Paris, D. G., Lomas, G. I., Guthmann, D., et al. (2021). *Deaf people in the criminal justice system: Selected topics on advocacy, incarceration, and social justice*. Gallaudet University Press.

McNeil, C. B., Hembree-Kigin, T. L., & Anhalt, K. (2010). *Parent-child interaction therapy*. Springer.

Mead, A. (2019). Enhancing Services for Deaf, Hard of Hearing, and Deafblind Patients in Rural America. *Rural Health Information Hub*. https://www.ruralhealthinfo.org/rural-monitor/enhancing-services-for-deaf#:~:text=There%20are%20two%20types%20of,effectively%20communicate%20with%20DHH%20patients

Mercado, K. C. (2022). *Parent-child interaction therapy: An examination of American sign language patterns*. Gallaudet University.

Morere, D. A., Dean, P. M., & Mompremoer, L. (2019). Mental health assessment of deaf clients: Issues with interpreters use and assessment of person with diminished capacity and psychiatric populations. *JADARA, 42*(4), 9.

Morisod, K., Malebranche, M., Marti, J., Spycher, J., Grazioli, V. S., & Bodenmann, P. (2022). Interventions aimed at improving healthcare and health education equity for adult d/deaf patients: A systematic review. *European Journal of Public Health, 32*(4), 548–556.

Najavits, L. (2002). *Seeking safety: A treatment manual for PTSD and substance abuse*. Guilford Press.

National Association of Social Workers. (2017). *National Association of Social Workers Code of Ethics*. https://www.socialworkers.org/About/Ethics/Code-of-Ethics/Code-of-Ethics-English

National Deaf Center on Postsecondary Outcomes. (2025). *Communicating with Deaf Individuals*. https://nationaldeafcenter.org/resource-items/communicating-deaf-people/

O'Hearn, A., & Pollard, R. Q., Jr. (2008). Modifying dialectical behavior therapy for deaf individuals. *Cognitive and Behavioral Practice, 15*(4), 400–414.

Pollard, R., & Dimeff, L. (2006). Opposite action: An adaptation from the Deaf perspective [Motion picture]. *Available from Behavioral Tech, 2133*.

Pollard, R. Q., & Dimeff, L. A. (2008). Dialectical behavior therapy with deaf clients. *Cognitive and Behavioral Practice, 15(4), 400–414.*.

Pollard, R. Q., Jr. (1996). Professional psychology and deaf people: The emergence of a discipline. *American Psychologist, 51*(4), 389.

Pollard, R. Q., Dean, R. K., O'Hearn, A., & Haynes, S. L. (2009). Adapting health education material for deaf audiences. *Rehabilitation Psychology, 54*(2), 232–238. https://doi.org/10.1037/a0015772

Previ, D. (2015). *Parent-child interaction therapy among deaf persons: A pilot study on PCIT used with American sign language*. Gallaudet University.

Previ, D. (2018). *Parent-child interaction therapy dyadic parent-child interaction coding system (DPICS): Interrater reliability with live versus video coding*. Gallaudet University.

Rayson, M. (1987). Psychological services for the deaf: A neglected area. *Journal of Rehabilitation, 53*(1), 45–49.

Reesman, J. H., Day, L. A., Szymanski, C. A., Hughes-Wheatland, R., Witkin, G. A., Kalback, S. R., & Brice, P. J. (2014). Review of intellectual assessment measures for children who are deaf or hard of hearing. *Rehabilitation Psychology, 59*(1), 99–106. https://doi.org/10.1037/a0035829

Schild, S., & Dalenberg, C. J. (2012). Trauma exposure and traumatic symptoms in deaf adults. *Psychological Trauma: Theory, Research, Practice, and Policy, 4*(1), 117.

Schooler, D., Day, L. A., Maynard, S., Rosier, R., Pabon, A., Miller, C. A., & Wagner, K. (2021). *Becoming Psychologists: Barriers and Bridges Encountered by Deaf and Hard of Hearing Students in Education and Training Settings.*

Shafaat, Z., Munawar, F., & Sharif, H. (2024). Cultural competence of social workers with deaf people. *Journal for Societal Issues, 6*(3), 290–300.

Shinn, M. M. (2013). Parent–child interaction therapy with a deaf and hard of hearing family. *Clinical Case Studies, 12*(6), 411–427. https://doi.org/10.1177/1534650113500065

Steinberg, A. G., Barnett, S., Meador, H. E., Wiggins, E. A., & Zazove, P. (2006). Health care system accessibility: Experiences and perceptions of deaf people. *Journal of General Internal Medicine, 21*, 260–266.

Tempel, A. B., Wagner, S. M., & McNeil, C. B. (2009). Parent-child interaction therapy and language facilitation: The role of parent-training on language development. *The Journal of Speech and Language Pathology—Applied Behavior Analysis, 3*(2–3), 216–232. https://doi.org/10.1037/h0100241

Tomaszewski, P., Krzysztofiak, P., Kowalska, J., & Hauser, P. C. (2025). Internalized oppression and deaf people's mental health. *Scientific Reports, 15*(1), 5268.

Tugg v. Towey, 864 F. Supp. 1201 (1994).

Vernon, M. (2006). The APA and deafness. *American Psychologist, 61*(8), 816.

Vernon, M., & Leigh, I. W. (2007). Mental health services for people who are deaf. *American Annals of the Deaf, 152*(4), 374–381.

Vernon, M., & Miller, K. R. (2005). Obstacles faced by deaf people in the criminal justice system. *American Annals of the Deaf, 150*(3), 283–291.

Warner, E., Finn, H., Westcott, A., & Cook, A. (2020). *Transforming trauma in children and adolescents: An embodied approach to somatic regulation, trauma processing, and attachment-building*. North Atlantic Books.

Weinstein, A., Jent, J. F., Cejas, I., & De La Asuncion, M. (2015). Improving behavior using child-directed interaction skills: A case study determining cochlear implant candidacy. *Cochlear Implants International, 16*(5), 285–289. https://doi.org/10.1179/1754762815Y.0000000007

Whitaker, R., & Morere, D. A. (2024). Deaf/hard of hearing ecological assessment form—Child (DEAF-C). *Journal of Deaf Studies and Deaf Education*, enae054. https://doi.org/10.1093/jdsade/enae054

Wilkins, A. M., Morere, D. A., Pick, L. H., Day, L. A., & Anderson, M. L. (2022). Characteristics of psychologists assessing deaf and hard of hearing clients. *The Journal of Deaf Studies and Deaf Education, 27*(2), 115–124. https://doi.org/10.1093/deafed/enab039

Chapter 2
The Role of Early Language Experience in Deaf and Hard of Hearing Children: Implications for Mental Health

Kimberly Ofori-Sanzo

Early Language Experience

During the first few years of life, children learn their first language (L1) from the adults in their immediate environment. This occurs through early exchanges with caregivers that promote linguistic growth and social interaction. Parent–child interaction is critical for language acquisition, and an infant's brain is shaped by the nature and quality of these early experiences (Donnelly & Kidd, 2021; Newman et al., 2015; Thompson, 2012). While there is a neurobiological basis for language acquisition, it is also a social process in which prompt and meaningful responses to infants serve as the foundation (Donnelly & Kidd, 2021; Levickis et al., 2022; Masek et al., 2021). A young child's language development is thus highly impacted by factors such as the amount of parental linguistic stimulation, parent–child bonding, parental teaching style, and parental attitudes and personality traits (Fox et al., 2010). Indeed, caregivers provide some of the most substantive stimuli to babies (Levitt & Eagleson, 2018), which is critical not only for brain development but for laying a foundation for the child's ability to learn (Rosemond, 2018). Linguistic development is also intertwined with cognitive, social, and emotional abilities (Im-Bolter & Cohen, 2007), and parent–child interactions play a profound role in the development of all these domains (Bick & Nelson, 2017; Komanchuk et al., 2023; Levitt & Eagleson, 2018; World Health Organization, 2004).

Interactions with parents allow for exposure to rich linguistic stimuli through a back-and-forth communicative exchange known as *serve and return* (Harvard University, 2007; Rosemond, 2018). For example, infants might "serve" by making sounds or smiling and caregivers "return" the serve by responding in prompt and meaningful ways (Chen et al., 2023). These back-and-forth interactions with

K. Ofori-Sanzo (✉)
Language First, Hardford,Vernon, CT, USA
e-mail: kimberly@language1st.org

T. Bone (ed.), *Deaf Mental Health*, Advances in Mental Health and Addiction,
https://doi.org/10.1007/978-3-032-06274-1_2

caregivers help infants develop communication and social skills and support the development of their neural circuitry (Bick & Nelson, 2017). Chen et al. (2023) found that children whose mothers provided meaningful responses to their child's serves at nine months had higher expressive language scores at 18 months.

Additionally, the positive nature of these interactions can "buffer impacts of stress on development and health over the lifespan" (Komanchuk et al., 2023, p. 413). On the contrary, a lack of caregiver–child interactions means that the brain does not receive the required positive stimulation, and the body's stress response is activated (Harvard University, 2007). An infant's brain changes in response to the stimuli in its environment, and an absence of necessary stimuli causes alterations in brain architecture that are evident on neuroimaging. Responsive and contingent interactions with parents are so crucial that their absence can alter neurodevelopment and result in atypical brain organization (Bick & Nelson, 2017; Komanchuk et al., 2023; Twardosz & Lutzker, 2010).

Beyond the importance of the interactions themselves, a key component of early communicative exchanges is the sensitivity and responsiveness of caregivers (Im-Bolter & Cohen, 2007). Masek et al. (2021) describe the concept of *contingency*, where parents who respond to their infants promptly and meaningfully help lay the foundation for fluent and connected communication. Within this concept of contingency, a *prompt* response is one that is timely and occurs soon after the infant's action, while a *meaningful* response is one that is relevant to the object or the infant's behavior (Chen et al., 2023; Masek et al., 2021). For example, if an infant smiles at their caregiver, a contingent response would be an immediate, relevant reaction such as, "Wow, what a pretty smile!" Komanchuk et al. (2023) provide an excellent example of a sensitive and responsive *serve-and-return* interaction:

> A caregiver and 3-year-old are out for a walk. The child sees a lilac bush and announces, "Look, flowers!" (serve). The caregiver stops and states, "Oh, yes, I see the lilac bush. The flowers are a pretty light purple. Can you smell them?" (return). The toddler leans forward to smell the flowers, claps their hands, and exclaims, "They smell pretty! I love purple!" (serve). The caregiver replies, "I like the color purple too. Should we find some other purple things?" (return). (p. 407)

If we consider this exchange in the context of a young deaf and hard of hearing (DHH) child with listening devices, it is likely that the child misheard or misperceived much of the spoken language in that interaction. Thus, even if the caregiver engages in serve-and-return with a DHH child, it is not guaranteed that the child accessed all the linguistic stimulation in the exchange.

Early Language Experience for DHH Children

Infants and toddlers do not have to be explicitly taught their L1; in fact, during typical language development, exposure to rich and high-quality caregiver–child communication interactions is typically enough to allow for fluent acquisition of an L1. For DHH children, however, the simple presence of spoken language input in their environment is not enough to presume that they are acquiring that language. To acquire language fluently, input must be addressed to the child and be accessible to the child (Chen Pichler et al., 2018). Thus, it is critical to make the distinction between exposure to linguistic input and access to that input. Hall (2020) defines *exposure* as the language signals being sent to the child and *access* as the language signals being received by the child's brain. Because language is often called "brain food," a meal analogy is fitting. If *exposure* to language is placing food on the table, then *access* is eating the food and allowing its nutrients to reach the bloodstream.

In typically developing hearing children, one can suppose that if they are exposed to a language (i.e., surrounded by it), they are accessing that language (i.e., taking it in). As it pertains to young DHH children, however, this is a hazardous assumption— even if the child has listening technology such as hearing aids or cochlear implants, language access is not guaranteed. To return to the meal analogy, simply placing food on the table (i.e., placing listening technology on a deaf child's head) does not guarantee that it will be eaten and be converted into energy and nutrients for the body. Wearing hearing technology does not make a DHH child hearing. In fact, DHH children who wear their devices with fidelity are still mishearing, misperceiving, and missing auditory input that is critical for spoken language development. Consequently, it is important to consider the linguistic signals that the child is *receiving* through those devices (Hall, 2020), and remember that the devices themselves are simply tools and do not guarantee any specific outcome (Szarkowski, 2019). As Ocuto (2024a) asserts, in a deaf child's early home language environment, language *access* is a critical factor in the child's linguistic development.

Unlike spoken languages transmitted through hearing technology, natural signed languages like American Sign Language (ASL) are fully accessible to sighted DHH children. As such, when exposed to a signed language, DHH children can fully access the linguistic signal. That is to say, they both receive food on the table and are able to consume it. They can readily "consume" this linguistic signal because it is being filtered through an unimpeded sense (i.e., vision), rather than a compromised sensory system (i.e., audition).

Language Deprivation

Language exposure without access places a DHH child at risk for not fully acquiring the ambient spoken language in their environment. If a DHH child cannot fully access their family's spoken language and they are also not exposed to a natural signed language such as ASL, then they may not develop a strong L1 in any language. Language deprivation, or the delayed or incomplete acquisition of an L1, is an epidemic among DHH children and creates a greater risk for various developmental consequences across the lifespan (Hall et al., 2018b).

Given what is known about the importance of language for overall development, it is perhaps not surprising that language deprivation has significant, irreversible, and long-lasting effects on not only language (Boudreault & Mayberry, 2006), but also on cognition (Marshall et al., 2015; Mayberry, 2002; Nelson, 2000; Szarkowski, 2019). While some cognitive skills are intertwined with language, many are independent of it. Hence, it is important to note that language deprivation does not necessarily cause difficulties in cognitive domains that are independent of language (Mayberry, 2002). This is illustrated in a study by Meinzen-Derr et al. (2018) in which the authors found that 62.5% of DHH children with nonverbal IQs within the normal range demonstrated verbal IQ scores below the average range.

It is evident that DHH children with an incomplete L1 can, and do, have intact cognition. However, a lack of early language access certainly impacts cognitive skills that are intertwined with language (i.e., cognitive-linguistic skills). These skills—such as executive functioning (EF), reasoning, and problem-solving—are mental abilities which require both linguistic processes and cognitive faculties. Executive functioning skills are those that are processed in the frontal lobe and include abilities like attention, working memory, planning, organization, and mental flexibility. In a study by Hall et al. (2017a), the authors found that DHH children with language deprivation were more likely to struggle with EF as compared to both hearing and DHH children who had accessible language from birth. Therefore, it was not their decreased auditory access that impacted their EF development, but their reduced early access to language (Hall et al., 2018a).

A delayed or incomplete L1 acquisition does not only impact language and cognition. It has also been linked to lower quality of life and difficulty with interpersonal relationships and emotional regulation (Gulati, 2019; Morgan et al., 2021; W. C. Hall, 2017). This may be unsurprising, as language helps us conceptualize problem-solving and provides verbiage for us to understand our emotions. Children with language deprivation may misbehave or appear oppositional because they lack the cognitive-linguistic skills and verbal reasoning to manage their feelings and self-regulate (Glickman, 2019). Additionally, an incomplete L1 may cause individuals to struggle with a conceptual model for conflict resolution skills (Glickman et al., 2020).

Inaccessible early language input may also be considered a form of neglect. As in other cases of neglect in which alterations in brain development are evident (Bick & Nelson, 2017), language deprivation manifests itself in anatomical changes of the linguistic system in the brain (Pénicaud et al., 2013). Cheng et al. (2019) found that deaf individuals who experienced language deprivation early in life developed less robust connections between neural language regions. Language deprivation is also associated with alterations in brain regions responsible for processing syntactic language (Skotara et al., 2012) as well as changes in gray and white matter in the visual cortex (Pénicaud et al., 2013). Additionally, deaf individuals with language deprivation who eventually learn a signed language process that linguistic input primarily in visual regions as opposed to language regions (Mayberry et al., 2011).

Communication Neglect

For the purposes of this chapter, the author makes the distinction between language deprivation and communication neglect. *Language deprivation* is a result of incomplete access to a natural language during the critical period for language acquisition, namely from birth to age five (Hall et al. 2017a, b), while *communication neglect* is the recurrent exclusion from family conversations and incidental learning that may occur across the lifespan (Kushalnagar et al., 2020). While both may be considered forms of stress that can impact the health of DHH children (Kushalnagar et al., 2020), they also represent distinct issues in DHH children's early language environments. Language deprivation refers to the lack of linguistic input to the brain, while communication neglect refers more to the social aspect of language. As Meek (2020) states, DHH individuals who experience communication neglect feel "loved yet disconnected" (p. 1682) when they chronically miss out on conversations with their hearing family members.

Family conversation facilitates the DHH child's access to an important aspect of home life (Bodner-Johnson, 1991). However, many DHH children are not experiencing fluent and bidirectional conversations with their hearing family members (Hall et al., 2018b). A *fluent* conversation is one in which both the child and the caregiver can easily express themselves in a dialogue that flows smoothly, without significant pauses or misunderstandings; *bidirectional* means that the conversation is a two-way interaction between two communication partners. DHH children who cannot fully access the spoken language in their home environment may struggle to become fluent in that language. Therefore, their opportunities for fluent and bidirectional conversations are greatly diminished.

Furthermore, DHH children are often not privy to the same conversations as the rest of their family members (Meek, 2020). In the early language experience of DHH children, rich family interactions may be present, but the child may not be accessing them. That is to say, a DHH child may not be able to fully hear or perceive the spoken language their family members are using in their interactions. As Ocuto (2024a) asserts, improving language access improves the quality of family interactions. Having contingent and reciprocal conversations between family members stimulates language and cognitive growth for a DHH child (Marschark et al., 2006), and their absence can lead to decreased conceptual knowledge development in DHH children (Ocuto, 2024a). A DHH child should be able to communicate fluently with all family members so that all can understand each other (Meek, 2020); yet caregivers of DHH children report that their child frequently misses out on family conversations (Patrick et al., 2018).

Within the context of communication neglect is the phenomenon of "Dinner Table Syndrome," or the common experience of deaf individuals in which they are surrounded by auditory conversations but unable to understand what is said, such as exchanges at the dinner table (Hall et al., 2018b). The term has come to represent any conversations among a group of hearing people that are not completely accessible to deaf individuals (Meek, 2020). These conversations involve rapid turn-taking and overlapping chatter, which makes them difficult for a deaf person to follow. Instead of asking for clarification or repetition, a deaf child learns to not participate in the conversation (Bodner-Johnson, 1991). Because of this, DHH children born to hearing families are often excluded from larger family conversations and thus from incidental learning (Meek, 2020).

Incidental learning, or unintentional, passive language acquisition, is vital for the acquisition of general and world knowledge (Convertino et al., 2014). Hearing children acquire nearly 70–90% of their knowledge through incidental learning (Marsick & Watkins, 2001, as cited in Wilkinson & Morford, 2020); however, DHH children often lack this opportunity because they are not able to overhear spoken conversations (Hall et al., 2018b; Hauser et al., 2010). These conversations can be innocuous discussions of everyday goings-on, sharing of memories, or looking ahead to future experiences (Ocuto, 2024b), or they can be more significant discussions about illness, treatment, and family medical history (Smith & Samar, 2016; Wilkinson & Morford, 2020).

Undoubtedly, access to indirect family communication is important for the development of general world knowledge, conceptual knowledge, and health literacy. When DHH individuals from hearing families do not have access to these opportunities, it can lead to a lack of access to health information resulting in decreased understanding of health-related topics and the vocabulary to discuss health-related issues. As Hall et al. (2018b) state, "the dinner table syndrome phenomenon, situated in context of the broader risks of language deprivation, likely has a significant impact on health outcomes of deaf people" (p. 3).

Early Language Experience and Mental Health

DHH children and adolescents are more vulnerable to all forms of abuse and neglect, placing them at increased risk for mental health problems (Glickman, 2019; Hindley, 2005; Kvam et al., 2007). In fact, Kvam et al. (2007) found that the risk of experiencing mental distress, including feeling fearful or hopeless, was more than doubled for DHH individuals as compared to hearing individuals. Importantly, it is not the reduced hearing itself that causes mental health issues, but rather the lack of communication in the home and the resultant incomplete acquisition of an L1. Embree et al. (2017) found that delayed L1 acquisition was linked to suicide attempts and mental illness, and Fellinger et al. (2009) found that DHH children who cannot make themselves understood by their family are four times more likely to be affected by mental health disorders than children who can successfully communicate with their caregivers. Not only may DHH children struggle to communicate their experiences with their parents, but their parents may struggle to understand them as well (Fellinger et al., 2009; Hindley, 2005; Kvam et al., 2007).

Kushalnagar et al. (2020) make the connection between Adverse Childhood Experiences (ACEs) and Adverse Childhood *Communication* Experiences (ACCEs), citing poor direct child–caregiver communication as a form of toxic stress that can have long-term health implications. Both ACEs and ACCEs are also linked to negative long-term effects on the brain, as seen in neuroimaging. While ACEs during childhood are associated with smaller sizes of certain brain regions, namely the hippocampus and amygdala (Luby et al., 2019), deprivation of early linguistic input is associated with reduced connectivity of the arcuate fasciculus (Cheng et al., 2019) and changes in brain tissue in the visual cortex (Pénicaud et al., 2013).

All the previously mentioned concerns with DHH children's early language environments—limited language access, language deprivation, and communication neglect—can be considered ACCEs, which are associated with increased risks for multiple chronic health outcomes (Kushalnagar et al., 2020). And, DHH adults are aware of this. In a study by Anderson et al. (2016), DHH participants reported an inability to communicate with their hearing parents as a source of stress and trauma. The inability to make oneself understood also increases the risk of being isolated or maltreated (Fellinger et al., 2009). On the contrary, DHH youth who are able to understand and communicate with their parents are more likely to have higher quality-of-life ratings and lower reported symptoms of depression (Kushalnagar et al., 2011).

Gulati (2019) discussed the impact of language deprivation on mental health, and interpersonal relationships and labeled this constellation of long-term consequences Language Deprivation Syndrome (LDS). Gulati emphasized multiple complications across the lifespan for deaf individuals with LDS, including cognitive delays, mental health difficulties, lower quality of life, and limited health literacy (Gulati, 2014). LDS is also linked to thought disorders (Black & Glickman, 2006; Black & Glickman, 2019; Glickman, 2007), and there are high levels of language deprivation and dysfluency in DHH prison populations (Glickman, 2019).

Implications

Exposing DHH infants and toddlers to a natural signed language in addition to a spoken language can help ensure that they acquire *at least one* complete language from birth (Hall et al., 2019). Bimodal bilingualism, or the acquisition of a signed and spoken (or written) language, yields similar cognitive benefits to spoken language bilingualism (Petitto & Ferraro, 2001), and signed language exposure is linked to improved overall language and cognitive skills in DHH children (Delcenserie et al., 2024). In fact, Clark et al. (2020) propose a default bimodal bilingual approach for early intervention practices for all DHH children to minimize the risk of language deprivation, and Wilkinson and Morford (2020) posit that bimodal bilingualism can serve as a protective factor to reduce the risk of poor health outcomes for DHH children. Additionally, exposure to a signed language is advantageous even for children with listening devices such as hearing aids and cochlear implants. This is because acquisition of a signed language facilitates and complements spoken language development (Sanzo, 2022; Secora & Smith, 2021). In fact, DHH children with cochlear implants who sign from birth demonstrate better *spoken language* outcomes than their peers who are not provided with a signed language (Davidson et al., 2014; Delcenserie et al., 2024; Hassanzadeh, 2012; Rinaldi & Caselli, 2014).

Given the evidence supporting the importance of caregiver–child interactions on DHH children's development, early intervention should focus on ensuring parents are well-equipped to provide their child with accessible language. Recent studies suggest that DHH children can acquire signed language even if their parents are not fluent (Caselli et al., 2021; Henner et al., 2016), and providing DHH children with both spoken and signed language at home can help create interactions that help establish the foundation for linguistic development (Gale & Martin, 2024; Ocuto, 2024a). The implementation of visual strategies utilized by Deaf adults as well as the use of family-centered ASL curricula can help enhance DHH children's early language environments (Gale & Martin, 2024; Lillo-Martin et al., 2023; Zarchy, 2023). Additionally, intervention that focuses on teaching parents communication strategies can increase their sensitivity, responsiveness, and involvement with their DHH child (Lam-Cassettari et al., 2015). Finally, continued investigation into the link between language acquisition and mental health is needed to inform best practices. Future research should focus on early childhood language experiences of deaf children to improve their overall health outcomes (Hall et al., 2018b).

Conclusion

The link between early language access and later mental health is becoming more evident. DHH children are at an increased risk for experiencing early language environments that are not fully accessible to them (Hall, 2017; Hall et al., 2018b). This reduced access to linguistic input, along with decreased involvement in family conversations, places DHH children at an increased risk for language dysfluency and mental health issues. Effective early communication in both spoken and signed language may help prevent many mental health problems in DHH individuals (Hindley, 2005), as the ability to make oneself understood at home can significantly reduce DHH children's adverse childhood experiences (Fellinger et al., 2009). Indeed, the importance of an accessible home language environment on DHH children's socio-emotional wellbeing cannot be understated (Embree et al., 2017; Fellinger et al., 2012; Ocuto, 2024a; Patrick et al., 2018).

References

Anderson, M. L., Wolf Craig, K. S., Hall, W. C., & Ziedonis, D. M. (2016). A pilot study of deaf trauma survivors' experiences: Early traumas unique to being deaf in a hearing world. *Journal of Child & Adolescent Trauma, 9*, 353–358.

Bick, J., & Nelson, C. A. (2017). Early experience and brain development. *Wiley Interdisciplinary Reviews: Cognitive Science, 8*(1–2), e1387.

Black, P. A., & Glickman, N. S. (2006). Demographics, psychiatric diagnoses, and other characteristics of North American deaf and hard-of-hearing inpatients. *Journal of Deaf Studies and Deaf Education, 11*(3), 303–321.

Black, P., & Glickman, N. (2019). Language Deprivation in the deaf inpatient population. *JADARA, 39*(1), 4.

Bodner-Johnson, B. (1991). Family conversation style: Its effect on the deaf child's participation. *Exceptional Children, 57*(6), 502–509.

Boudreault, P., & Mayberry, R. I. (2006). Grammatical processing in American Sign Language: Age of first-language acquisition effects in relation to syntactic structure. *Language and Cognitive Processes, 21*(5), 608–635. https://doi.org/10.1080/01690960500139363

Caselli, N., Pyers, J., & Lieberman, A. M. (2021). Deaf children of hearing parents have age-level vocabulary growth when exposed to ASL by six-months. *The Journal of Pediatrics, 232*, 229.

Chen Pichler, D., Lillo-Martin, D., de Quadros, R. M., & Stumpf, M. R. (2018). *Sign language acquisition by deaf and hearing children*. Gallaudet University Press.

Chen, Y., Cabrera, N. J., & Reich, S. M. (2023). Mother-child and father-child "serve and return" interactions at 9 months: Associations with children's language skills at 18 and 24 months. *Infant Behavior and Development, 73*, 101894.

Cheng, Q., Roth, A., Halgren, E., & Mayberry, R. I. (2019). Effects of early language deprivation on brain connectivity: Language pathways in deaf native and late first-language learners of American Sign Language. *Frontiers in Human Neuroscience, 13*.

Clark, M. D., Cue, K. R., Delgado, N. J., Greene-Woods, A. N., & Wolsey, J. L. A. (2020). Early intervention protocols: Proposing a default bimodal bilingual approach for deaf children. *Maternal and Child Health Journal, 24*, 1339–1344.

Convertino, C., Borgna, G., Marschark, M., & Durkin, A. (2014). Word and world knowledge among deaf learners with and without cochlear implants. *Journal of Deaf Studies and Deaf Education, 19*(4), 471–483. https://doi.org/10.1093/deafed/enu024

Davidson, K., Lillo-Martin, D., & Chen Pichler, D. (2014). Spoken English language development among native signing children with cochlear implants. *Journal of Deaf Studies and Deaf Education, 19*(2), 238–250.

Delcenserie, A., Genesee, F., & Champoux, F. (2024). Exposure to sign language prior and after cochlear implantation increases language and cognitive skills in deaf children. *Developmental Science, 27*(4), e13481.

Donnelly, S., & Kidd, E. (2021). The longitudinal relationship between conversational turn-taking and vocabulary growth in early language development. *Child Development, 92*(2), 609–625.

Embree, J. A., Kinzeler, N. R., Fraker, S., Castle, S., & Wilson, J. F. (2017). Age of language acquisition and prevalence of suicidal behavior in a deaf population with co-occurring substance use disorder. *JADARA, 51*(3), 1–24.

Fellinger, J., Holzinger, D., Sattel, H., Laucht, M., & Goldberg, D. (2009). Correlates of mental health disorders among children with hearing impairments. *Developmental Medicine & Child Neurology, 51*(8), 635–641.

Fellinger, J., Holzinger, D., & Pollard, R. (2012). Mental health of deaf people. *The Lancet, 379*(9820), 1037–1044.

Fox, S. E., Levitt, P., & Nelson, C. A. (2010). How the timing and quality of early experiences influence the development of brain architecture. *Child Development, 81*(1), 28–40.

Gale, E., & Martin, A. (2024). Deaf gain: Visual communication for all young children. *Discover Education, 3*(1), 66.

Glickman, N. (2007). Do you hear voices? Problems in assessment of mental status in deaf persons with severe language deprivation. *Journal of Deaf Studies and Deaf Education, 12*(2), 127–147. https://doi.org/10.1093/deafed/enm001

Glickman, N. S. (2019). Language deprivation syndrome. In N. S. Glickman & W. C. Hall (Eds.), *Language deprivation and deaf mental health* (pp. 47–53). Routledge.

Glickman, N. S., Crump, C., & Hamerdinger, S. (2020). Language deprivation is a game changer for the clinical specialty of deaf mental health. *JADARA, 54*(1), 54.
Gulati, S. (2014). *Language Deprivation Syndrome*. Retrieved from http://www.northeastern.edu
Gulati, S. (2019). Language deprivation syndrome. In N. S. Glickman & W. C. Hall (Eds.), *Language deprivation and deaf mental health* (pp. 24–53). Routledge.
Hall, W. C. (2017). What you don't know can hurt you: The risk of language deprivation by impairing sign language development in deaf children. *Maternal and Child Health Journal, 21*(5), 961–965. https://doi.org/10.1007/s10995-017-2287-
Hall, M. L. (2020). The input matters: Assessing cumulative language access in deaf and hard of hearing individuals and populations. *Frontiers in Psychology, 11*(1407).
Hall, M. L., Eigsti, I. M., Bortfeld, H., & Lillo-Martin, D. (2017a). Auditory deprivation does not impair executive function, but language deprivation might: Evidence from a parent-report measure in deaf native signing children. *The Journal of Deaf Studies and Deaf Education, 22*(1), 9–21.
Hall, W. C., Levin, L. L., & Anderson, M. L. (2017b). Language deprivation syndrome: A possible neurodevelopmental disorder with sociocultural origins. *Social Psychiatry and Psychiatric Epidemiology, 52*, 761–776.
Hall, M. L., Eigsti, I. M., Bortfeld, H., & Lillo-Martin, D. (2018a). Executive function in deaf children: Auditory access and language access. *Journal of Speech, Language, and Hearing Research, 61*(8), 1970–1988. https://doi.org/10.1044/2018_JSLHR-L-17-0281
Hall, W. C., Smith, S. R., Sutter, E. J., DeWindt, L. A., & Dye, T. D. V. (2018b). Considering parental hearing status as a social determinant of deaf population health: Insights from experiences of the "dinner table syndrome.". *PLoS One, 13*(9), e0202169.
Hall, M. L., Hall, W. C., & Caselli, N. K. (2019). Deaf children need language, not (just) speech. *First Language, 39*(4), 367–395.
Harvard University Center on the Developing Child. (2007). *The Science of Early Childhood Development* (InBrief). Retrieved from www.developingchild.harvard.edu
Hassanzadeh, S. (2012). Outcomes of cochlear implantation in deaf children of deaf parents: Comparative study. *The Journal of Laryngology and Otolaryngology, 126*, 989–994.
Hauser, P. C., O'Hearn, A., McKee, M., Steider, A., & Thew, D. (2010). Deaf epistemology: Deafhood and deafness. *American Annals of the Deaf, 154*(5), 486–492.
Henner, J., Caldwell-Harris, C. L., Novogrodsky, R., & Hoffmeister, R. (2016). American Sign Language syntax and analogical reasoning skills are influenced by early acquisition and age of entry to signing schools for the deaf. *Frontiers in Psychology, 7*.
Hindley, P. A. (2005). Mental health problems in deaf children. *Current Paediatrics, 15*, 114–119.
Im-Bolter, N., & Cohen, N. J. (2007). Language impairment and psychiatric comorbidities. *Pediatric Clinics of North America, 54*, 525–542.
Komanchuk, J., Letourneau, N., Duffett-Leger, L., & Cameron, J. L. (2023). History of "serve and return" and a synthesis of the literature on its impacts on children's health and development. *Issues in Mental Health Nursing, 44*(5), 406–417.
Kushalnagar, P., Topolski, T. D., Schick, B., Edwards, T. C., Skalicky, A. M., & Patrick, D. L. (2011). Mode of communication, perceived level of understanding, and perceived quality of life in youth who are deaf or hard of hearing. *Journal of Deaf Studies and Deaf Education, 16*(4), 512–523.
Kushalnagar, P., Ryan, C., Paludnevicience, R., Spellun, A., & Gulati, S. (2020). Adverse childhood communication experiences associated with an increased risk of chronic diseases in adults who are deaf. *American Journal of Preventative Medicine, 59*(4), 548–554.
Kvam, M. H., Loeb, M., & Tambs, K. (2007). Mental health in deaf adults: symptoms of anxiety and depression among hearing and deaf individuals. *Journal of Deaf Studies and Deaf Education, 12*(1), 1–7.
Lam-Cassettari, C., Wadnerkar-Kamble, M. B., & James, D. M. (2015). Enhancing parent–child communication and parental self-esteem with a video-feedback intervention: outcomes with

prelingual deaf and hard-of-hearing children. *Journal of Deaf Studies and Deaf Education, 20*(3), 266–274.

Levickis, P., Conway, L., Smith, J., & Bennetts, S. (2022). Parent–Child Interaction and Its Impact on Language Development. In J. Law, S. Reilly, & C. McKean (Eds.), *Language Development: Individual Differences in a Social Context* (pp. 166–192). Cambridge University Press.

Levitt, P., & Eagleson, K. L. (2018). The ingredients of healthy brain and child development. *Journal of Law and Policy, 57*(75).

Lillo-Martin, D. C., Gale, E., & Chen Pichler, D. (2023). Family ASL: An early start to equitable education for deaf children. *Topics in Early Childhood Special Education, 43*(2), 156–166.

Luby, J. L., Tillman, R., & Barch, D. M. (2019). Association of timing of adverse childhood experiences and caregiver support with regionally specific brain development in adolescents. *JAMA Network Open, 2*(9), e1911426–e1911426.

Marschark, M., Schick, B., & Spencer, P. E. (2006). Understanding sign language development of deaf children. In B. Schick, M. Marschark, & P. E. Spencer (Eds.), *Perspectives on deafness. Advances in the sign language development of deaf children* (pp. 3–19). Oxford University Press.

Marshall, C., Jones, A., Denmark, T., Mason, K., Atkinson, J., Botting, N., & Morgan, G. (2015). Deaf children's non-verbal working memory is impacted by their language experience. *Frontiers in Psychology, 6*(527). https://doi.org/10.3389/fpsyg.2015.00527

Marsick, V. J., & Watkins, K. J. (2001). Informal and incidental learning. *New Directions for Adult and Continuing Education, 89*, 25–34. https://doi.org/10.1002/ace.5

Masek, L. R., McMillan, B. T., Paterson, S. J., Tamis-LeMonda, C. S., Golinkoff, R. M., & Hirsh-Pasek, K. (2021). Where language meets attention: How contingent interactions promote learning. *Developmental Review, 60*, 100961.

Mayberry, R. I. (2002). Cognitive development in deaf children: The interface of language and perception in neuropsychology. *Handbook of neuropsychology, 8*(Part II), 71–107.

Mayberry, R. I., Chen, J. K., Witcher, P., & Klein, D. (2011). Age of acquisition effects on the functional organization of language in the adult brain. *Brain and Language, 119*(1), 16–29.

Meek, D. R. (2020). Dinner table syndrome: A phenomenological study of deaf individuals' experiences with inaccessible communication. *The Qualitative Report, 25*(6), 1676–1694.

Meinzen-Derr, J., Sheldon, R., Grether, S., Altaye, M., Smith, L., Choo, D. I., & Wiley, S. (2018). Language underperformance in young children who are deaf or hard-of-hearing: Are the expectations too low? *Journal of Developmental and Behavioral Pediatrics, 39*(2), 116.

Morgan, G., Curtin, M., & Botting, N. (2021). The interplay between early social interaction, language, and executive function development in deaf and hearing infants. *Infant Behavior and Development, 64*. https://doi.org/10.1016/j.infbeh.2021.101591

Nelson, C. A. (2000). Neural plasticity and human development: The role of early experience in sculpting memory systems. *Developmental Science, 3*(2), 115–136. https://doi.org/10.1111/1467-7687.00104

Newman, L., Sivaratnam, C., & Komiti, A. (2015). Attachment and early brain development – Neuroprotective interventions in infant–caregiver therapy. *Translational Developmental Psychiatry, 3*(1), 28647.

Ocuto, O. L. (2024a). Deaf children, home language environments, and reciprocal-contingent family interactions. *Journal of Deaf Studies and Deaf Education, 29*, 322–334.

Ocuto, O. L. (2024b). Understanding deaf children and their home language environments. *Journal of Deaf Studies and Deaf Education, 29*, 434–435.

Patrick, D. L., Edwards, T. C., Kushalnagar, P., Topolski, T., Schick, B., Skalicky, A., & Sie, K. (2018). Caregiver-reported indicators of communication and social functioning for young children who are deaf or hard of hearing. *The Journal of Deaf Studies and Deaf Education, 23*(3), 200–208.

Pénicaud, S., Klein, D., Zatorre, R. J., Chen, J. K., Witcher, P., Hyde, K., & Mayberry, R. I. (2013). Structural brain changes linked to delayed first language acquisition in congenitally deaf individuals. *NeuroImage, 66*, 42–49.

Petitto, L. A., & Ferraro, V. (2001). Bilingual signed and spoken language acquisition from birth: Implications for the mechanisms underlying early bilingual language acquisition. *Journal of Child Language, 28*, 453–496.

Rinaldi, P., & Caselli, M. C. (2014). Language development in a bimodal bilingual child with cochlear implant: A longitudinal study. *Bilingualism: Language and Cognition, 17*(4), 798–809.

Rosemond, Z. (2018). The importance of serve and return in the infant classroom settings. *Training and Practice, 16*(3), 45–50.

Sanzo, K. (2022). Benefits of visual language: How acquisition of a signed language complements spoken language development. *Perspectives of the ASHA Special Interest Groups*, 1–8.

Secora, K., & Smith, D. (2021). The benefit of the "and" for considerations of language modality for deaf and hard-of-hearing children. *Perspectives of the ASHA Special Interest Groups, 6*, 397–401.

Skotara, N., Salden, U., Kügow, M., Hänel-Faulhaber, B., & Röder, B. (2012). The influence of language deprivation in early childhood on L2 processing: An ERP comparison of deaf native signers and deaf signers with a delayed language acquisition. *BMC Neuroscience, 13*, 1–14.

Smith, S. R., & Samar, V. J. (2016). Dimensions of deaf/hard-of-hearing and hearing adolescents' health literacy and health knowledge. *Journal of Health Communication, 21*(sup2), 141–154.

Szarkowski, A. (2019). Language development in children with cochlear implants: Possibilities and challenges. In N. S. Glickman & W. C. Hall (Eds.), *Language deprivation and deaf mental health* (pp. 235–262). Routledge.

Thompson, R. (2012). Bridging developmental neuroscience and the law: Child-caregiver relationships. *Hastings Law Journal, 63*(6).

Twardosz, S., & Lutzker, J. R. (2010). Child maltreatment and the developing brain: A review of neuroscience perspectives. *Aggression and Violent Behavior, 15*, 59–68.

Wilkinson, E., & Morford, J. P. (2020). How bilingualism contributes to healthy development in deaf children: A public health perspective. *Maternal and Child Health Journal, 24*(11), 1330–1338.

World Health Organization. (2004). *The importance of caregiver-child interactions for the survival and healthy development of young children: A review.*

Zarchy, R. (2023). *Effects of family-centered ASL instruction on hearing parents' child-directed signing* [Unpublished doctoral capstone]. Rocky Mountain University of Health Professions.

Chapter 3
Understanding and Teaching Theory of Mind in DHH Children

Cathy J. Chovaz and Emnette Tesfamariam

Theory of Mind and Deaf and Hard-of-Hearing Children

Understanding the development of ToM in DHH children is one of the main tenets of this chapter and is a complicated construct. To untangle this, we will begin by providing some contextual background on deafness in children and the salient concepts potentially intersecting with ToM.

Theory of Mind

Theory of Mind (ToM) is the ability to attribute mental states to oneself or another. It is an important social-cognitive skill typically emerging by 18 months, with competence established between the ages of three and five years. Cognitive ToM encompasses the ability to understand and reason about beliefs, intentions, and knowledge. The classic Sally-Anne task shows Anne moving a marble out of Sally's basket and placing it in her own box while Sally is out of the room (Baron-Cohen et al., 1985). A child with ToM determines Sally will *first* look for the marble in her basket, recognizing people's perspective or mental state may differ from their own or from objective truth (see Fig. 3.1). Affective ToM focuses on recognizing and understanding the emotions and feelings of oneself or another (Westby & Robinson, 2014). Emotion recognition involves the ability to match facial expressions to

C. J. Chovaz (✉)
Department of Psychology, King's College at Western University, London, ON, Canada
e-mail: Cathy.chovaz@uwo.ca

E. Tesfamariam
Emnette Tesfamariam, King's College at Western University, London, ON, Canada

T. Bone (ed.), *Deaf Mental Health*, Advances in Mental Health and Addiction,
https://doi.org/10.1007/978-3-032-06274-1_3

Fig. 3.1 Sally-Anne Task

feelings, predict someone's primary emotions in a situation, and understand that people may conceal their true emotions.

Development of ToM

Although ToM develops on a continuum, distinct developmental markers are evident throughout childhood and adolescence. Early precursors to mental state reasoning involve pretend play and joint attention (Doherty, 2009). Pretend play emerges at 18 months and facilitates ToM abilities through the extensive modelling of various mindsets. Furthermore, joint attention activities equip 3-year-old children with an explicit understanding that seeing/not seeing differs and reflects individual thought. Mastery in specific ToM skills tends to follow consecutive realizations that others have unique desires, beliefs, knowledge, and emotions (Wellman & Liu, 2004). Particularly, metarepresentational thought, identified through the false belief (FB) task, is widely acknowledged as a "tipping point" in ToM development. Whereas 3-year-old children struggle with the metarepresentational nature of FB tasks, typically developing children acquire this skill at around age 4 (Wellman et al., 2013). More advanced ToM tasks such as second-order FB and sarcasm develop throughout elementary school (Westby & Robinson, 2014). Second-order FB skills imply a child's realization that it is possible to hold a FB about someone else's belief. Sarcasm, double bluffs, and faux pas require a child to understand that a literal meaning can contrast with an intended meaning, people might not mean what they say, and interpretative cues can be gleaned from context or tone of voice (Westby & Robinson, 2014).

Language Acquisition in the Development of ToM

Decades of compelling research has shown that language and ToM are clearly intertwined, and yet the exact mechanism by which language engenders ToM development continues to be explored. Does language precede ToM, does ToM precede language or do both constructs develop together? Although beyond the scope of this chapter, it is well accepted that language acquisition is particularly important for ToM development as it provides a system for the child to think and converse about mental states (Doherty, 2009). There also appears to be strong positive associations between early language development and stronger ToM performance (Farrar & Maag, 2002).

Effective communication demands the anticipation of a listener's mental state and inference of a speaker's mental state (i.e., pragmatics; Doherty, 2009). Mental-state recognition is fostered through dialogic references to words like *think* and *pretend.* Schick et al. (2007) note that language is a specific way in which the mind is conveyed in actionable terms. Mental states, abstract or concrete, are often represented through complements which are dependent and embedded under communication verbs (e.g., say, tell, ask, etc.) or mental-state verbs (e.g., think, believe, know, etc.). For instance, the mental-state verb *believe* allows for a false proposition in the complement clause "Marge believed her chair giggled" by contextualizing the state-specificity of Marge's mental world. Thus, language, through conversational exposure, becomes one primary way children are habituated to differences in perspective.

In summary, children with ToM can predict another's behaviour by inferring their desires, beliefs, knowledge, intentions, and/or emotions. A child's ability to separate their internal mind from the external world serves as a foundational basis for inter- and intrapersonal interactions. Their ability to sense what others are thinking and formulate a response to it greatly impacts their overall emotional/social functioning and well-being, especially their capacity to perspective-take in social relationships.

Atypical ToM Development

Children denied or blocked neurodevelopmentally from opportunities that develop ToM skills tend to have lifelong difficulties. These may include misunderstanding the intentions of others, lacking insight into how their behaviour affects others, struggling with social reciprocity, developing abstract language, and relationship skills. Indeed, studies done in a clinical population assert ToM is a dynamic construct impacted by individual experience (Sprung, 2010). A child's understanding of mental states can be impaired/delayed or derailed/biased from a typical range (e.g., bullies with advanced ToM). While some ToM deficits can be overcome, one may fail to ever understand certain aspects of ToM (Sprung, 2010).

Baron-Cohen et al. (1985) were among the first researchers to suggest that deficits or delays in ToM in children with autism may be the reason for their difficulties with social interactions. These deficits in social-cognitive skills generate difficulties with FB understanding (Baron-Cohen et al., 1985), sometimes more so than advanced tasks targeting affective ToM (Peterson et al., 2005). Likewise, social functioning challenges associated with attention-deficit hyperactivity disorder may cause deficits in social cognition. Although not well understood in all contexts, dysfunctional ToM has been identified in over 30 different mental disorders (Sprung et al., 2022).

Deaf and Hard-of-Hearing Children (DHH) and Language Acquisition

DHH children are a very diverse group with different abilities, different challenges, and different outcomes. These differences include hearing threshold (i.e., mild to profound hearing loss), age of identification, medical history, educational history, family composition, and cultural identity. DHH children, though not confined to, may use signed and/or spoken language with (or without) a technological aid (cochlear implants, hearing aids). Moreover, DHH children are often at a higher risk of mental health disorders relative to their hearing peers (Aanondsen et al., 2023; Du Feu & Chovaz, 2014).

The common factors within this diversity include the critical need for early and consistent access to a full language (signed, spoken or both) which may be challenging within some families. Hearing parents of DHH children are far more common than Deaf parents with Deaf children. Research on the families with hearing parents/DHH children has well described the elevated stress factors and communicative barriers (Hintermair, 2006; Pipp-Siegel et al., 2002; Quittner et al., 2010), as well as the significant behavioural and emotional difficulties often experienced by the children. The reader should note that, despite the literature typically focusing on the negative challenges facing hearing parents of DHH children, Szarkowski and Brice (2016) provided qualitative descriptions of these families that also reflect enriched parenting experience and overall improved life satisfaction.

The salient issue relevant to the development of ToM (and this chapter) is the DHH child's language acquisition. All babies (hearing and deaf) are born with an innate ability to learn language. Language acquisition is a subconscious, instinctive process which is both amazingly simple and amazingly complex. The simplicity is that, barring catastrophic events or genetic anomalies, babies are born with brains hardwired and structured for language acquisition (Ambridge & Lieven, 2011; Kuhl, 2000). The complexity is that this acquisition is very much dependent on the successful and necessary connections made between brain cells. These connections are highly impacted by experiences provided by the child's environment. The linguistic experiential exposure needs to happen during a neurodevelopmentally critical time, which is approximately the first five years of development (Hall et al., 2017). Lack of, or delays in, language exposure during this early time of brain development affects neurolinguistic structures, resulting in an irreversible biological impact on both the brain and healthy development (Hall et al., 2017; Pénicaud et al., 2013; Skotara et al., 2012).

Although language acquisition happens naturally with accessible exposure, the constellation of diverse circumstances may be vastly different for DHH children. Deaf parents of Deaf children are native signers and enjoy conversational opportunities to the same extent as their hearing peers (Humphries et al., 2012; Woolfe et al., 2002), whereas hearing parents of DHH children often experience a disconnect. Spoken language despite cochlear implants, intensive auditory-therapy and full immersion in a spoken environment may not be easily accessible to some DHH children (Spellun & Kushalnagar, 2018).

Currently, most children born deaf in the developed world receive cochlear implants to hopefully ensure consistent and accessible exposure to sound (Brentari, 2010). However, the outcomes of cochlear implants are variable, and a significant number of studies have documented serious and significant concerns with first-language acquisition in implanted Deaf children (Humphries et al., 2024). This, however, continues to be a controversial point in both the literature as well as clinical paradigms. Certainly, many implanted DHH children continue to be seriously delayed or deprived of early exposure to a *fully* accessible language.

Language Deprivation

The acquisition of language can be one of the most significant challenges DHH children face (Du Feu & Chovaz, 2014; Glickman & Hall, 2018). Gulati (2018) applied the term *language deprivation* to DHH children who experienced less than necessary/sufficient access to a first language (either spoken or signed). Environments deprived of language hinder the DHH child from accessing mentalistic conversation. Therefore, delayed ToM development in DHH children may be partly explained by suboptimal exposure to a fully accessible language (Schick et al., 2007). Furthermore, any degree of language deprivation is often accompanied by additional challenges with executive functioning, social-emotional skills and relationships, and learning (Hall et al., 2017). More specifically, DHH children with language delays present with significant psychological distress, including inattention, distractibility, symptoms of mood disruption, lack of empathy, difficulties with emotional regulation, and inability to engage in perspective-taking. This clinically complex presentation may result in multiple misdiagnoses or accurate mental health diagnoses. It is disconcerting and devastating that language deprivation in DHH children, which significantly affects ToM development has been described as a neurodevelopmental disorder with sociocultural origins (Hall et al., 2017).

Mental Health Counselling of DHH Children

Our mental health clinic near a large Canadian city provides a variety of counselling services to DHH children and their families. These services include screening for mental health disorders, formulating appropriate and accessible intervention plans, and evaluating outcomes. Provided services match the first and preferred language of the child, with most children presenting as users of American Sign Language (ASL). The frontline staff are all Deaf clinicians.

During a review of our services, it became apparent that a number of our young clients were not making progress in counselling. We recognized that the children presenting to our clinic were typically complex, often presenting with multiple diagnoses (some of which we did not confirm with our own internal psychological assessments), and many with delayed identification of deafness and subsequent exposure to language. Through many clinical discussions, we began to wonder if delays in the development of ToM may be a critical factor in the success of counselling. Like Glickman and Hall's (2018) recommendation of pre-therapy for deaf adults who are linguistically, cognitively, and developmentally unprepared to use therapy, we wondered if our clients were (1) presenting with delays in Theory of Mind and (2) if this could potentially be a block to the efficacy of accessible counselling?

A search of the literature indicated that tools assessing mental-state understanding posed a two-part problem for DHH children: lack of conceptual range and language dependency. Many of our non-native signing DHH children presented with significantly impaired or dysfluent sign and/or spoken language skills. Dysfluent language is unclear, poorly developed, and insufficient for routine conversational use by native signers and is a common result of language-deficient environments (Glickman & Hall, 2018). This presents challenges as most ToM tasks require considerable language skills regardless of linguistic modality.

A search for nonverbal ToM measures revealed a singular focus on FBs and/or tasks requiring low verbal responses (Schick et al., 2007; Woolfe et al., 2002). The sentence structures used to present FB tasks uniquely require mastery of mental-state verbs. It can be difficult then to use pictures to convey the same meaning. Language-dependent tasks that require language-based responses also demand visual coordination from the child. Together then, this may prohibit language-delayed DHH children from adequately relaying their understanding of mental states. Therefore, late-signing DHH children may have been underestimated in their ToM capabilities (Woolfe et al., 2002), especially when ToM is assessed with a single point of measure (Marschark et al., 2000). Within a narrative task, 87% of DHH children demonstrated an understanding that mental states have a causal effect on behaviour, cautioning against preliminary claims of ToM deficits due to failing FB tasks (Marschark et al., 2000). Our search further confirmed DHH children lacked an accessible opportunity to relay mental states through ToM tasks. This prompted the novel development of a nonverbal ToM assessment spanning a range of topics.

Development of a Non-verbal ToM Screener for DHH Children

To address the need for a more accessible ToM screener for DHH children, we modified Wellman and Liu's (2004) 5-item scale covering a range of ToM abilities, including desires, beliefs, ignorance, FB, and emotion reasoning. Given that Peterson et al. (2005) confirmed DHH children follow the same developmental ToM progression, we elected to minimize language demands using animated scenes via a digital software *Storyboard* that:

1. Verbal cues were made visual using thought bubbles, facial/body expressions, opened/closed doors, on/off lights, and room transitions.
2. Gender, age, and name changes were made when appropriate to diversify characters (non-Anglicized names) and/or due to available props in software.
3. Open-ended questions were structured to include a pool of "choose" options from a related collection of props (e.g., crayon box duplicates with pens/crayons/

glue sticks). The final task targeting hidden emotions employed a locker door to mimic the seen/not seen element of child internal/external feeling.

4. Task objectives, target, and control questions were appropriately retained. Short, simple pre-recorded ASL directives were used to prime question understanding and cue responses. Side-by-side animated scenes (see Fig. 3.2) utilize ASL to cue pointing (e.g., "Which snack will he choose, the carrot or cookie?"). No language-based response was required (pointing only).
5. Final animations were organized in PowerPoint presentations with associated ASL phrases (signed by a Deaf therapist) embedded via picture-in-picture (PIP).

We conducted a pilot study using our nonverbal ToM screener with 26 DHH children/youth aged 8 to 19 ($M_{age} = 13.31$, $SD = 3.60$; see Table 3.1). DHH children/youth were recruited during the clinic intake process, where informed consent was provided by parents and/or children aged 12 + .

To assign levels of ToM understanding we developed categorical scoring: lack of ToM (0), preliminary ToM (1–2), a foundation of ToM (3–4), and advanced ToM (5). Categories were determined with the sequential reasoning of Wellman and Liu's (2004) scale. For instance, grasping differences in desire and belief precedes recognizing that someone can hold a FB. Therefore, foundational ToM is often anchored in successful FB performance, while emotion recognition tasks establish advanced ToM capabilities. Based on this rating scale, our results showed that 53.8% of the sample was considered as having preliminary ToM (scored 1–2) meaning roughly the other half of the group did not (barring 2: failed all tasks).

Notably, 50% of the sample diverged from the developmental sequence established in Wellman and Liu's (2004) study and previous replications. Typical progression arranges successful task performance in a hierarchy where passing a later task conveys similar success on prior tasks (e.g., passing FB implies passing **all**

Fig. 3.2 Frame from Diverse Desires Task

Table 3.1 Demographic information (n = 26)

Variable	Characteristic	n	%
Racial/ethnicity	White/Caucasian	14	53.8
	Black/African American	3	11.5
	Asian/Pacific Islander	3	11.5
	South Asian	3	11.5
	Multiracial/Biracial	2	7.7
	Indigenous	1	3.8
Gender	Male	15	57.7
	Female	11	4.3
Parent hearing status	Both hearing	23	88.5
	Both deaf	3	11.5
Parental communication with child	ASL	10	38.5
	Oral	7	26.9
	ASL/Oral	6	23.1
	Pen/paper	2	7.7
	Other	1	3.8
Child's communication preference	ASL	19	73.1
	Spoken	4	15.4
	ASL/spoken	3	11.5
Child's level of hearing loss	Moderate	6	23.1
	Moderately severe	1	3.8
	Severe	5	19.2
	Profound	14	53.8
Additional disability	Psychological	9	34.6
	Developmental	2	7.7
	Combination	5	19.2
	Other	1	3.8
	None known	9	34.6
Technological aid	Cochlear implant	9	34.6
	Hearing aids	9	34.6
	Bone anchored hearing aid	1	3.8
	Bimodal CI/hearing aid	3	11.5
	None	4	15.4
Educational settings	Deaf/ASL environment/	19	73.1
	schoolmainstreamed (deaf)	7	26.9

previous tasks). See Table 3.2 for a breakdown of our sample's distinct task performance.

Development of Clinic ToM Modules

In response to these results, we developed two levels of foundational ToM skills for children showing delays in ToM development. The first module builds on the classic Sally-Anne tasks, and the second module focuses on thoughts, feelings, actions, knowledge, beliefs, and respect. We consider this essential pre-work prior to counselling (Fig. 3.3).

Table 3.2 Brief description of ToM tasks and pass/fail rate

ToM task	Brief description	Pass	Fail
Diverse desires (69.2%)	Child judges a character can have a different desire than them toward same objects	18	8
Diverse beliefs (34.6%)	Child judges a character can have different beliefs than them about the same object, when unaware of which belief is true or false	9	17
Knowledge access (34.6%)	Child judges a character's knowledge of what is in a box, when they have seen inside it and the character has not	9	17
False belief (30.8%)	Child judges a character's false belief about a distinctive container (crayon box), when aware of what is in the container	8	18
Real-apparent emotion (38.5%)	Child judges a character's internal feelings can differ from their displayed emotion	10	16

Percentages denote pass rate.

Fig. 3.3 Example of Clinic ToM Level 1 Module

Development of Family ToM Guide

We feel it is helpful to have parents work with their DHH child within the family environment, parallel to what the therapists are doing within the clinic. As such, we have developed Family ToM Guides that target the main tenets of ToM interventions: exposure to mental-state vocabulary, linguistic structures, and perspective-taking discourse via group discussion and/or storybooks. These family modules will provide an information package for parents regarding the concept of Theory of Mind as well as strategies for how to incorporate this in everyday life.

Summary

Ultimately, language acquisition is comparable to a doorway. Language is critical for the development of ToM, yet this can only happen when the child is consistently in the metaphorical language room with a willing communicative partner. Lacking an awareness of the world, knowledge about the self and others, as well as behavioural and cognitive strategies are among the sequelae of delayed ToM acquisition in DHH children who lack a fluent conversational partner.

The challenge is how can we best support DHH children without first language fluency in monitoring mental states effectively? We feel training programmes for DHH children that target ToM via language-focused exercises need to be readily accessible to families, teachers, and counsellors working with DHH children. Given the vital role early social exchanges play in ToM acquisition, we have developed family-focused strategies that coincide with clinical or educational paradigms. These family modules are shared with parents of DHH children who are referred to our mental health clinic. These modules are intentionally designed to be readily understood so that parents learn natural ways of incorporating mental-state-rich conversations in their everyday interactions with their DHH child. We have included online resources for parents, such as relevant storybooks, movies, and videos in ASL as well as provided access to ASL emotion rich signs such as think, wonder, dream, scared, happy, and curious. Indeed, it is essential that hearing parents engage in intentional mental-state language, as DHH children need to be brought into the room for healthy and adaptive developmental growth.

References

Aanondsen, C. M., Jozefiak, T., Lydersen, S., Heiling, K., & Rimehaug, T. (2023). Deaf and hard-of-hearing children and adolescents' mental health, quality of life and communication. *BMC Psychiatry, 23*(1), 297–297. https://doi.org/10.1186/s12888-023-04787-9

Ambridge, B., & Lieven, E. V. M. (2011). *Language acquisition: Contrasting theoretical approaches*. Cambridge University Press.

Baron-Cohen, S., Leslie, A. M., & Frith, U. (1985). Does the autistic child have a "theory of mind"? *Cognition, 21*(1), 37–46. https://doi.org/10.1016/0010-0277(85)90022-8

Brentari, D. (Ed.). (2010). *Sign Languages*. Cambridge University Press. https://doi.org/10.1017/CBO9780511712203

Doherty, M. J. (2009). *Theory of mind: How children understand others' thoughts and feelings*. Psychology Press.

Du Feu, M., & Chovaz, C. J. (2014). *Mental health and deafness*. Oxford University Press.

Farrar, M. J., & Maag, L. (2002). Early language development and the emergence of a theory of mind. *First Language, 22*(2), 197–213. https://doi.org/10.1177/014272370202206504

Glickman, N. S., & Hall, W. C. (2018). Pre-therapy with deaf people with language and learning challenges. In *Language deprivation and deaf mental health* (1st ed.). Routledge. https://doi.org/10.4324/9781315166728

Gulati, S. (2018). Language deprivation syndrome. In S. Glickman & W. C. Hall (Eds.), *Language deprivation and deaf mental health* (pp. 24–53). Routledge. https://doi.org/10.4324/9781315166728

Hall, W. C., Levin, L. L., & Anderson, M. L. (2017). Language deprivation syndrome: A possible neurodevelopmental disorder with sociocultural origins. *Sociology, Psychiatry, Psychology, Epidemiology, 52*(6), 761–776. https://doi.org/10.1007/s00127-017-1351-7

Hintermair, M. (2006). Parental resources, parental stress, and socioemotional development of deaf and hard of hearing children. *Journal of Deaf Studies and Deaf Education, 11*(4), 493–513.

Humphries, T., Kushalnagar, P., Mathur, G., Napoli, D. J., Padden, C., Rathmann, C., & Smith, S. R. (2012). Language acquisition for deaf children: Reducing the harms of zero tolerance to the use of alternative approaches. *Harm Reduction Journal, 9*(1), 16. https://doi.org/10.1186/1477-7517-9-16

Humphries, T., Mathur, G., Napoli, D. J., & Rathmann, C. (2024). An approach designed to fail deaf children and their parents and how to change it. *Harm Reduction Journal, 21*(1), NA. http://dx.doi.org.proxy1.lib.uwo.ca/10.1186/s12954-024-01039-1

Kuhl, P. K. (2000). A new view of language acquisition. *Proceedings of the National Academy of Sciences of the United States of America, 97*(22), 11850–11857. https://doi.org/10.1073/pnas.97.22.11850

Marschark, M., Green, V., Hindmarsh, G., & Walker, S. (2000). Understanding theory of mind in children who are deaf. *Journal of Child Psychology and Psychiatry, 41*(8), 1067–1073. https://doi.org/10.1111/1469-7610.00694

Pénicaud, S., Klein, D., Zatorre, R. J., Chen, J. K., Witcher, P., Hyde, K., & Mayberry, R. I. (2013). Structural brain changes linked to delayed first language acquisition in congenitally deaf individuals. *NeuroImage, 66*, 42–49. https://doi.org/10.1016/j.neuroimage.2012.09.076

Peterson, C. C., Wellman, H. M., & Liu, D. (2005). Steps in theory-of-mind development for children with deafness or autism. *Child Development, 76*(2), 502–517. https://doi.org/10.1111/j.1467-8624.2005.00859.x

Pipp-Siegel, S., Sedey, A. L., & Yoshinaga-Itano, C. (2002). Predictors of parental stress in mothers of young children with hearing loss. *Journal of Deaf Studies and Deaf Education, 7*(1), 1–17.

Quittner, A. L., Barker, D. H., Cruz, I., Snell, C., Grimley, M. E., Botteri, M., & CDaCI Investigative Team. (2010). Parenting stress among parents of deaf and hearing children: Associations with language delays and behavior problems. *Parenting: Science and Practice, 10*(2), 136–155.

Schick, B., de Villiers, P., de Villiers, J., & Hoffmeister, R. (2007). Language and theory of mind: A study of deaf children. *Child Development, 78*(2), 376–396.

Skotara, N., Salden, U., Kügow, M., Hänel-Faulhaber, B., & Röder, B. (2012). The influence of language deprivation in early childhood on L2 processing: An ERP comparison of deaf native signers and deaf signers with a delayed language acquisition. *BMC Neuroscience, 13*(1), 44–44. https://doi.org/10.1186/1471-2202-13-44

Spellun, A., & Kushalnagar, P. (2018). Sign language for deaf infants: A key intervention for a developmental emergency. *Clinical Pediatrics*. https://doi.org/10.1177/0009922818778041

Sprung, M. (2010). Clinically relevant measures of children's theory of mind and knowledge about thinking: Non-standard and advanced measures. *Child and Adolescent Mental Health, 15*(4), 204–216. https://doi.org/10.1111/j.1475-3588.2010.00568.x

Sprung, M., Burghardt, J., Mazza, M., & Riffer, F. (2022). Editorial: Misunderstanding others: Theory of mind in psychological disorders. *Frontiers in Psychology, 13*, 838853–838853. https://doi.org/10.3389/fpsyg.2022.838853

Szarkowski, A., & Brice, P. J. (2016). Hearing parents' appraisals of parenting a deaf or hard-of-hearing child: Application of a positive psychology framework. *Journal of Deaf Studies and Deaf Education, 21*(3), 249–258. https://doi.org/10.1093/deafed/enw007

Wellman, H. M., & Liu, D. (2004). Scaling of theory-of-mind tasks. *Child Development, 75*, 523–541. https://doi.org/10.1111/j.1467-8624.2004.00691.x

Wellman, H. M., Peterson, C. C., & Eccles, J. S. (2013). Deafness, thought bubbles, and theory-of-mind development. *Developmental Psychology, 49*(12), 2357–2367. https://doi.org/10.1037/a0032419

Westby, C., & Robinson, L. (2014). A developmental perspective for promoting theory of mind. *Topics in Language Disorders, 34*(4), 362–382. https://doi.org/10.1097/TLD.0000000000000035

Woolfe, T., Want, S. C., & Siegal, M. (2002). Signposts to development: Theory of mind in deaf children. *Child Development, 73*(3), 768–778. https://doi.org/10.1111/1467-8624.00437

Chapter 4
The Biopsychosocial Assessment of the Patient Who Is Deaf or Hard of Hearing

Kimberly K. Mathos and Jennifer Macioce

Introduction

Hearing loss affects 15–26% of the world's population (Fellinger et al. 2012). It is a very heterogeneous condition. Hearing loss has far-reaching impact on social, emotional, and cognitive functioning. In the United States, 2 out of every 1000 babies are born with detectable hearing loss in one or both ears. In the United States, 27% of Deaf and hard-of-hearing children between the ages of 6 and 19 years of age have additional disabilities (www.nidcd.nih.gov).

The degree of hearing loss and age of onset of hearing loss will influence the language, communication, and the formation of a person's identity. The onset of hearing loss before language development happens in about 1 per 1000 people. Language development typically begins between 10 and 14 months.

An audiologist can quantify the degree of hearing loss that a person has at different decibels of loudness and at various sound pitches. A person must have the capacity to appreciate sounds in the 20–30 decibel range to discern spoken language (Fig. 4.1).

The most common type of hearing loss is called presbycusis and is a type of hearing loss that occurs late in a person's life (www.nidcd.nih.gov). Many senior citizens lose their hearing as they age, and most frequently the loss is in the high-frequency range sounds. This means that a person might struggle to make out specific words that end in soft sounds, or they may have great difficulty hearing a

K. K. Mathos, D.O, M.P.H. (✉)
Department of Psychiatry, Univerisity of Pittsburgh Medical Center, Pittsburgh, PA, USA

University of Pittsburgh Medical Center, UPMC, Pittsburgh, United States
e-mail: Mathoskk2@upmc.edu

J. Macioce
Jennifer Macioce LCSW, ICGC-11, Pittsburgh, PA, USA

T. Bone (ed.), *Deaf Mental Health*, Advances in Mental Health and Addiction,
https://doi.org/10.1007/978-3-032-06274-1_4

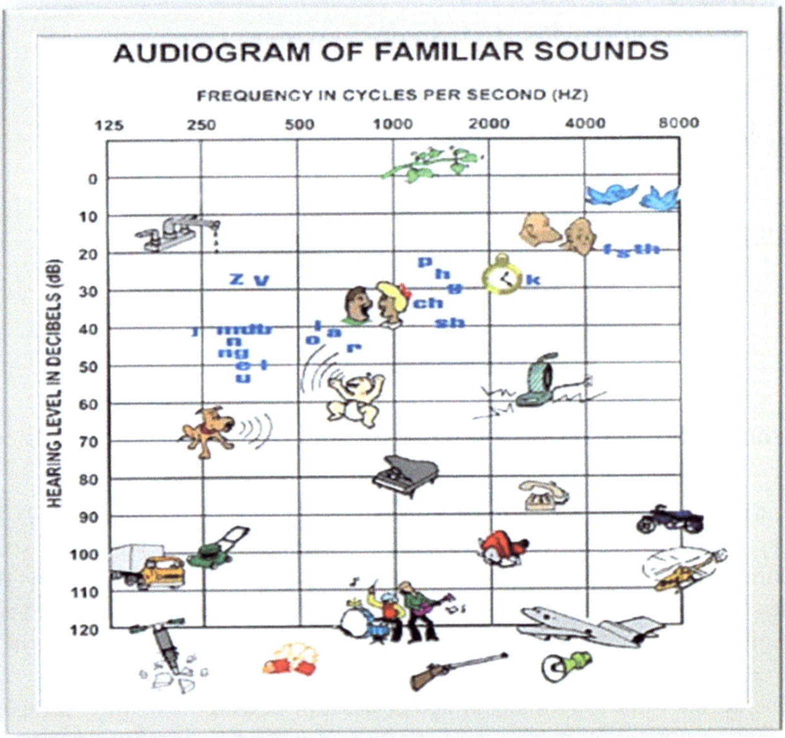

Fig. 4.1 Representation of a graphic image of the various levels of hearing loss (Mathos, 2019)

child's voice, which is typically of higher pitch. The kind of hearing loss that a senior citizen may develop is often related to degeneration of the inner ear or auditory nerve.

Senior citizens who are born with normal hearing usually socialize with people who also have normal hearing throughout their lifetime. Their friends and family do not typically know American Sign Language (ASL). Seniors may prefer adopting communication strategies that use their residual hearing. They benefit from visual cues to assist with their failing speech recognition. They prefer to socialize in an environment where there is less background noise and better lighting so that they can lip read more easily. They may benefit from technology such as amplified sound systems, voice-to-text applications on their phone, or TV with captions or amplification to help them feel more connected to other people.

Among people who do not rely on their hearing for communication, there is a group of individuals who use ASL to communicate. Many people who use ASL are members of a Deaf community. In referencing this community, it is common to capitalize the word "Deaf." This group maintains social connectedness through Deaf organizations, unique art forms, and social events. Deaf culture is a rich and beautiful celebration of the cherished language and kindred experiences made possible through ASL. A person who learns and adopts this visual language will want to be with others who share that language.

In the examples below, we will begin to describe the diversity of communication strategies, reliance on hearing, or adoption of ASL that can shape identity development.

Case Scenarios

Case #1

Helen is a 60-year-old female from a rural area in eastern Pennsylvania. She is the only person with hearing loss in her family. She lost her hearing due to contracting meningitis at age 2. She went to a school with hearing children when she was young. She had only one friend who also had hearing loss. She chose to go to the National Technical Institute for the Deaf in Rochester, New York, when she chose a college. She wanted to pick a college where there is a greater number of Deaf and hard-of-hearing people. Helen speaks but also uses ASL.

Case #2

Joan is a 30-year-old female who has experienced profound hearing loss since birth. Her parents communicate in ASL. Her parents are both proud members of the Deaf community. Joan attended a local residential school for the Deaf. At this school, she met her future husband. Her husband also communicates in ASL. Joan now works with other people who are Deaf and use ASL.

Case #3

John is a 40-year-old male who developed hearing loss in elementary school following an attack of meningitis as a toddler. He attended an oral school for the Deaf. He was diagnosed with a hearing loss in his left ear and a moderate loss in his right ear. He learned to read and use amplification when he was young. He went on to college and got a degree in architectural engineering. He made use of preferential seating, notetaking, and used an FM system[1]in college and graduate school. John decided to

[1]An FM system is a wireless assistive listening device that helps people with hearing loss hear more effectively in noisy environments by transmitting a speaker's voice directly to the listener's

get a cochlear implant when he was 30 years old and his hearing loss had become more profound. His fiancée and his peer group do not use American Sign Language.

Case #4

Tanya is a 40-year-old female who has intellectual disabilities. She has been identified as having CHARGE syndrome as the etiology of her deafness (). Because she has CHARGE syndrome, she also has a plethora of other health conditions. She has had a heart transplant, and she now has renal failure and visual loss. Her language is limited, and she has developed what is called "home signs." This means that she communicates by using gestures and fingerspelling of simple words, which are mostly nouns, to communicate. She went to a school where sign language was not encouraged. Her parents also have intellectual disabilities. Her parents therefore also needed more parent training and advocacy support to learn about community resources, and assistive technology that would help their adult daughter stay connected to peers.

The Initial Encounter

The first task in a mental health assessment is to ask the patient to describe their preferred language and accommodation needs. A person might request a Sign Language interpreter if their native language is ASL. If they are hard of hearing, they may prefer using a voice-to-text application or an FM system. Some may request an oral interpreter or a transcript of a meeting.

The language and accommodation strategies that a person prefers must be documented in the medical chart and utilized at each visit. This is crucial for several reasons, including ensuring continuity of care, facilitating communication among healthcare professionals, and supporting legal and reimbursement needs (Fig. 4.2).

History Gathering

The mental health clinician should gather information about such things as whether deafness was identified at birth, prior to the onset of language, or thereafter.

The timing of the hearing loss, the degree of hearing loss, and whether changes in hearing were acute or progressive is important to note. Some hearing loss comes

---

hearing aid through a dedicated radio frequency. The speaker wears a microphone (transmitter) and the listener wears a receiver connected to their hearing aids.

Panel 1: How to interact with deaf patients

- Ask the patient about his or her preferred communicative approach. If it is sign language, collaborate with a signing professional or with a qualified interpreter.
- Engage the patient warmly and directly, with eye-contact as often and for as long as possible. Make it clear when focus needs to shift away—eg, to the computer.
- Be aware of the restricted effectiveness and fatigue of lip reading. Add clear visual elements to discourse—eg, gestures; writing notes; and use of simple, key words and grammar, drawings and many visual aids.
- When speaking, ensure that the patient has the best possible view of your face . Do not stand in front of a light source (eg, a window or lamp).
- When speaking, use simple language and short sentences. Speak at a natural speed and volume. Give clear, concrete examples, and avoid vague, general terms and jargon.
- Avoid simultaneous comments during examination of a deaf patient. Communicate first, then act.
- Accept that good communication with deaf patients takes more time than it does with hearing patients. Plan for long patient visits because of large communication and education needs.
- Check for comprehension. Ask the patient to summarise essential points. Do not ask a patient whether he or she understood, because nodding might not mean comprehension.

Fig. 4.2 Interacting with deaf patients from Fellinger et al. (2012)

in later life because of aging, chemotherapy, recurrent ear infections, chronic noise exposure, or artillery fire, to name a few possible etiologies. Some causes of hearing loss may be due to an infection and present at birth. Toxoplasmosis, rubella, cytomegalovirus, herpes, and other infections can be passed from the mother to the child during pregnancy, delivery, or birth. These infections called the "TORCH" infections can cause later development of conditions such as ADHD, learning disabilities, and even psychosis. Cytomegalovirus is the second most common cause of deafness in children. Meningitis is another condition which is inclined to lead to acquired hearing loss. An attack of meningitis also places a person at risk of developing learning disabilities or attention deficit disorder. Many times, the etiology of a hearing loss is never identified conclusively.

Clinicians should inquire about the presence of other health conditions and be vigilant for specific syndromes that confer risk for other medical and mental health sequelae.

Unique Risks and Vulnerabilities

Most Deaf and hard-of-hearing people are born to hearing parents. It is common that few people in the Deaf child's family learn American Sign Language fluently. Since most parents of deaf people are hearing and do not sign fluently, the relationship that a culturally Deaf person has with their parents and siblings can be strained or superficial. Insecure attachment because of language deprivation can have a devastating impact on social and emotional development and lead to chronic feelings of isolation and devaluation.

Although exclusion may not be intentional, many people who are deaf or hard of hearing feel lonely, angry, and unimportant with their family members. The painful accumulation of being left out over their lifetime leads many deaf and hard-of-hearing people to avoid holiday gatherings with their family. Because people with deafness or hearing loss are often largely excluded from family conversations due to communication barriers, they may not be informed about genetic risks such as a family history of alcoholism or mental illness.

Deaf or hard-of-hearing people are inclined to face oppression and chronic interpersonal devaluation. They have higher rates of unemployment, trauma exposure, sexual abuse, domestic violence and substance abuse (Fellinger et al. 2012).

Most deaf and hard-of-hearing people face barriers to accessing good physical health care. Health care providers may not comply with the request to arrange interpreters (Mathos et al. 2009). Gaps in knowledge about health and mental health topics are the norm (Fellinger et al. 2012).

It is important to assess financial stressors and make note of how a person entertains themselves. It is important to screen for Internet and gaming addiction, gambling, and, for some, victimization from scams due to the heightened use of Internet and social media in the population (Wohl & Niehaus, 2019).

There also continues to be inequities in housing and employment opportunities for deaf and hard-of-hearing people. This discrimination is likely due to a combination of factors including communication barriers, lack of accessibility, negative stereotypes and an unwillingness of landlords or employers to make necessary accommodations like installing visual smoke alarms or alternative entry and security systems.

Review of Symptoms: Important Points to Consider

Mental health clinicians use the Diagnostic and Statistical Manual, which was first published in 1952, to classify and diagnose mental disorders. Inventory checklists in the manual are English-based. Timelines and the chronicity of symptoms are of paramount importance to establish a correct diagnosis. The words for anxiety and depression in ASL do not convey the longitudinal nature of the condition. Patients may need education about the clinical phenomena of depression and other mental health conditions. They may not know that depression is a biologically driven illness that responds to therapy and pharmacotherapy, for example. The interpreter should be instructed to expand on words or concepts which seem to be unfamiliar to the patient who is Deaf.

Contextual cues are very important to convey in ASL as a review of symptoms is conducted. For example, the word "suicide" can be signed as if a person is slashing their wrist. This would be an inquiry only if the clinician wishes to learn whether a person has tried to commit suicide by slashing their wrist and would not translate to include a person who tried to commit suicide by another method such as drug overdose. It is best to spell out the word "suicide" and then cite specific modalities of suicide that a person might consider. Time should be allotted in the appointment to explain symptoms or to provide rationale for the line of questions being posed.

Relevant Treatment Considerations

People who have hearing loss but do not use American Sign Language face different challenges as they attempt to access mental health services. Hard of hearing and people who are "Oral Deaf" often struggle to find accessible mental health care. "Oral Deaf" people have typically focused on developing listening and spoken language skills and do not use ASL. Their needs are quite distinct from the needs of culturally Deaf individuals.

Hard-of-hearing patients report that they benefit when a mental health clinician is informed about assistive technology and interpersonal stressors related to communication breakdowns. This group of people benefits from learning coping strategies related to adjusting to hearing loss. Topics such as innovative technologies about hearing aids, virtual platforms to include captioning, new voice-to-text applications, the importance of taking mental breaks after prolonged periods of lipreading are a few important points of discussion in therapy. Collaboration with an audiologist is important for people who are hard of hearing. The audiologist can diagnose the cause and extent of hearing loss, prescribe personalized treatment recommendations, and manage conditions like tinnitus and balance disorders.

Therapeutic Interventions

Deaf people who use ASL often benefit from seeing a therapist who is also Deaf or fluent in ASL. Deaf, DeafBlind, and hard-of-hearing people are inclined to trust and turn to those who share their language, cultural background, and life experiences. Hence, they may preferentially align with advocates and other members of their own community. Case management and advocacy, therapy, and peer support should be sought by native signers if such services exist in the community.

ASL is a unique and visually descriptive language and is not simply "English on the hands." Graphics and visual descriptors are of paramount importance to ensure common ground in discussing, evaluating, and treating mood, thought and emotional disorders. Graphics can also be utilized as a sort of diary card to help a person track their moods and identify with feeling states. "Feeling cards," such as the ones below, can also provide a starting point to begin conversation about mood states (Fig. 4.3).

Fig. 4.3 Graphic description to illustrate talking points (Glickman, 2012)

Therapeutic Issues That Arose for the Four Cases Introduced Previously

Helen (Case #1) presented for care of recurrent depression. She identifies as being culturally Deaf but prides herself on her ability to read English. Her parents did not believe she could find a job on her own, go to college, or marry. She attended a college in Rochester, New York. She married a man who was culturally Deaf as well. He never went to college. They had a child who was hearing. They lived in a rural area, where there was a shortage of interpreters. Her family members are only able to fingerspell or use hand shapes that represent letters. They cannot generate full sentences in ASL. Helen's family members often came to interpret at doctor's appointments and school meetings for their hearing son. The family members did not debrief Helen after the meetings to ensure she understood the discussion. Helen felt consistently devalued. She learned to depend on hearing people, though this reliance on them made her angry and depressed. In treatment, one therapeutic goal has been to report on her own accomplishments and to self-advocate when she feels stifled or oppressed.

Joan (Case # 2) comes from a culturally Deaf family. She can communicate well with her family members in ASL. She is married to a Deaf man. She lives in a more urban area of Pennsylvania, where there are many other culturally Deaf individuals. She has a history of bipolar illness. Joan's mother also had bipolar illness. Joan did not know much about bipolar illness when she first came for treatment. Early in her life, she used cocaine, which led her to experience more frequent episodes of mania. Psychoeducation was provided about the dangers of cocaine use. Joan no longer uses cocaine. She has been hospitalized for psychiatric care in the past, but now her mood has been stable. Recently she began to gamble. Joan was unaware of how gambling can become an addiction (ncpgambling.org). In therapy, she has learned to manage her bipolar illness, to establish consistent sleep patterns, and to take medications consistently. She has learned how to identify triggers related to addiction and mental health relapse. Joan celebrates her Deaf cultural identity. She often joins an ocean-liner cruise which is a celebration held annually with former Deaf classmates. Joan is now in sustained recovery. She has a job that she enjoys very much. She is a group-home supervisor at a facility for Deaf individuals who have mental health and intellectual disabilities.

John (Case # 3) was educated as an architect. He previously worked for a large housing firm prior to the COVID-19 pandemic. He has moderate-to-profound hearing loss. He never learned American Sign Language. He is reliant on speechreading. He had a major decline in his mental health during the COVID-19 pandemic when wearing a mask became a public mandate. His workplace began to have remote meetings during COVID. His boss did not recognize his need to have meetings captioned nor did he offer summary sheets of John's job expectations. John also did not self-advocate for these accommodations. Colleagues always wore masks. John left his job because he was overwhelmed, suicidal, and severely depressed and anxious. When he was at work, he often became filled with rage. He had frequent suicidal thoughts. He moved with his brother to Montana, where he found that there were fewer social demands and people were less inclined to wear a mask. John now drives a truck for his brother's company. He continues to receive treatment for anxiety, but he has not returned to his baseline level of functioning.

Tonya (Case #4) lives with her mother and stepfather in a rural part of Pennsylvania. Her parents both have intellectual disabilities. She attended a residential school for the Deaf in her high school years. In special studies classes, there was emphasis on her learning independent-living skills, which were prioritized over communication skills. She did not socialize much with Deaf people in her adult years. She presented for therapy when she began to become aggressive toward her mother. Her mother noted that she felt bad that Tonya did not meet with other Deaf people more often. She enrolled Tonya in a Deaf social-skills group in the nearby city. About 4 months after she began to attend the group, she began to experience nightmares and extreme mood lability. She reported to the leader of the group that her neighbor was demanding that she have sex with him. In therapy, her mother was encouraged to cease contact with this neighbor and to report this crime immediately to the police. Her mother had difficulty setting limits with the neighbor initially because she depended on him for small tasks, such as reading her mail and making small repairs on her home. Tonya's language was quite limited, but she was able to draw pictures about what had happened to her. Tonya and her mother sought treatment at a victim-support agency. Tonya was treated for PTSD and anxiety.

Even though people with hearing differences have an equal, if not greater, risk of having mental health issues, very few people seek treatment (Fellinger et al. 2012). The clinician should be aware that a Deaf or hard-of-hearing person faces many barriers to obtaining mental health care.

Kilbourne et al. (2006) define vulnerable populations as ones that face discrimination and healthcare inequities compared to the general population. Figure 4.4 illustrates key potential determinants of health including, individual, provider, and health care system variables that can impact access to care.

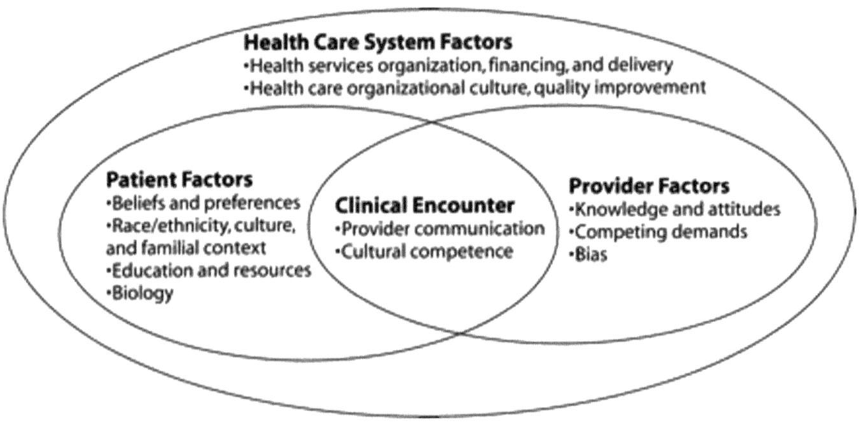

Fig. 4.4 Analyzing health care disparities from Kilbourne et al. (2006)

One barrier is that Deaf and hard-of-hearing people often attribute stress and mental health issues solely to social isolation and communication breakdowns. They may not seek treatment because they do not have information that mental health issues can be treatable.

There have been efforts in some cities to make public service announcements in ASL for the Deaf community. In Western Pennsylvania, a website was created to advertise ASL-fluent and "Deaf friendly" resources (www.healthbridges.info). Mental health clinicians have gone to hearing-loss support groups (www.hearing-loss.org) to present information about mental health and substance abuse challenges and to inform participants as to where intervention can be found.

Lack of knowledge about best-practice strategies for serving Deaf people is an obstacle among many hearing clinicians. Many times, the first encounter may not go well because the clinician is ill-prepared to provide the accommodation needed for the assessment. If the interpreter cannot be arranged, the patient may lose interest in seeking treatment. In the United States, the Americans with Disabilities Act defines that in the healthcare setting, Deaf people who use ASL must be provided an interpreter if their native language is ASL. Payment for the interpreter is the responsibility of the agency that provides the service and is tax deductible (Mathos, 2019). Mental health facilities may be unfamiliar with laws surrounding this topic.

Deaf and hard-of-hearing people are often turned away from mental health services because facilities are unwilling to pay for interpreters or to obtain requested accommodations. A preferential option for the Deaf patient who is seeking care may be to work with a clinician who is fluent in ASL if this option exists. Clinicians who are Deaf or hard-of-hearing themselves or who are ASL fluent are, however, a small group.

The American Deafness and Rehabilitation Association (www.adara.org) is an organization that fosters awareness about the need for specialized mental health services for Deaf and hard-of-hearing people in the United States. Membership includes counselors for people who are Deaf or hard-of-hearing. ADARA has a biannual conference and a journal where members can appreciate innovative practice ideas shared by colleagues.

Interagency networking with other agencies that serve Deaf and hard-of-hearing people is extremely important. Agencies that support Deaf and hard-of-hearing people, such as schools for the Deaf, offices of vocational rehabilitation, employment supports for the Deaf, audiology clinics, and advocacy groups, are important collaborative partners.

In the United States, telehealth has become extremely important and more common as a modality to provide mental health care. This modality of treatment became commonplace following the COVID-19 pandemic. Virtual therapy is uniquely suited for Deaf people who are fluent in ASL and who need a linguistically and culturally attuned skilled provider who may not be available in their own local community.

While there has been great expansion of private practice providers who work on virtual platforms with culturally Deaf people, when patients need more intense services, they often encounter many obstacles related to interpreter costs for hospital stays, rehabilitation, group therapies, support groups, and all levels of ongoing outpatient care.

In some areas of the United States, a small number of agencies, schools, and group homes have developed specifically to care for people who are Deaf or hard of hearing and who struggle with serious mental illness or intellectual disabilities. These agencies are therapeutic because patients are in an environment where they can fully engage with people who share their language and life experience. Patients there can learn coping strategies to deal with their illness effectively.

Points to Ponder

Globally, there is a need to expand mental health services for people who are Deaf and hard of hearing. There is a need for research about mental health in this minority community. There is a need for specialized outreach and for research on the efficacy of specific intervention strategies for this population.

There is a growing interest in addressing behavioral health service delivery to people with hearing differences. Mental health service development for Deaf consumers has been fostered by the formation of task forces comprised of invested stakeholders in some regions and lawsuits in other areas of the country (Mathos & Pollard, 2016). One task force, chaired by the co-author, has been together in western Pennsylvania since 2008. This work group surveys members annually to establish collective goals and action items. Goals in the group have always been set by consensus vote (Butterfoss, 2007). The initial goals were about eight broad topics: resource awareness, information gathering about consumer need, public outreach, community education about mental health, necessary accommodations and social supports, direct service development, workforce development, and the need to establish mentoring opportunities for professionals in training.

It is important in analyzing efforts to improve mental healthcare for minority populations that the ideas for service development come from within the community. We as hearing healthcare providers can be allies to the cause. Clinicians with lived experience must be encouraged to pursue careers in the mental health field.

Fred "Mister" Rogers is a Pittsburgh native; he pioneered TV programming related to altruism and acceptance of diversity. He said, "our job is to help people to realize how rare and valuable each one of us really is and that each one of us has something that no one else has or will ever have. It is our job to encourage each other and to discover that uniqueness" (*Mister Rogers It's a Beautiful Day Book of Quotes*, 2020).

References

Butterfoss, F. (2007). *Coalitions and partnerships in community health*. Jossey-Bass.

Fellinger, J., Holzinger, D., & Pollard, R. (2012). Mental health of deaf people. *The Lancet, 379*(9820), 1037–1044.

Glickman, N. (Ed.). (2012). *Deaf mental health care*. Routledge.

Kilbourne, A., Switzer, G., Hyman, K., Crowley-Matoka, M., & Fine, M. (2006). Advancing health disparities research within the health care system: A conceptual framework. *American Journal of Public Health, 12*(96), 2113–2121.

Mathos, K. (2019). The psychiatric assessment of people who are deaf or hard of hearing. *Psychiatric Times, 36*(6), 16+. https://link-gale-com.uml.idm.oclc.org/apps/doc/A593801068/HRCA?u=univmanitoba&sid=bookmark-HRCA&xid=f3095e68

Mathos, K. K., & Pollard, R. Q. (2016). Capitalizing on community resources to build specialized behavioral health services together with persons who are deaf, deafblind or hard of hearing. *Community Mental Health Journal, 52*(2), 187–193. https://doi-org.uml.idm.oclc.org/10.1007/s10597-015-9940-y

Mathos, K., Kilbourne, A., Myers, R., & Post, E. (2009). Disparities in mental health for persons who are deaf: Advancing research towards action. *Journal of the American Deafness and Rehabilitation Association, 42*(3), 152–166.

Wohl, A., & Niehaus, M. (2019). Internet addiction and the deaf community: A case study on risk, treatment implications and the need for more research. *JADARA, 35*(1) Art. 4, 1-7. Retrieved from https://nsuworks.nova.edu/jadara/vol35/iss1/4

Part II
Specialized/Unique Circumstances

Chapter 5
The Practice of Forensic Psychology and the Deaf Community: Key Issues for Clinical Practice and the Legal System

David M. Feldman, Tomina Schwenke, Paul Silvasi, and Tali M. Shir

The Deaf Community

The Forensic Psychologist's role is to aid the court in answering a psycho-legal question by providing specialized knowledge and opinions related to the psychological and cognitive functioning of defendants. In the case of a deaf or hard-of-hearing defendant, this can include cultural and linguistic phenomena rarely understood or accommodated by the legal system. This may include information regarding how hearing loss affects development, language, and communication abilities, and how cultural customs and norms influence deaf and hard-of-hearing individuals' thoughts and behaviors. These factors can have a profound effect on how well deaf and hard-of-hearing defendants are able to navigate the legal system and the fairness of any legal procedures and outcomes.

Competent forensic assessment and treatment of deaf and hard-of-hearing individuals requires that evaluators, providers, attorneys, judges, and legal personnel have a foundational knowledge of deafness and Deaf culture. While deaf and hard-of-hearing individuals make up a significant proportion of the criminal justice system, there has been little effort to understand the cultural, linguistic, and mental health challenges associated with this population (Feldman et al., 2023b; Vernon, 2006). However, the proportion of deaf or hard-of-hearing defendants, or those

D. M. Feldman (✉) · T. M. Shir
College of Psychology, Nova Southeastern University, Fort Lauderdale, FL, USA
e-mail: dfeldman@nova.edu; ts2321@mynsu.nova.edu

T. Schwenke
Emory School of Medicine, Atlanta, GA, USA
e-mail: Tomina.j.schwenke@emory.edu

P. Silvasi
Utah State Hospital, Provo, UT, USA
e-mail: pmsilvasi@utah.gov

T. Bone (ed.), *Deaf Mental Health*, Advances in Mental Health and Addiction,
https://doi.org/10.1007/978-3-032-06274-1_5

involved in some stage of the arrest-to-trial process, at any given time is more fluid and is generally unknown.

The term "deaf/Deaf" is important to define at this early point, as the context of the word(s), and to note that not all deaf people are members of the Deaf community or utilize sign language as a means of communication. The word *deaf* can refer both to the physical ability to hear and to cultural and linguistic identification (Napier et al., 2006). More traditional models of deafness have focused on the inability to hear from a medical or audiological perspective (Branson & Miller, 2002) with little regard to identity and community (Ladd, 2003; Lane et al., 1996). More modern models emphasize culture and sign language (Lane, 1999). An individual's perceptions of their deafness will, among other things, guide their use of language, identity, and role in society. Those who identify as part of the Deaf community and express that identity from a cultural perspective will likely use the term *Deaf*. As both deaf and Deaf identifying persons can be involved with the legal system, we generalize by using *deaf* as a broader representation of the issues and concerns of these individuals involved in various legal stages.

The Deaf community also varies across socioeconomic status, ethnicity, religion, and many other demographics (Foss, 2014; Pray & Jordan, 2010). There is also a wide range in sign language fluency among individuals who are deaf, which may be based on age at hearing-loss onset, early access to language, education, and social factors. The cause of deafness may also have a significant effect on development, and many etiologies of deafness may also include factors associated with intellectual disability and cognitive functioning. For instance, etiologies such as maternal rubella, cytomegalovirus, spinal meningitis, and prematurity can all result in brain damage (Kuntz et al., 2023). In addition, these may affect language development, which in turn could affect such things as understanding legal rights, the ability to provide informed consent, or the demonstration of knowledge of legal information.

It is important to consider here how cultural and language differences are important for the forensic psychologist or other professionals working in the legal system. Culture and language often play a crucial role in the individual's understanding of the world around them, interactions with that world, perceptions of those interactions, and accommodations needed to facilitate accessibility. Deaf individuals are less likely to benefit from the incidental learning that happens when a person can automatically access auditory information within the environment such as communication with attorneys, and the ability to navigate the criminal justice system.

The Legal System and the Deaf Community

In navigating the legal system, deaf suspects and defendants are guaranteed the same rights as their hearing counterparts. The Americans with Disabilities Act (1990) "requires all state and local courts to be accessible to deaf individuals and requires the provision of interpreters, transcription, or other appropriate auxiliary aids for deaf people in court" (National Association of the Deaf, 2015, pp. 161–162).

Generally, these take the form of sign language interpreters, although other accommodations (e.g., assistive technology) may also be provided.

However, the application of these rights is often denied due to misunderstandings, ignorance of needs and rights, or even intentional abuse. The legal system was not designed with deaf individuals in mind and may be inefficient and negligent in its ability to fairly and efficiently process deaf suspects through a myriad of complex procedures and policies. In many cases, this will leave the deaf individual at a significant disadvantage when interacting with the justice system. Police may be unable to effectively communicate with deaf suspects who are left unable to provide information or comply with (verbal) legal orders. The complexities of the legal system may be difficult to translate into sign language and leave the deaf defendant unaware of their rights and unable to make informed decisions.

The recognition of the special circumstances surrounding the interactions of deaf defendants and the legal system is not a new concept. An 1856 article in the American Journal of Insanity entitled "On the Legal Rights and Responsibilities of the Deaf and Dumb" (Peet, 1856) makes several references to the theoretical association between hearing ability, language, intelligence, legal rights, and theology and goes on to cite several cases involving deaf defendants. In all of these cases, no attempts appear to have been made to facilitate communication with, or effort to obtain input from, the deaf defendant.

Around the turn of the century, the Bill of Rights was not well enforced, leading to the conviction of many deaf suspects and defendants who had no concept of their rights (Sheprow, 1999). Although not specific to deaf suspects alone, the cases of *Escobedo v. Illinois* (1964) and *Miranda v. Arizona* (1966) also emphasized communication and the more modern concept of accessibility. By the 1970s, the right to an interpreter in U.S. Court was established in the federal courts with a case involving Rogelio Negrón, who was a Puerto Rican defendant living in New York and working as a farm laborer. He spoke Spanish; however, no interpreter was provided at the trial, and he was convicted of murder. The U.S. Court of Appeals overturned the conviction based on the lack of access to language he could comprehend, and the Court Interpreters Act of 1978 was passed by Congress (Kuntz et al., 2023).

More recent studies have expanded into other areas of the criminal justice system, including interactions with law enforcement and linguistic diversity. Miller and Vernon (2001) investigated due process and found that "between 25 and 40 percent of prelingually deaf persons were at risk for being found incompetent to stand trial" due to what he defined as an "insufficient primitive linguistic level" (King & Vernon, 1999, p. 99). Young et al. (2001) examined the mental health needs of deaf suspects in the UK criminal justice system and the difficulty "to describe adequately this population and to provide appropriate and targeted response to its needs" (p. 567).

The legal system may be divided into three stages or phases (enforcement, justice, and corrections) and the needs of the Deaf individual at each stage may require different types of accommodations. For example, while the provision of sign language interpreters may be a consistent accommodation, the purpose and complexity of what is being communicated may vary; a law enforcement officer arriving at the scene of a crime, the forensic evaluator determining competency, or the correctional officer managing inmates may all require an interpreter with different skill sets and experience.

Interpreters in Legal Settings

It is important to recognize that "interpreting English into ASL and vice-versa requires a great deal of skill; and relying on amateurs who know some sign language is a frequent error" (Dubow et al., 1986, p. 2). Professional criteria for certification as an ASL interpreter have been established by the National Registry of Interpreters for the Deaf (RID, 1979). This certification includes not only training in American Sign Language and translation but also the RID Code of Ethics (1979) and NAD-RID Code of Professional Conduct (2005). However, interpreters alone are not a guarantee of full and equal access (LaVigne & Vernon 2003; Olsen & Kermit, 2014).

It is often assumed that in the case of deaf defendants, simply providing a sign language interpreter will provide equal access to court proceedings. However, "for a number of reasons, nothing could be farther from the truth" (Vernon & Andrews, 2011, p. 6). While there are certainly deaf individuals who would prefer the provision of an ASL interpreter, many deaf defendants have such limited language ability that just providing an ASL interpreter would be inadequate. Vernon and Miller (2001) suggest that "such cases represent linguistic incompetence to stand trial, just as mental retardation and legal insanity represent psychological incompetence" (pp. 429–434) and reference *Holmes v. Florida* (1986) as a case example. It is also important for clinicians to be mindful that when a deaf defendant exhibits low language ability, additional accommodations are needed. For instance, a Certified Deaf Interpreter (CDI) should be retained in many complex legal cases, and when the defendant is not a fluent sign language user, to further break down concepts and facilitate communication.

There are many challenges to deaf individuals in accessing language in legal situations, and misunderstandings and miscommunications are not uncommon (Feldman et al., 2023b). It is not unusual for a deaf suspect to be unaware that an officer is speaking to them or, while detained being grabbed or shouted at to get their attention. In some cases, deaf individuals are asked to wait for long periods of time for interpreters or are provided with insufficiently skilled signers (du Feu & Chovaz, 2014). Finally, even qualified ASL interpreters may *unintentionally* miss some of the nuances and subtleties of legal questioning and testing, add to or change responses based on their understanding of the question, overexplain, or use signs that give away an answer. For optimal results, interpreters and clinicians should discuss the evaluation and communication process before testing to familiarize the clinician with the role of the interpreter and to familiarize the interpreter with the nature and process of the evaluation (Landsberger et al., 2013). Clinicians and evaluators should be aware of challenges within the interpreting process, such as signs that have multiple meanings and English words that do not have signed equivalents.

The civil rights outlined in the Americans with Disabilities Act specifically pertaining to inmates with disabilities are often ignored, or at least not enforced by correctional officials, law enforcement agencies, and the courts (Vernon, 2009). Accommodations for deaf inmates are frequently unavailable, either because of costs or due to staff not being familiar with the need, or existence, accommodations. Despite federal laws dictating the use of interpreters in correctional settings, a 1993 survey found that almost 40% of the responding correctional agencies did not provide interpreters even though 72% indicated they had incarcerated Deaf inmates (McEntee, 1993).

The lack of available and qualified interpreters in correctional facilities may leave the deaf inmate unaware and uninformed of critical information needed for both navigating the correctional system and their personal safety (Miller & Vernon, 2001; Vernon, 2009). Without an interpreter, the deaf inmate may not have the ability to communicate with correctional officers, administrators, and other inmates. They may not be able to fully participate in rehabilitation, educational, religious, and social activities, including visitation with attorneys and loved ones. Unfortunately, the commonly used "easy" solution that is utilized is often worse than having no communication. In an effort to save money and time, many correctional facilities will enlist the aid of a (hearing) inmate who claims to "*know*" sign language, without any verification, to serve as an inmate interpreter. Miller and Vernon (2001) reported at least one documented case where an inmate interpreter put a deaf inmate in physical danger when they leaked information about the deaf inmate's crime to the general population. Second, inmate interpreters may not have the sign language skills to accurately facilitate communication. Third, inmate interpreters may intentionally distort communication between correctional staff and the deaf inmate for their own needs (Vernon, 2010).

Deaf Suspects, Defendants, and Inmates

The US Department of Justice regulates the provision of interpreters for law enforcement and state: "law enforcement agencies should provide for qualified interpreters to assist agencies when dealing with hearing-impaired persons" and "the law enforcement agency has an obligation under federal law to offer an interpreter to the arrestee without cost" (National Association of the Deaf, 2015, pp. 171–172). Furthermore, "complainants and victims are also entitled to have interpreters" (McEntee, 1995, p. 186).

Research on interactions between Law Enforcement Officers and deaf suspects is scarce, and few law enforcement training programs on interacting with individuals who are deaf exist (Feldman et al., 2025). However, attempts have been made to assist law enforcement to more effectively interact with the Deaf community (Engelman et al., 2013; Feldman et al., 2025; Garner, 2019). Deaf suspects and victims "face significant barriers in their interactions with the police" and "these barriers can have a detrimental effect not only on deaf individuals but also in law enforcement efforts to prosecute cases" (McAnnany & Shaw, 2011, p. 878).

In most cases, the first interaction between a deaf individual and law enforcement will occur when an officer has either observed some infraction (e.g., traffic violation) or is called to investigate an alleged crime. It is important to note that deafness is not a visible condition, and law enforcement officers may not be aware that a suspect is deaf until attempts at communication are attempted. For deaf suspects, the initial contact with law enforcement officers may be disorienting, challenging, and even frightening, considering communication barriers and limited access to information. Silvasi (2020) found that communication difficulties contributed to a highly stressful situation for both police officers and deaf suspects and can escalate the situation. The difficulties or inability to hear, and therefore respond, to verbal commands made by officers has been noted, resulting in negative outcomes for the deaf suspect (Andone, 2017).

Historically, the Miranda warnings, when given to a deaf suspect, have rarely been presented in a manner that is fully accessible (Andrews et al., 2007). While more recent information is scarce, original studies of the comprehension of the Miranda Warnings and deaf suspects have found that approximately 30% "are not properly informed of their rights" (Anon, 1992). ASL and English are not mutually translatable, and making an English word-for-word to ASL translation of the warnings will likely be confusing for many deaf suspects.

Judges, attorneys, and other courtroom personnel often lack an awareness of the accommodations entitled to deaf defendants to assure equal and fair justice (Dubow et al., 1986). Unfortunately, this results in the protective laws designed to ensure rights of deaf defendants are overlooked or not enforced, albeit unintentionally (Andrews et al., 2007; Frumkin, 1998; Musumeci, 2006; Terhune, 2004–2005). Many examples exist of the negative consequences for the deaf defendant when courts do not provide adequate accommodations (Feld Thomas & Gasten, 2009; Vernon, 2010).

The Psychological Evaluation of Deaf Defendants

In legal situations, psychological evaluations are often used to help determine competency or criminal responsibility. As with any psychological testing, it is important to consider how culture and language influence administration, scoring, and interpretation, which, in the case of the deaf defendant, presents a unique set of challenges for forensic evaluators (Pollard & Berlinski, 2017). The forensic examiner, before even beginning an evaluation, must also consider their own level of cultural and linguistic awareness, as well as individual client variables, such as language (differences, preferences, deprivation); cultural and community affiliation; and level, and type, of education (O'rouke & Grewer, 2005). Unfortunately, few psychologists exist who possess these skills and knowledge, and few evaluative resources have been developed that are specifically developed for the needs of deaf examinees (Landsberger et al., 2013; Morere et al., 2019).

Tests with normative data, standardized administration, or even guidelines for deaf examinees are rare, which leaves the interpretation of scores based on "hearing" norms. Test instructions may even present a challenge as some terms and concepts may not readily be translatable into ASL or other forms of signed communication with the same intent or meaning, or the sign gives away the answer. Many tests are based on reading and self-report, and the reading level of the deaf examinee, often lower than hearing peers, must be considered. It is also important to consider how hearing loss, language, and culture may skew the questions, responses, and interpretation.

Cultural factors such as personal disclosure, eye contact, physical space, body movement, and head nodding may be interpreted with "hearing bias" and incorrectly pathologize a deaf defendant. Deaf examinees may score artificially high on measures of paranoid symptomology due to oppression and real experiences with hearing society (Williams & Ables, 2004). Glickman (2007) notes that Deaf individuals who have not developed language proficiency may demonstrate behavioral and language traits mistakenly appearing as symptoms of psychosis. Cognitive limitations may be due to deficits in language development, poor education, or language acquisition and not necessarily an underlying cognitive deficit (Woolfe et al., 2002). A lack of information or knowledge about personal or family history, due to poor communication with hearing family, may be interpreted as memory or cognitive impairment. Deaf defendants may have a difficult time with words and concepts that have no signed equivalent or with terms that are unfamiliar in common discourse (e.g., "charges" or "range of possible penalties"). Some legal terms have no signed equivalent (e.g., jury), and when a substitution is utilized (e.g., "decision group"), it may not fully convey the same meaning.

Psychologists evaluating deaf defendants may have to break with administration and protocol to accommodate the deaf examinee (Maller, 2003). However, any modifications or adaptations to test materials must be done with caution and noted in the report with rationale and potential effect on interpretation.

Deaf Defendants and Competency to Proceed

Many deaf individuals have experienced less access to education and therefore have a lower fund of knowledge regarding legal terminology and concepts. Miller and Vernon (2001) looked specifically at linguistic diversity and the legal system and noted that "between 25 and 40 percent of prelingually deaf or hard-of-hearing persons are at risk for being found incompetent to stand trial" due to what Vernon and Daigle-King (1999) defined as "insufficient primitive linguistic level" (p. 99). Additionally, Miller (2004) found that 50% of deaf inmates in a Texas prison had limited reading and language abilities severe enough to question their understanding of due process during their arrest and trial. Miller et al. (2005) also found that

20.2% of violent deaf offenders in a prison population possessed minimal language skills severe enough to argue that they should have been deemed incompetent to stand trial.

Considering these limitations, it becomes extremely difficult to establish if the deaf defendant has a minimum fund of knowledge as required by law to demonstrate competency, and, if not, to determine if competency is a restorable condition.

Competency Restoration

For those deaf defendants deemed not competent, but restorable, consideration must be made for an appropriate restoration environment. This should include a professional with sign language ability, or if no such person is available, use of interpreters or other accommodations as *preferred by the deaf individual.* Individual training may also be more effective as competency groups typically means hearing facilitators and participants and spoken English. Furthermore, restoration training should include actual knowledge as opposed to rote memorization of English-based legal terms, as memorization would not likely be enough to demonstrate competency under *United States v. Duhon* (2000).

Understanding how quickly and effectively defendants restore to competency is important, as competency restoration treatment is time limited. In 1972, the Supreme Court of the United States (SCOTUS) held that defendants cannot be held indefinitely for competency restoration treatment (*Jackson v. Indiana,* 1972). The defendant in this case, Theon Jackson, was a deaf man who was described to be unable to "read, write, or otherwise communicate through limited sign language." It was further discussed in this case that Mr. Jackson had undergone communication skills training with the Indiana School for the Deaf "without noticeable success." Based on this discussion of Mr. Jackson's history and limited communicative abilities, it can be presumed that he was a deaf individual with a history of language deprivation, similar to a large proportion of deaf and hard-of-hearing (DHH) defendants involved in the criminal justice system. The expert who evaluated the defendant in this case opined that it was "extremely unlikely that [Jackson] could ever learn to read or write and questioned whether [Jackson] even had the ability to develop any proficiency in sign language." SCOTUS ruled that the indefinite commitment of a criminal defendant solely on account of their lack of capacity violates due process and that they "cannot be held more than the reasonable period of time necessary to determine whether there is a substantial probability that he will attain competency in the foreseeable future" (p. 1). If it is determined that the defendant will not attain competency, "the State must either institute civil proceedings applicable to indefinite commitment of those not charged with a crime or release the defendant." (p. 10).

Sadly, although a case involving a deaf man was influential in establishing parameters around how long someone can undergo competency restoration treatment, there has been little research focused on restoration with this population. Consequently, many programs are ill-equipped and ill-informed on how to effectively work with incompetent DHH defendants. According to Vernon et al. (1997), incompetent DHH defendants charged with serious offenses are often indefinitely committed to state hospitals as a result of their "irreversible deficits in linguistic and mental functioning," (p. 375) indicating that SCOTUS's decision in *Jackson v. Indiana* (1972) had not been adequately implemented.

A particular concern relates to DHH defendants who have a history of language deprivation, resulting in limited language fluency and a decreased capacity to acquire language as an adult. In discussing this population, Eckes (2006) wrote, "There is no easy solution for what to do with a defendant, particularly a linguistically incompetent one, once that defendant is declared incompetent. The next step for any incompetent defendant, regardless of the basis for incompetency, is to attempt to restore the defendant to competency. However, due to the nature of the incompetence for linguistically deprived defendants, which is caused by an irreversible physical condition, most if not all of linguistically deprived defendants are not restorable." (p. 1660).

In his review, Eckes (2006) describes two types of cases involving DHH defendants with a history of language deprivation. The first set of cases were those that resulted in a dismissal of charges and release. The rationale of courts in many of these circumstances related to the nature of the defendants' deficits, and how they did not meet criteria for civil commitment. However, criticism of these decisions has related to the lack of consideration of community safety, particularly for DHH defendants charged with serious offenses. The second set of cases involved defendants who were committed for competency restoration treatment. In Illinois and Louisiana, it was held that any defendant who was found to be incompetent to proceed was considered mentally ill under their respective state codes and, therefore, could be involuntarily committed. In New York, an appellate court held that a defendant's language deprivation was considered to be a "mental defect," (p. 1669) which then qualified them to be civilly committed under New York law.

Existing methods of competency restoration treatment have not been developed with DHH defendants in mind, especially those with experiences of language deprivation. In their article, Pollard and Berlinski (2017) discussed a curriculum developed by Florida State Hospital, which defendants with typical hearing are able to successfully complete within 2.5 to 3 months. However, DHH defendants "with significant language deprivation and fund of information deficits," (p. 266) undergoing the same curriculum have not achieved competency despite several years of instruction. Despite the decision in *Jackson v. Indiana* (1972) occurring more than 50 years ago, there has been limited progress in tailoring competency restoration treatment for DHH defendants.

In some jurisdictions, alternatives to state hospitals for competency restoration have been explored, resulting in some states establishing outpatient competency restoration programs (OCRPs). OCRPs may be a useful alternative for deaf defendants as they may allow for more specialized treatment. A proposed benefit of OCRPs is that they are more cost efficient and operate at a lower cost than inpatient restoration programs. There are additional benefits, such as more rapidly resolved cases within the outpatient setting, which then significantly reduces the waitlists for inpatient restoration services. Following the case of *Trueblood* et al. *v. Washington State Department of Social and Health Services* et al. (2023), states are under pressure to restore incompetent defendants in a timely way but generally have limited spaces at forensic state hospitals.

There has been a specialized treatment program established for those with intellectual disabilities, known as the Slater Method (Wall et al., 2003). The Slater Method consists of five modules that are completed sequentially. Modules are completed a minimum of three times, and when all answers are fair or good, one would proceed to the next module. The program is designed to be completed within 6 months. A study comparing restoration rates for defendants with intellectual disabilities revealed that significantly more defendants exposed to the Slater Method attained restoration (61.1%) compared to those who received treatment as usual (16.7%) (Wall & Christopher, 2012). Based on the result of this study, it can be argued that specialized competency restoration protocols developed for use with specific populations are capable of being effective.

Research illustrating the effectiveness of the Slater Method (Wall et al., 2003) in restoring those with intellectual disability to competency suggests that specialized competency restoration programs tailored to specific populations can be successful, even if the nature of their deficits relates to a condition that is chronic, not amenable to change, and cannot be treated with medications. As such, it is recommended that a competency restoration program developed for use with DHH defendants is an avenue that is being explored. In the nascent stages, independent efforts are underway to develop training methods that build off of the benefits found by using the Slater Method to accommodate the linguistic and visual needs of DHH defendants.

The Correctional System and the Deaf Inmates

According to the U.S. Bureau of Justice Statistics, an estimated 32% of state and federal inmates have a disability (Bronson et al., 2016). Although the experiences of many minority groups in the correctional system have been examined, little attention has been given to the experiences of deaf inmates (Kelly, 2017). While it has been estimated that over ten thousand deaf inmates are in the correctional system (Lewis, 2014), the broad definition of "deaf," lack of hearing evaluation during intake, and fear of victimization make any accurate count of deaf inmates or their location difficult to establish (Gibbs & Ackerman, 1999). As being deaf makes an inmate more vulnerable to assault, many deaf inmates may attempt to conceal their hearing loss from the staff and inmate population (Vernon, 2010).

Prison can be an extremely difficult process for the deaf inmate as correctional facilities are not designed or equipped for their needs (Gibbs & Ackerman, 1999). Deaf individuals held within the correctional system also present a unique challenge for staff and various facets of correctional life will likely be impacted.

Some deaf inmates may be unaware of the conditions of their incarceration (Ridgeway, 2012). Interpreters may not be provided at orientation and intake, and distributed handbooks may be beyond the reading level of many deaf inmates (Goben et al., 2009). Without access to such information, deaf inmates may have difficulty navigating the correctional institution, resulting in conflict with correctional staff and fellow inmates (Miller & Vernon, 2001). According to Vernon and Miller (2005), the two most serious problems deaf inmates face are physical danger and isolation. Deaf inmates are often more vulnerable to assault by other inmates who see them as isolated and unable to report offenses (Feldman, 2017). Feldman (2017) also noted that because deaf inmates cannot hear what is going on around them and identify potentially dangerous situations, they are likely at a higher risk of rape and other forms of assault. It is also more difficult for deaf inmates, due to language barriers, to make friends and form alliances with other inmates for mutual protection (Feldman, 2017).

The deaf inmate may also experience higher levels of isolation from family, attorneys, and friends than their hearing counterparts. Educational, vocational, religious, and mental health programs may also be inaccessible to the deaf inmate due to accommodation restrictions (Vernon, 2010). An inmate who is deaf is often the only deaf inmate in the facility, isolated and with few opportunities for socialization leading to depression, anxiety, and paranoia (Novic, 2018). Accessible mental health services, or social support, available to hearing inmates may not be available for deaf inmates as there are few professionals who can communicate directly (Feldman, 2017).

Conclusion

Clearly, the ability of the deaf suspect, defendant, or inmate to navigate the legal system is challenging with much depending on language, communication, accommodations, and accessibility. This is further complicated by misunderstandings among many forensic psychologists who have little knowledge of deafness or the Deaf community. However, we must consider the realities of the mental health, legal, and criminal justice systems. For example, it is not likely that the majority of mental health or legal professionals will learn ASL with enough proficiency to provide effective communication, and there are too few professionals with this expertise. It is also impossible to predict when a deaf examinee, suspect, defendant, or inmate may be arrested, referred, or incarcerated. Therefore, many mental health and legal professionals deal with these challenges in real time with little prior thought about, or time to prepare for, deaf individuals.

The best solution appears to be providing educational and training resources for professionals involved in various aspects of the legal and correctional systems. This may include training to become familiar with the role of interpreters and a general understanding of accommodations that are entitled to the deaf examinee, suspect, defendant, or inmate. It is also recommended that professionals in forensic and legal settings are encouraged to "know what they don't know" and recognize the need to seek consultation with experts familiar with psychological evaluations, legal settings, and the Deaf community. Many professional ethical codes and guidelines refer to individual competency and good judgment in assessing one's ability to effectively communicate, conduct evaluations, provide services, advocate, and form opinions based on their existing skills, abilities, experience, and training.

It is also important that forensic and legal professionals remember that "deaf people" are not a homogeneous group. For accommodations to be effective they should be based on multiple factors, such as individual preferences, and cultural identification and affiliation. Deaf suspects, defendants, and inmates should be encouraged and allowed to navigate the legal system utilizing the accommodations that they feel are most useful, as opposed to accommodations being imposed without their input. While many may prefer communication utilizing a sign language interpreter, others may prefer live captioning, video conferencing, speech-lip reading, or a combination of systems and this should be evaluated for each individual. One suggestion would be to have forensic psychologists, law enforcement agencies, and courts to build a relationship with local interpreting agencies and Deaf Service Centers who can provide services, training, and consultation.

Those professionals who do have knowledge, or at least recognition of the unique needs of deaf examinees, suspects, defendants, and inmates should also have a role in advocating for the competent and effective provision of services to their peers to ensure the adherence to appropriate services. They should encourage other forensic psychologists, law enforcement agencies, courts, and correctional facilities to become familiar with the needs of, and accommodations entitled to, individuals who are deaf that come into contact with the legal and correctional systems.

Finally, more current research is needed which addresses the challenges faced by deaf suspects, defendants, and inmates and the consequences of the failure to provide needed, required, and effective accommodation. These should include the development of more linguistically and culturally appropriate forensic evaluation tools and techniques. Furthermore, policy and solution-focused projects should be developed to disseminate knowledge of evidence-based best practices for forensic evaluations, interventions, training, and to ensure and expand the provision of culturally appropriate law enforcement, legal, and correctional services.

References

Andone, D. (2017, September 21). 'He can't hear you': Officers shoot, kill deaf man after giving verbal orders. *CNN*. https://www.cnn.com/2017/09/21/us/police-shoot-deaf-manoklahoma-citytrnd/index.htm

Andrews, J. F., Vernon, M., & LaVigne, M. (2007). The Bill of Rights, due process and the deaf suspect. *Journal of Interpreting, 2007*, 9–38.

Anon, L. (1992). *Annual survey of deaf and hard of hearing children and youth*. Gallaudet University Press.

Branson, J., & Miller, D. (2002). *Damned for their difference: The cultural construction of deaf people as "disabled": A sociological history*. Gallaudet University Press. https://doi.org/10.1080/15017410510032244

Bronson, J., Maruschak, L., & Alper, M. (2016). *Disabilities reported by prisoners: Survey of prison inmates*. Bureau of Justice Statistics, U. S. Department of Justice, 252642.

Dubow, S., & Greer, S. (1992). *Legal rights: The guide for deaf and hard of hearing people* (pp. 15–45). Gallaudet University Press.

Dubow, S., Goldberg, L., Geer, S., Gardner, F., Penn, A., Conlon, S., & Charmatz, M. (1986). *Legal rights of hearing impaired persons* (3rd ed., p. 2). Gallaudet University Press.

Du Feu, M., & Chovaz, C. (2014). Legal and forensic issues. In M. du Feu & C. Chovaz (Eds.), *Mental health and deafness* (pp. 232–246). Oxford University Press.

Eckes, E. (2006). The incompetency of courts and legislatures: Addressing linguistically deprived deaf defendants. *University of Cincinnati Law Review, 75*, 1649.

Engelman, A., Ilvey, S., Tseng, W., Dahrogue, D., Brune, J., & Neurhauser, L. (2013). Responding to the deaf in disasters: Establishing a need for systematic training for state-level emergency management agencies and community organizations. *BMC Health Services Research, 13*, 84. https://doi.org/10.1186/1472-6963-13-84

Escobedo v. Illinois, 378 U.S. 478 (1964).

Feldman, D. (2017). Deaf inmates. In K. Kearly (Ed.), *The encyclopedia of corrections*. Wiley-Blackwell.

Feldman, D. M., Caggiano, C., & Beldon-Feldman, J. (2023a). Why language matters: What forensic psychologists need to know about the deaf community, American Sign Language, and interpreters. *Practice Innovations, 8*(3), 249–264. https://doi.org/10.1037/pri0000219

Feldman, D. M., Silvasi, P. M., Rotshtyn, D., & Covell, C. (2023b). *Intersections of the Legal System and the Deaf Community From Law Enforcement to Incarceration. Springer International Publishing AG.*

Feldman, D., Miller, M., & Shir, T. M. (2025). First responders and the deaf community. In V. Van Hasselt & M. Bourke (Eds.), *Advances in first responder mental health: Research, training, and practice*. [Manuscript in preparation]. Springer Publishing.

Foss, K. A. (2014). Constructing hearing loss or "deaf gain?" Voice, agency, and identity in television's representations of d/deafness. *Critical Studies in Media Communication, 31*(5), 426–447.

Frumkin, I. B. (1998). *Competency to waive Miranda Rights* (pp. 8–9). NLADA Indigent Defense.

Garner, J. L. (2019). *The Deaf & law enforcement listening through Deaf eyes: A grounded theory approach* [Doctoral dissertation, Nova Southeastern University]. NSUWorks, Abraham S. Fischler College of Education. https://nsuworks.nova.edu/fse_etd/228

Gibbs, A., & Ackerman, N. (1999). Deaf prisoners—Needs, services and training issues. *Prison Service Journal*, 32–33. https://doi.org/10.1353/aad.2005.0036

Glickman, N. (2007). Do you hear voices? Problems in assessment of mental status in deaf persons with severe language deprivation. *Journal of Deaf Studies and Deaf Education, 12*, 127–147.

Goben, B., Enos, K., & Andrews, J. (2009). *What to do? In jail but can't read the inmate handbook: Solutions for the deaf offender* [Unpublished manuscript, Lamar University].

Holmes v. Florida, 438 U.S. 1052 (1986).

Jackson v. Indiana, 406 U.S. 715 (1972).

Kelly, M. (2017). Sounding out d/deafness: The experiences of d/deaf prisoners. *Journal of Criminal Psychology, 8*(1), 22–32.

King, N., & Vernon, M. (1999). Unique legal issues facing deaf defendants. *The Florida Defender, VII*(#1), 11–15.

Kuntz, L. A., Pratt, J., & Cotterell, M. (2023). Working with persons involved in the legal system who are deaf. *Journal of the American Academy of Psychiatry and the Law*. Advance online publication. 10.29158/JAAPL.220079-22.

Ladd, P. (2003). Understanding deaf culture: In search of Deafhood. *Multilingual Matters*. https://doi.org/10.21832/9781853595479

Landsberger, S. A., Sajid, A., Schmelkin, L., Diaz, D. R., & Weiler, C. (2013). Assessment and treatment of deaf adults with psychiatric disorders: A review of the literature for practitioners. *Journal of Psychiatric Practice, 19*(2), 87–97.

Lane, H. (1999). *The mask of benevolence: Disabling the deaf community* (Rev. ed.). Dawn Sign Press.
Lane, H., Hoffmeister, R., & Bahan, B. (1996). *A journey into the deaf world.* Dawn Sign Press.
LaVigne, M., & Vernon, M. C. (2003). An interpreter isn't enough: Deafness, language, and due process. *Wisconsin Law Review, 5*, 844–936.
Lewis, T. (2014). Police brutality and deaf people. Speak freely. *American Civil Liberties Union (ACLU).* Retrieved 2022, from https://www.aclu.org/blog/national-security/police-brutality-and-deaf-people
Maller, S. J. (2003). Intellectual assessment of deaf people: A critical review of core concepts and issues. In M. Marschark & P. E. Spencer (Eds.), *Oxford handbook of deaf studies, language, and education* (pp. 451–463). Oxford University Press. https://doi.org/10.1093/oxfordhb/9780199750986.013.0033
McAnnany, K., & Shah, A. K. (2011). With their own hands: A community lawyering approach to improving law enforcement practices in the deaf community. *Valparaiso University Law Review, 45*(3), 875–925.
McEntee, M. K. (1993). Accessibility of mental health services and crisis intervention to the deaf. *American Annals of the Deaf, 138*(1), 26–30. https://doi.org/10.1353/aad.2012.0569
McEntee, M. (1995). Deaf and hard-of-hearing clients: Some legal complications. *Social Work, 40*(2), 183–187.
Miller, K. R., & Vernon, M. (2001). Linguistic diversity in deaf defendants and due process rights. *The Journal of Deaf Studies and Deaf Education, 6*(3), 226–234. https://doi.org/10.1093/deafed/6.3.226
Miller, K. (2004). Linguistic diversity in a deaf prison population: Implications for due process. *Journal of Deaf Studies and Deaf Education, 9*(1), 112–119.
Miller, K. R., Vernon, M., & Capella, M. E. (2005). Violent offenders in a deaf prison population. *Journal of Deaf Studies and Deaf Education, 10*(4), 417–425.
Miranda v. Arizona, 384 U.S. 436 (1966).
Morere, D. A., Dean, P. M., & Mompremoer, L. (2019). Mental health assessment of deaf clients: Issues with interpreters use and assessment of person with diminished capacity and psychiatric populations. *JADARA, 42(4), 9.*
Musumeci, M. B. (2006). Confronting sentences that silence: The Americans with Disabilities Act: Effective communication mandate for prisoners and probationers who are deaf. *Clearinghouse Review Journal of Poverty, Law and Policy, 2006*, 627–638.
Napier, J., McKee, R. L., & Goswell, D. (2006). *Sign language interpreting: Theory and practice in Australia and New Zealand.* Federation Press.
National Association of the Deaf. (2015). *Legal rights: The guide for deaf and hard of hearing people* (6th ed., pp. 161–162). Gallaudet University Press. 171–172.
National Association of the Deaf, & Registry of Interpreters for the Deaf. (2005). *NAD-RID code of professional conduct.* National Association of the Deaf.
Novic, S. (2018, June 21). Deaf prisoners are trapped in frightening isolation. *CNN.* https://edition.cnn.com/2018/06/21/opinions/aclu-georgia-deaf-abuse-lawsuit-novic/index.html
Olsen, T., & Kermit, P. (2014). Sign language, translation, and rule of law – Deaf peoples experiences from encounters with the Norwegian criminal justice system. *Scandinavian Journal of Disability Research, 17*(Sup1), 23–41.
O'Rourke, S., & Grewer, G. (2005). Assessment of deaf people in forensic mental health settings: A risky business! *The Journal of Forensic Psychiatry & Psychology, 16*(4), 671–684. https://doi.org/10.1080/14789940500279877
Peet, H. P. (1856). On the legal rights and responsibilities of the deaf and dumb. *American Journal of Insanity, XII*(2).
Pollard, R. Q., Jr., & Berlinski, B. T. (2017). Forensic evaluation of deaf individuals: Challenges and strategies. *Journal of Social Work in Disability & Rehabilitation, 16(3–4), 261–275.* https://doi.org/10.1080/1536710X.2017.1372240

Pray, J. L., & Jordan, I. K. (2010). The deaf community and culture at a crossroads: Issues and challenges. *Journal of Social Work in Disability & Rehabilitation, 9*(2), 168–193. https://doi.org/10.1080/1536710X.2010.493486

Registry of Interpreters for the Deaf. (1979). *RID Code of ethics*. Registry of Interpreters for the Deaf.

Ridgeway, J. (2012). The silent treatment. *Mother Jones, 37*(2), 56–59.

Sheprow, G. J. (1999). *Interpreting for the Miranda warnings. American sign language interpreting resources*. National Association of the Deaf.

Silvasi, P. M. (2020). *Warnings that fell on deaf ears: A three-pronged analysis of encounters between Deaf individuals and law enforcement* (Publication No. 27838166) [Doctoral dissertation, Gallaudet University]. *ProQuest Dissertations & Theses Global.*

Terhune, K. L. (2004–2005). Deaf criminal defendants: Is the system just? *National Association of the Deaf Magazine, 4*(5), 20–21.

Thomas, V. L., & Gastin, L. A. (2009). The Americans with Disabilities Act: Shattered aspirations and new hope. *Journal of the American Medical Association, 301*(1), 95.

Trueblood et al. v. Washington State Department of Social and Health Services et al., No. 14-cv-01178-MJP (W.D. Wash. 2023).

U.S. Congress. (1990). *The Americans with Disabilities Act of 1990, Pub. L. No. 101–336, 104 Stat. 327 (1990).* https://www.congress.gov/bill/101st-congress/house-bill/2273/text

United States v. Duhon, 104 F. Supp. 2d 663 (W.D. La. 2000).

Vernon, M. (2006). The APA and deafness. *American Psychologist, 61*(8), 816–824. https://doi.org/10.1037/0003-066X.61.8.816

Vernon, M. (2009). ADA routinely violated by prisons in the case of deaf prisoners. *Prison Legal News, 20*(7), 14–15.

Vernon, M. (2010). The horror of being deaf and in prison. *American Annals of the Deaf, 155*(3), 311–321. https://doi.org/10.1353/aad.2010.0018

Vernon, M., & Andrews, J. (2011). *Basic legal issues in handling cases of defendants who are deaf.* The Champion. National Association of Criminal Defense Lawyers.

Vernon, M., & Miller, K. (2001). Interpreting in mental health settings: Issues and concerns. *American Annals of the Deaf, 146(5), 429–434.* https://doi.org/10.1353/aad.2012.0200

Vernon, M., & Miller, K. (2005). Obstacles faced by deaf people in the criminal justice system. *American Annals of the Deaf, 150*(3), 283–291.

Vernon, M., & Daigle-King, B. (1999). Historical overview of inpatient care of mental patients who are deaf. *American Annals of the Deaf, 144*(1), 51–61. https://doi.org/10.1353/aad.2012.0134

Vernon, M., Raifman, L., & Greenberg, S. (1997). The Miranda warnings and the deaf suspect. *Behavioral Sciences and the Law, 14*, 122–128.

Vernon, M., Raifman, L., Greenberg, S., & Monteiro, B. (2009). Forensic pretrial police interviews of deaf suspects avoiding legal pitfalls. *Journal of Law and Psychiatry, 24*(2021), 43–59.

Wall, B. W., & Christopher, P. P. (2012). A training program for defendants with intellectual disabilities who are found incompetent to stand trial. *Journal of the American Academy of Psychiatry and the Law, 40*(3), 366–373. https://jaapl.org/content/40/3/366

Wall, B. W., Krupp, B. H., & Guilmette, T. (2003). Restoration of competency to stand trial: A training program for persons with mental retardation. *Journal of the American Academy of Psychiatry and the Law, 31*(2), 189–201. https://jaapl.org/content/40/3/366

Williams, C., & Abeles, N. (2004). Issues and implications of deaf culture in therapy. *Professional Psychology: Research & Practice, 35*(6), 643–648.

Woolfe, T., Want, S. C., & Siegal, M. (2002). Siblings and theory of mind in deaf native signing children. *Journal of Deaf Studies and Deaf Education, 5*(3), 342–347.

Young, A., Howarth, P., Ridgeway, S., & Monteiro, B. (2001). Forensic referrals to the three specialist psychiatric units for deaf people in the UK. *The Journal of Forensic Psychiatry, 12*(1), 19–35. https://doi.org/10.1080/09585180122591

Chapter 6
Mental Health and Deaf LGBTQ Adults

Kathryn Wagner, Cara A. Miller, and Margalit Roitman

Chapter Aims and Objectives

This chapter introduces readers to historical, contemporary, and emerging issues in mental health, illness, and wellness among Deaf and Hard-of-Hearing (DHH) lesbian, gay, bisexual, transgender, and queer-identified (LGBTQ) people and communities. Through a discussion of research, practice, and anecdotal findings, the authors aim to increase readers' knowledge and understanding of psychological health risks and protective factors among DHH LGBTQ adults. The authors first introduce personal, economic, cultural, and societal factors influencing mental health among DHH LGBTQ people and communities. The authors then discuss pertinent research on commonly presenting psychological issues, diagnostic presentations, challenges in finding support, health outcome disparities, and particular issues that clinicians may encounter (Kushalnagar & Miller, 2019; Miller et al., 2019). The authors highlight barriers that transgender and gender nonconforming DHH people commonly encounter when seeking gender- and culturally affirmative care as well as education on sex and gender (Lund et al., 2021; Miller et al., 2019). For example, the widespread impacts of stigma and discrimination contribute to unfavorable mental health outcomes for many DHH LGBTQ adults. Finally, the authors conclude with recognizing support systems that facilitate mental health and well-being, including family and community acceptance, positive media portrayal, increasing cultural awareness in Deaf spaces, and inclusive shifts in professional health research and practice (Miller & Clark, 2019; Young et al., 2023). Acknowledging the complexities of identity development and social affiliation, the authors close this chapter with a discussion of future directions.

K. Wagner (✉) · C. A. Miller · M. Roitman
Clinical Psychology Program, Gallaudet University, Washington, DC, USA
e-mail: Kathryn.wagner@gallaudet.edu; Cara.miller@gallaudet.edu

T. Bone (ed.), *Deaf Mental Health*, Advances in Mental Health and Addiction,
https://doi.org/10.1007/978-3-032-06274-1_6

Introduction

As noted in this chapter aims and objectives, the authors describe the unique issues that Deaf LGBTQ people face when seeking mental health services. This chapter begins with a historical overview of how DHH LGBTQ people have faced discrimination in seeking and obtaining mental health care. The authors then explore current issues relevant to mental health care for DHH LGBTQ individuals. In addition, the authors showcase the lived experience of professionals working with DHH LGBTQ people and communities. The authors conclude by highlighting potential treatment approaches and suggest clinical recommendations for future work with this population.

Historical Context: Mental Health Among DHH LGBTQ People and Communities

While valuing unity through shared language experiences, Deaf and Hard-of-Hearing communities have maintained a complex relationship with the diversity of human sexualities and gender identities (Klein, 2021; Mauldin, 2018). Historically, the Deaf community in the United States has been influenced by dominant sociocultural norms regarding LGBTQ identities. Many Deaf advocacy groups have long omitted or excluded issues of LGBTQ civil rights in their priorities, missions, and efforts, thereby marginalizing Deaf LGBTQ people (Leigh, 2017). Conversely, the predominantly hearing LGBTQ community has historically overlooked DHH people and issues of relevance within large-scale advocacy efforts and practices, such as not including interpreters as a budget line item for LGBTQ cultural events (Miller & Clark, 2019). Thus, it has been challenging for many DHH LGBTQ people to find inclusion and community within predominantly hearing LGBTQ spaces. DHH LGBTQ persons have encountered challenges in seeking and receiving mental health care, as described in this section.

Research suggests that DHH people, as compared to hearing peers, may be significantly less likely to access healthcare and mental health services despite higher documented, diagnostic rates of mental health conditions (Gallagher, 2022; Hernandez, 2024; Kushalnagar et al., 2019; Sanfacon et al., 2021). Historically, from personal and community experience, many DHH people have offered that mental health professionals have limited Deaf cultural awareness of critical issues; these include language differences, frequent family dynamics, common educational experiences, and knowledge of small community dynamics, among others (Leigh & Gutman, 2010; Miller et al., 2019). The fear that hearing professionals will not understand or consider these issues when providing services is just one of the many factors that contribute to mental health resource disparities among DHH individuals, including those who are LGBTQ identified. However, as American society and the mental health field continue evolving, mental health resources have become increasingly available and relatively more accessible to more DHH people. A growing body of research, along with corresponding policy changes, has contributed to a general attitude shift toward seeking and receiving mental health services in the DHH community (Kuehne et al., 2022; Mathos et al., 2009). Even further, legislation mandating equal access as well as new research into adapting mental health resources for the specific needs of DHH people has improved accessibility and efficacy of mental healthcare (Anderson et al., 2021; Kuehne et al., 2022; Mathos et al., 2009).

With similarity to DHH people, LGBTQ people have historically been pathologized or ostracized in mental health spaces and thus may share a historical sense of distrust. For many years, the Diagnostic and Statistical Manual of Mental Disorders (DSM), published by the American Psychiatric Association, was used as a tool to pathologize LGBTQ people's identities (Martos et al., 2017). The DSM listed homosexuality as a mental disorder until as recently as 1974 (Wolfe & Fogwell, 2022). Gender Identity Disorder, a similarly pathologizing label, was introduced to the DSM III in 1980 to mixed responses, including praise from those who noted that the diagnosis could enable more individuals to receive and access insurance-covered healthcare. Currently, the most recent iteration of the DSM (DSM-5-TR) includes Gender Dysphoria, which is described as the distress a person experiences when their gender identity differs from assigned sex at birth. Given a longstanding history of pathologizing LGBTQ identities, as well as conversion practices, mistrust has developed between the LGBTQ population and mental health service providers (Owens et al., 2007; Shipherd et al., 2010). As society moves to be more accepting of LGBTQ identities, mental health services have become more accessible and more affirming for the community (Martos et al., 2017).

Several milestones highlight the progression of advocacy and awareness for Deaf and LGBTQ people's mental health care needs within the area of mental health services. The Americans with Disabilities Act (ADA), published in 1990, mandates accessible communication services for DHH people, including providing American Sign Language (ASL) interpreters and other access accommodations in mental health settings, if requested (Americans with Disabilities Act, 1990). Similarly, The World Professional Association for Transgender Health (WPATH) has improved its standards to be more inclusive for DHH people; WPATH now provides guidelines for working with DHH people (Coleman et al., 2022). In addition to growing resources for DHH LGBTQ people, social media has facilitated the development of community and visibility for DHH LGBTQ people (Leigh et al., 2022; Miller & Clark, 2019; Saunders, 2016). Numerous digital networking groups, blogs, and social media accounts explore DHH LGBTQ people's lives and often provide support and advocacy for DHH and LGBTQ people (Paglieri et al., 2022; Saunders, 2016).

Current Issues: Mental Health of DHH LGBTQ Individuals

In this section, the authors discuss commonly presenting psychological issues that DHH LGBTQ individuals face, including psychological issues; personal, cultural, social, and family issues; and disparities and barriers to mental health care access.

Psychological Issues

Psychological issues and concerns of relevance to DHH LGBTQ people are as multifaceted and nuanced as is each person in their environment. While research in this area is historically limited, recent studies are exploring diagnostic trends, examining social factors for risk and resilience, and highlighting experiences of marginalized communities within the DHH LGBTQ population. The following is a brief overview of recent literature examining psychological concerns, diagnostic presentations, and commonly identified risk and protective factors.

Depression and Anxiety Disorders

Depression and anxiety top the list of the most commonly reported mental health concerns among DHH LGBTQ individuals. A 2019 study by Kushalnagar and colleagues found that 25% of Deaf adults reported being diagnosed with depression or anxiety disorders, compared with 22% of hearing adults (Kushalnagar et al., 2019). Minority stress, limited social support, and communication challenges may contribute to functional impairment in daily living, as well as feelings of sadness and hopelessness (Gallagher, 2022). Deaf people, including those with late-onset hearing loss, may also report feelings of greater isolation compared to their hearing peers, which can exacerbate depressive symptoms (Gallagher, 2022; Hernandez, 2024). Among this group, social anxiety may be particularly pronounced, given the communication challenges experienced in hearing LGBTQ spaces.

Trauma and Post-traumatic Stress

Much has been written in the literature about stress and traumatic stress among DHH people (Anderson et al., 2016; Hall et al., 2023). Post-Traumatic Stress Disorder is a significant mental health concern for DHH LGBTQ individuals, particularly youth and among those who have experienced violence, bullying, or abuse. As noted, DHH LGBTQ individuals may encounter difficulties accessing trauma-informed, culturally responsive, and language-concordant care, which can exacerbate trauma symptoms, lead to inaccurate diagnoses, and result in ineffective or harmful care (Aldalur et al., 2025; Holcomb, 2022).

Substance Use Disorders

Deaf and hard-of-hearing LGBTQ individuals experience comparable or higher rates of substance use disorders compared with hearing individuals, with mental health comorbidities often going unaddressed (Aldalur et al., 2024; Aldalur et al., 2025). Contributing and exacerbating factors may include social isolation, stigma, communication barriers, and limited preventive and educational resources for DHH LGBTQ people, as well as limited knowledge and experience among providers with different and disparate areas of specialty (Anderson et al., 2021; Hernandez, 2024). Recent clinical efforts include adaptation of substance use treatment approaches with DHH people (Anderson et al., 2021). In psychology, counseling, social work, and rehabilitation education curricula, there is a push by educators to include substance use disorder treatment for DHH people (Biskupiak et al., 2018; James et al., 2022).

Gender Dysphoria

Finally, transgender, nonbinary, and gender-nonconforming DHH individuals have experienced ongoing challenges to receiving supportive care in medical and mental health contexts, even as best practices and standards of care continue to evolve (Martos et al., 2017; Pachankis et al., 2021). Given that Deaf individuals often already face barriers to communication, the aforementioned challenges may be compounded by societal rejection or discrimination related to gender identity, sexual orientation, or gender presentation (Sanfacon et al., 2021).

Personal, Cultural, Social, and Familial Challenges

Social Isolation and Minority Stress

Combined and compounded experiences of multiple identities in formation and social navigation can engender unique forms of "minority stress," wherein individuals, including those who identify as DHH and LGBTQ, may experience marginalization within multiple affiliated communities (Miller & Clark, 2019; Schaad, 2015). This compounded minority stress may contribute to higher levels of anxiety, depression, and reduced quality of life.

Identity Development

Processes of identity development among DHH LGBTQ individuals may be complicated by compounding experiences of exploring Deaf and Hard-of-Hearing identity as well as LGBTQ identities along with lived experiences of race, ethnicity, geographic origin, religion, disability, and so on. Individuals may experience feelings of incongruence especially in environments that do not fully acknowledge or support multiple aspects of their identities (Miller & Clark, 2019). This can generate challenges in forming a cohesive sense of self and navigating social and familial expectations. Identities of DHH people of varying backgrounds, including among marginalized groups, are part of a fast-growing body of research (Dunne, 2013; Moges, 2017; Schmitz, 2021).

Challenges in Family Relationships

Experiences of limited familial support and a heightened risk of emotional distress are historically noted in the psychological literature on deaf children in hearing families (Yuen et al., 2022). Deaf and hard-of-hearing LGBTQ individuals report challenges in family dynamics (Dunne, 2013), and the Trevor Project (2022) recently noted that DHH youth were "less likely to report having high levels of family support for their sexual orientation or gender identity (35%) compared to their hearing peers (27%)" (para. 5). Experiences linked to deafness and sexual or gender identity may contribute to within-family conflicts, including issues around parental and sibling acceptance as well as religious and faith community involvement (Leigh, 2017). Such challenges may be further compounded with experiences of discrimination and stigma for DHH LGBTQ individuals, as commonly reported by Black, Indigenous, and People of Color (BIPOC) DHH LGBTQ individuals (for a personal narrative on this topic, see Morris, 2023).

Difficulty in Finding Support and Acceptance

Deaf and hard-of-hearing LGBTQ people report limited experiences of meaningful understanding and support within their Deaf and LGBTQ communities. For example, DHH LGBTQ individuals may find it difficult to find LGBTQ support or social networks that are culturally informed and linguistically accessible, or large enough to present a pool of potential partners beyond those already in one's social circles (Beese & Tasker, 2022; Cheslik & Wright, 2021).

Disparities and Barriers to Mental Health Care Access

As stated above, DHH LGBTQ individuals frequently encounter challenges to accessing effective mental health care for reasons including communication barriers, limited access to services, histories of mistrust, and cultural misunderstandings, among others (Hernandez, 2024). As mental health providers may have limited opportunities to obtain further training in cultural competency, patient-provider discordance may contribute to underreporting of mental health issues and unmet needs for care (Aldalur et al., 2025; Heiman et al., 2015; Kushalnagar et al., 2019).

Discrimination and Stigma

Deaf and hard-of-hearing LGBTQ individuals report experiences of discrimination in healthcare settings, both covert and overt (Argenyi & Kushalnagar, 2019; Biskupiak et al., 2018). Cultural barriers and provider oversight in patient-provider relationships may contribute to experiences of marginalization, misunderstanding, misdiagnosis, and sometimes inadequate treatment of mental health concerns such as depression, anxiety, and suicidal ideation (Williams & Adams, 2021). These experiences may be compounded by the lack of visibility of DHH LGBTQ individuals in healthcare training and continuing education programming for providers (Hoang et al., 2011; Yu et al., 2023).

Barriers to Safe and Inclusive Spaces

Historically, DHH LGBTQ people have struggled to find and build inclusive spaces which can contain the fullness of identities composed of multiple lived experiences. Many social LGBTQ spaces, such as social clubs and bars, are often inaccessible to Deaf individuals, just as many Deaf or signing spaces are normed on cisgender and heterosexual identities of members (Miller & Clark, 2019). The limited choices of inclusive spaces can contribute to feelings of alienation and difficulty forming meaningful social connections or relationships.

Clinician Approaches to Treatment and Case Examples

Having highlighted mental health issues that many DHH LGBTQ individuals face, including psychological disorders; cultural, social, and family challenges; and disparities in mental health care access, we now turn to the pertinent discussion of treatment approaches. We draw from published study findings and clinicians' reported experiences.

Clinicians Who Work with DHH LGBTQ Populations

A number of publications highlight the importance of therapist training and skill in the assessment and treatment of gender concerns and transgender-specific mental health concerns (Bockting, 2008). Additionally, study findings emphasize the importance of cultural and language competence when working with DHH clients

(Leigh & Gutman, 2010; Williams & Adams, 2021). However, there are fewer publications that highlight the experience of clinicians who work with populations who are both DHH and LGBTQ. Those publications emphasize the importance of the clinician receiving training in two areas: (1) that of understanding the lived experience of culturally Deaf individuals (and awareness of mental health disparities and ASL and/or interpreter use) and (2) awareness regarding barriers that LGBTQ people face, especially transgender persons. This dual training is especially important given that Deaf LGBTQ people often have higher rates of PTSD, depression, suicidality, and substance use (Kushalnagar et al., 2019). In a personal narrative, Patrick Tully (2018) discusses his experiences seeking out a culturally competent provider:

> I remember coming into therapy for the first time and my partial hearing loss was never discussed. I felt ashamed by the hearing loss and didn't have the courage to bring up my shame. I would have welcomed any questions or comments but that didn't happen. I was curious what my therapist thought about a client with these intersecting identities. I was worried the old assumption that hearing loss meant an intellectual disability was present would interfere with therapy. I don't have an intellectual disability but I knew the assumption existed in society. I had so many curiosities [...] Being gay has had challenges of its own, but being both gay and hard-of-hearing is quite a unique situation (Tully, 2019, para. 1).

Tully recognizes the need to assess personal assumptions about what it means to be DHH and LGBTQ identified. He suggests that an efficacious approach for a therapist is to directly enquire about the client's experiences about being Deaf and/or LGBTQ and to approach each client with curiosity. Moreover, clinicians have highlighted the importance of marketing services that are LGBTQ affirming and ASL accessible when applicable so that clients can find a good fit (Gutman & Zangas, 2010).

Virginia Gutman and Thomas Zangas' chapter, "Therapy issues with lesbians, gay men, bisexuals, and transgender individuals who are Deaf" in Irene Leigh's 2010 *Psychotherapy with Deaf Clients from Diverse Groups* text highlights the necessity of clinicians being versed in the struggles and insular world issues that Deaf LGBTQ persons face. Issues of unique relevance include confidentiality and boundaries; clients coming out in therapy with DHH or signing LGBTQ providers; accessing LGBTQ resources in ASL and other accessible means; and recognizing communication barriers that may impede LGBTQ identity disclosure to hearing family members (Gutman & Zangas, 2010).

More recently, researchers discuss the importance of clinicians recognizing the difficulties that Deaf LGBTQ clients often experience when trying to receive accessible healthcare services (Miller et al., 2019). Even when a psychotherapist may not directly address a client's physical health symptoms, therapists may be called on to advocate for the client if needed or to provide consultation. Doing so effectively requires thorough and competent training. Below the authors provide two personal narratives.

Case Example 1: Deaf Transgender Individual Seeks Affirming Healthcare

"Jae" is a 25-year-old Deaf, transgender individual, seeking a letter for top surgery approval after being on testosterone for 2 years. He scheduled appointments with two different reputable surgeons for the initial consultation. At the first clinic, the surgeon refused to provide an ASL interpreter so Jae cancelled the appointment when he realized the clinic would not sufficiently address his accessibility-related request. "I felt demoralized," he shared with his therapist, a Deaf clinician who had written a letter to support Jae's justification for top surgery, a gender-affirming procedure that many trans and nonbinary folks seek to minimize gender dysphoria. At the second clinic, the provider, Dr. Williams, agreed to provide an ASL interpreter but did not provide, upon request, a person with the appropriate qualifications; instead, the clinic chose a telehealth provider without medical qualifications. The Internet connection was also choppy, and Jae missed out on pertinent information and left the office "feeling confused" about the medical recovery process. He said he wanted to persist with seeking accommodations because he liked the doctor, whose surgical techniques he preferred. When he shared his experience with his therapist, the therapist (with Jae's consent) contacted the clinic and explained the importance of providing qualified ASL interpreters who were trained in mental health interpreting. The therapist also reminded the clinic that due to ADA, they were required to fund the interpreters themselves, and that ideally, given the sensitive nature of this request, the interpreter should appear in person. Over three appointments before the surgery date, Dr. Williams's office implemented protocols for securing qualified ASL interpreters with LGBTQ healthcare terminology experience, documented Jae's communication preferences, extended appointment times to accommodate interpretation, and sought Deaf cultural competency training from Jae's therapist and through continuing education credits (CEUs). Dr. Williams even learned basic ASL greetings to establish rapport directly with Jae. These accommodations enabled Jae to successfully seek gender-affirming top surgery. Both Jae and the therapist's persistence led to improvements in Jae's overall experience; that said, the burden of seeking accessibility should not rest on Jae, which is why his therapist, with Jae's permission, advocated on his behalf. Jae's case illustrates the importance of ensuring communication accessibility at every appointment, demonstrates the unfairness of Deaf transgender individuals often serving as educators while simultaneously seeking healthcare, and highlights the importance of advocacy from all persons working with DHH LGBTQ folks.

Case Example #2: Deaf Lesbian Client Navigates Relationship and Family Issues

Other therapeutic issues that may emerge in clinical contexts include those around family, language, and communication. "Cas" is a 48-year-old signing Deaf lesbian woman who has been working with her therapist, a CODA ASL-fluent clinician, for the past year. Cas initially came to therapy seeking support in navigating family of origin relationships within her large family as she prepares for her forthcoming wedding with her partner of three years, "Therese." With her therapist's support, Cas considers the various logistics she and Therese are managing as they plan, and other issues that she anticipates will come up during the wedding. These include "typical queer wedding issues," Cas tells her therapist—like deciding who to invite, managing family members' discomfort with LGBTQ relationships, addressing financial and logistical issues with venues, and so on. Additional issues which Cas is managing include those related to accessibility, communication, language, and culture, all related to and inextricable from her DHH LGBTQ identities. For example, Cas and Therese hope to work with ASL interpreters with whom they have previously worked, while trying to identify interpreters with whom they and their signing family members have minimal or past or potential future relationship or professional conflicts. Further, the interpreters that signing family members have expressed a communication preference for have previously made a number of disparaging comments about LGBTQ people, and Cas is uncomfortable working with those interpreters but would like to ensure her family members can fully understand and participate. Cas expresses to her therapist that in mixed DHH-hearing spaces, she typically finds that her DHH peers and hearing peers tend to self-segregate; she is particularly anxious about this dynamic happening at their wedding as the majority of Cas' family is Deaf, while Therese's family members are predominantly hearing non-signers. The therapist works with Cas to explore these issues individually and in tandem, taking care to attend to DHH-relevant aspects while considering the fuller aspects of identity, family, and culture. As the wedding approaches, Cas extends a wedding invitation to her therapist, expressing that she very much hopes her therapist will attend. The therapist considers a number of relevant issues, including those of ethical and professional practice, limiting potential harms while maintaining the therapeutic relationship, maintaining professional boundaries, and navigating issues of small communities, such as the high likelihood that other clients will be attending the wedding. Cas and the therapist discuss these issues with great care.

Approaches to Treatment with DHH LGBTQ Population

As Leigh and Gutman (2010) note, when working with DHH people, "the client's language, culture, values, and goals can influence the effectiveness of particular therapeutic approaches and the ways in which they are applied" (p. 11). Clinicians must consider how all clients' experiences, including those of socialized privilege and minoritization, may impact the efficacy and outcomes of an evidence-based approach—for example, a clinician who is educated and trained in culturally responsive mental health care with DHH people may overlook a transgender client's hesitation in disclosing their gender identity if the client does not feel affirmed by the clinician in this regard.

Research suggests that clinicians working with DHH LGBTQ populations, especially with transgender and nonbinary people, typically approach treatment from an affirmation perspective (Glickman & Harvey, 1996; Hinrichs & Donaldson, 2017). Affirmative therapy, a psychotherapeutic philosophy that validates sexual and gender minority clients' experiences and advocates for their needs, supports clients in coming to a place of self-actualization, realizing one's full potential (D'Souza & Gurin, 2016; Hinrichs & Donaldson, 2017). Gutman and Zangas (2010) note that therapists should help clients "internalize a sense of pride and wholeness as LGBT Deaf people" regardless of the therapist's theoretical approach (p. 94). Such an approach is also effective with DHH persons who may be contemplating, developing, or exploring their identity as D/deaf or Hard of Hearing (Glickman & Harvey, 1996).

In addition to affirmative therapy, other best practices require that the therapist be trained in evidence-based practices applied to specific mental health concerns, such as Eye Movement Desensitization and Reprocessing (EMDR) or Cognitive Processing Therapy (CPT) for PTSD, or Cognitive Behavior Therapy (CBT) for Substance Use or Alcohol Use Disorder, to name a few. Similarly, when working with transgender Deaf clients who may be seeking gender affirming care, the therapist must not only know the WPATH Standards of Care, but also be able to integrate such knowledge with their training in evidence-based practices in the context of the presenting needs and life history of the particular client (Coleman et al., 2022). In addition to or compounded by isolated or co-occurring mental health concerns, DHH LGBTQ people may report experiences of systemic and interpersonal violence, both acute and chronic, that can span "childhood to adulthood, covert to overt, and interpersonal to systematic" (Lund et al., 2021, p. 1). Thus, clinicians should be trained to provide culturally responsive, trauma-informed, and, when possible, language-concordant care when working with clients who have experienced personal and systemic violence.

Finally, therapists offering evidence-based psychotherapy (EBP) must have knowledge (or at minimum seek consultation) on adapting such approaches to fit the needs of DHH clients of varying identities. For example, regarding the use of EMDR with DHH clients, therapist Alana Roy writes: "Deaf people store memories visually and kinesthetically rather than linguistically – EMDR makes use of bilateral stimulation which commonly involves eye movements related to REM sleep, but can also use tactile, auditory or kinesthetic stimuli" (The Signs of Life Psychology, 2020, para. 8). When providing EMDR to DHH clients, asking them to close their eyes and listen to the clinician may not be optimal if the client relies on fully visual communication means such as sign language or lipreading—rather, the therapist must modify the approach to fit the client's needs (Freeman, 2019; Jhai, 2024).

Deaf and Hard-of-Hearing clients often struggle to find therapists who are fluent in ASL and/or who can meet their communication needs (Boness, 2016). Can the clinician communicate with the DHH client in ASL, if this is the client's preferred language? Is the clinician aware that not all DHH people use ASL and some may prefer to speak and/or lipread? If the clinician does not sign, do they have the resources to provide a culturally competent ASL interpreter trained in mental health interpreting for a client if requested, and furthermore, are they aware that such accommodations are mandated under ADA? As many DHH clinicians know, bringing in an interpreter for a client's first psychotherapy session is a matter of careful thought and preparation—the clinician should identify an interpreter who ideally has training and experience in mental health interpreting (Coleman et al., 2022; National Association of the Deaf, 2025). Further, the clinician should ascertain that all parties, including interpreter and clinician, do not have dual roles such that therapy is compromised (Cohen, 2019). Additionally, therapists should strive to be aware of their own areas of personal and systemic ignorance, bias, and likely countertransference (Kuehne et al., 2022). These are just a few considerations of clinicians who work with DHH LGBTQ clients. Extending beyond the scope of this chapter, one must also consider the multifaceted considerations to using interpreters in sessions, and we encourage readers to view the National Association for the Deaf (NAD) Position Statement on Mental Health Interpreting Services for People Who are Deaf for a list of relevant, in-depth resources (National Association of the Deaf, 2025).

In sum, regardless of specific approaches used, the culturally responsive clinician should be well-versed in the ways in which the multi-directional experience of identities may show up for a client (Anders et al., 2021).

Conclusion

Mental health concerns and diagnoses common among DHH LGBTQ people may include mood and anxiety disorders, PTSD, substance use disorders, and symptoms and diagnoses of gender dysphoria. Deaf and Hard-of-Hearing LGBTQ people seeking effective mental health care may encounter complex challenges that include social isolation, barriers to access, systemic and institutional discrimination, and a dearth of culturally responsive or language-concordant support systems with competence or capacity to meet clients' specific needs. Clients' varied identities may shape and be shaped by the challenges noted above, while the limited availability of culturally responsive mental health services may exacerbate presenting issues.

Irrespective of language and identity concordance or non-concordance, mental health care providers should consider the mental health needs of DHH LGBTQ people, using nuanced, culturally responsive, and trauma-informed approaches to improve therapy outcomes and client well-being. Understanding the complexity of individual experiences within the broader social context and evolving landscape of mental health care is crucial for providing effective mental health care and support to Deaf LGBTQ people (Cook et al., 2014). As noted by Jackson et al. (2022), future research and clinical training would do well to focus on the elimination of structural racism and transphobia and to "avoid the injustice of burdening marginalized individuals with the task of building the resilience to endure oppressive systems that are not of their making" (p. 22). Providers are encouraged to consider how the intersection of systemic change and individual resiliency could lead to better health outcomes and equity for DHH LGBTQ populations.

References

Aldalur, A., Dillon, K. M., Rotoli, J. M., Stecker, T., & Conner, K. R. (2024). Deaf perceptions about treatment for alcohol use and mental health. *Journal of Substance Use and Addiction Treatment, 158*, 209–233. https://doi.org/10.1016/j.josat.2023.209233

Aldalur, A., Anderson, M. L., Van Orden, K. A., & Conner, K. R. (2025). Mental health treatment engagement among deaf individuals. *Psychiatric Services*, appi-ps. https://doi.org/10.1176/appi.ps.20240079

Americans With Disabilities Act of 1990, 42 U.S.C. § 12101 et seq. (1990). https://www.ada.gov/pubs/adastatute08.htm

Anders, C., Kivlighan, D. M., Porter, E., Lee, D., & Owen, J. (2021). Attending to the intersectionality and saliency of clients' identities: A further investigation of therapists' multicultural orientation. *Journal of Counseling Psychology, 68*(2), 139–148. https://doi.org/10.1037/cou0000447

Anderson, M. L., Wolf Craig, K. S., Hall, W. C., et al. (2016). A pilot study of deaf trauma survivors' experiences: Early traumas unique to being deaf in a hearing world. *Journal of Child and Adolescent Trauma, 9*, 353–358. https://doi.org/10.1007/s40653-016-0111-2

Anderson, M. L., Glickman, N. S., Wolf Craig, K. S., Sortwell Crane, A. K., Wilkins, A. M., & Najavits, L. M. (2021). Developing signs of safety: A deaf-accessible counselling toolkit for trauma and addiction. *Clinical Psychology & Psychotherapy, 28*(6), 1562–1573. https://doi.org/10.1002/cpp.2596

Argenyi, M., & Kushalnagar, P. (2019). Social media use and HIV screening uptake among deaf adults in the United States: Cross-sectional survey study. *JMIR Public Health and Surveillance, 5*(4), e13658. https://doi.org/10.2196/13658

Beese, L. E., & Tasker, F. (2022). Toward an understanding of the experiences of deaf gay men: An interpretative phenomenological analysis to an intersectional view. *Journal of Homosexuality, 69*(14), 2412–2438. https://doi.org/10.1080/00918369.2021.1940015

Biskupiak, A., Smith, S., & Kushalnagar, P. (2018). Pre-exposure prophylaxis knowledge and perceived effectiveness to prevent HIV among deaf gay, bisexual, and queer men. *LGBT Health, 5*(8), 469–476. https://doi.org/10.1089/lgbt.2018.0102

Bockting, W. O. (2008). Psychotherapy and the real life experience: From gender dichotomy to gender diversity. *Sexologies, 17*(4), 211–224. https://doi.org/10.1016/j.sexol.2008.08.001

Boness, C. L. (2016). Treatment of deaf clients: Ethical considerations for professionals in psychology. *Ethics and Behavior, 26*(7), 562–585. https://doi.org/10.1080/10508422.2015.1084929

Cheslik, B., & Wright, S. J. (2021). The impact of gay social networking applications on dating in the deaf gay community. *Sexuality & Culture, 25*(3), 1025–1040. https://doi.org/10.1007/s12119-020-09807-4

Cohen, C. (2019). Confidentiality in mental health with deaf populations: Perceptions of the consumer. *JADARA, 36*(1) Retrieved from https://repository.wcsu.edu/jadara/vol36/iss1/5

Coleman, E., Radix, A. E., Bouman, W. P., Brown, G. R., de Vries, A. L. C., Deutsch, M. B., Ettner, R., Fraser, L., Goodman, M., Green, J., Hancock, A. B., Johnson, T. W., Karasic, D. H., Knudson, G. A., Leibowitz, S. F., Meyer-Bahlburg, H. F. L., Monstrey, S. J., Motmans, J., Nahata, L., Nieder, T. O., & Arcelus, J. (2022). Standards of Care for the Health of transgender and gender diverse people, version 8. *International Journal of Transgender Health, 23*(Suppl 1), S1–S259. https://doi.org/10.1080/26895269.2022.2100644

Cook, J. E., Purdie-Vaughns, V., Meyer, I. H., & Busch, J. T. A. (2014). Intervening within and across levels: A multilevel approach to stigma and public health. *Social Science & Medicine, 103*, 101–109. https://doi.org/10.1016/j.socscimed.2013.09.023

D'Souza, J., & Gurin, M. (2016). The universal significance of Maslow's concept of self actualization. *The Humanistic Psychologist, 44*(2), 210–214. https://doi.org/10.1037/hum0000027

Dunne, C. M. (2013). *Deaf/LGBTQ intersectional invisibility in schools: The lived experiences of deaf lesbian students of color at a school for the deaf.* University of Pennsylvania.

Freeman, A. (2019). Eye movement desensitization and reprocessing (EMDR) as an effective technique for post traumatic disorders in hearing impaired persons. *JADARA, 37*(1) Retrieved from https://repository.wcsu.edu/jadara/vol37/iss1/6

Gallagher, G. M. (2022). *Prevalence of self-reported communication experiences and common DSM-5 diagnoses among a clinical sample of Deaf and Hard of Hearing university students.* (Publication No. 2845001115) [Doctoral dissertation, Gallaudet University]. ProQuest Dissertations & Theses Global. Gallaudet University.

Glickman, N., & Harvey, A. (1996). *Culturally affirmative psychotherapy with deaf persons.* Routledge Press.

Gutman, V., & Zangas, T. (2010). Therapy issues with lesbians, gay men, bisexuals, and transgender individuals who are deaf. In I. W. Leigh (Ed.), *Psychotherapy with deaf clients from diverse groups* (pp. 85–108). Gallaudet University Press.

Hall, W. C., Dye, T. D., & Siddiqi, S. (2023). Associations of childhood hearing loss and adverse childhood experiences in deaf adults. *PLoS One, 18*(6), e0287024. https://doi.org/10.1371/journal.pone.0287024

Heiman, E., Haynes, S., & McKee, M. (2015). Sexual health behaviors of deaf American sign language (ASL) users. *Disability and Health Journal, 8*(4), 579–585. https://doi.org/10.1016/j.dhjo.2015.06.005

Hernandez, B. (2024). *Prevalence and impact of discrimination on marginalized Deaf and Hard of Hearing individuals' access to mental health care.* [Doctoral dissertation, Gallaudet University]. ProQuest Dissertations & Theses Global.

Hinrichs, K. L. M., & Donaldson, W. (2017). Recommendations for use of affirmative psychotherapy with LGBT older adults. *Journal of Clinical Psychology, 73*(8), 945–953. https://doi.org/10.1002/jclp.22505

Hoang, L., LaHousse, S. F., Nakaji, M. C., & Sadler, G. R. (2011). Assessing deaf cultural competency of physicians and medical students. *Journal of Cancer Education: The Official Journal of the American Association for Cancer Education, 26*(1), 175–182. https://doi.org/10.1007/s13187-010-0144-4

Holcomb, T. (2022). *Utilizing the Childhood Trauma Questionnaire with Deaf adults: Translation and validation of an ASL-English bilingual survey.* (Publication #: 29326490) [Doctoral dissertation, Gallaudet University]. ProQuest Dissertations & Theses Global.

Jackson, S. D., Wagner, K. R., Yepes, M., Harvey, T. D., Higginbottom, J., & Pachankis, J. E. (2022). A pilot test of a treatment to address intersectional stigma, mental health, and HIV risk among gay and bisexual men of color. *Psychotherapy, 59*(1), 96–112. https://doi.org/10.1037/pst0000417

James, T. G., Argenyi, M. S., Guardino, D. L., McKee, M. M., Wilson, J. A. B., Sullivan, M. K., Schwartzman, E. G., & Anderson, M. L. (2022). Communication access in mental health and substance use treatment facilities for deaf American sign language users. *Health Affairs, 41*(10), 1413–1422.,1422A-1422L. https://doi.org/10.1377/hlthaff.2022.00408

Jhai, Z.-T. (2024). The impact and adaptation of EMDR therapy on the Taiwanese deaf university students. *Journal of EMDR Practice and Research, 18*(1), 10.1891/EMDR-2023- 0043.

Klein, B. A. (2021). *Aging deaf lesbians: A study of stigmatization, marginalization, resistance and resilience from 1945 to 2020.* American University.

Kuehne, J., Joy, M., Deacon, M., Higgins, B., & Roberts, N. (2022). Law and Ethics in Counseling with the Deaf Community (2022). Faculty Publications and Presentations. 219. https://digitalcommons.liberty.edu/ccfs_fac_pubs/219

Kushalnagar, P., & Miller, C. A. (2019). Health disparities among mid-to-older deaf LGBTQ adults compared with mid-to-older deaf non-LGBTQ adults in the United States. *Health Equity, 3*(1), 541–547. https://doi.org/10.1089/heq.2019.0009

Kushalnagar, P., Reesman, J., Holcomb, T., & Ryan, C. (2019). Prevalence of anxiety or depression diagnosis in deaf adults. *Journal of Deaf Studies and Deaf Education, 24*(4), 378–385. https://doi.org/10.1093/deafed/enz017

Leigh, I. W. (2017). The complexities of deaf identities. In S. Bagga-Gupta, A. L. Hansen, & J. Feilberg (Eds.), *Identity revisited and reimagined: Empirical and theoretical contributions on embodied communication across time and space* (pp. 207–220). Springer International Publishing/Springer Nature.

Leigh, I. W., & Gutman, V. (2010). Psychotherapy with deaf people: The ethical dimension. In I. W. Leigh & V. Gutman (Eds.), *Psychotherapy with deaf clients from diverse groups* (2nd ed., pp. 3–17). Gallaudet University Press.

Leigh, I. W., Andrews, J. F., Harris, R. L., & Ávila, G. T. (2022). Deaf community: Past and present. In *Deaf culture: Exploring deaf communities in the United States* (pp. 3–29). Plural Publishing.

Lund, E. M., Burgess, C., & Johnson, A. J. (2021). Queer violence: Confronting diverse forms of violence against LGBTQ+ persons and communities. In E. M. Lund, C. Burgess, & A. J. Johnson (Eds.), *Violence against LGBTQ+ persons: Research, practice, and advocacy* (pp. 1–4). Springer Nature. https://doi.org/10.1007/978-3-030-52612-2_1

Martos, A. J., Wilson, P. A., & Meyer, I. H. (2017). Lesbian, gay, bisexual, and transgender (LGBT) health services in the United States: Origins, evolution, and contemporary landscape. *PLoS One, 12*(7), e0180544. https://doi.org/10.1371/journal.pone.0180544

Mathos, K. K., Kilbourne, A. M., Myers, R. R., & Post, E. P. (2009). Disparities in mental health services for persons who are deaf: Advancing research towards action. *Journal of the American Deafness & Rehabilitation Association (JADARA), 42*(3), 152–166.

Mauldin, L. (2018). "Coming out" rhetoric in disability studies: Exploring the limits of analogy by looking at its fit with the deaf experience. *Disability Studies Quarterly, 38*(2) https://dsqsds.org/index.php/dsq/article/view/5863/4900

Miller, C., & Clark, K. (2019). Deaf and queer at the intersections: Deaf LGBTQ people and communities. In I. W. Leigh & D. O'Brien (Eds.), *Deaf identities: Exploring new frontiers* (pp. 305–335). Oxford University Press. https://doi.org/10.1093/oso/9780190887599.003.0013

Miller, C. A., Biskupiak, A., & Kushalnagar, P. (2019). Deaf LGBTQ patients' disclosure of sexual orientation and gender identity to health care providers. *Psychology of Sexual Orientation and Gender Diversity, 6*(2), 194–203. https://doi.org/10.1037/sgd0000319

Moges, R. (2017). Cripping deaf studies and deaf literature: Deaf queer ontologies and intersectionality. In A. Kusters, M. De Meulder, & D. O'Brien (Eds.), *Innovations in deaf studies: The role of deaf scholars* (pp. 215–239). Oxford University Press.

Morris, B. A. (2023, November 4). *Black Deafhood: A journey at the intersection of sexuality, disability, race*. Washington Blade. https://www.washingtonblade.com/2023/11/04/bobbi-angelica-morrisprofile/

National Association of the Deaf. (2025). *Position statement on mental health interpreting services with people who are deaf.* https://www.nad.org/about-us/position-statements/position-statement-on-mental-health-interpreting-services-with-people-who-are-deaf/

Owens, G. P., Riggle, E. D., & Rostosky, S. S. (2007). Mental health services access for sexual minority individuals. *Sexuality Research & Social Policy, 4*, 92–99. https://doi.org/10.1525/srsp.2007.4.3.92

Pachankis, J. E., Clark, K. A., Jackson, S. D., Pereira, K., & Levine, D. (2021). Current capacity and future implementation of mental health services in U.S. LGBTQ community centers. *Psychiatric Services, 72*(6), 669–676. https://doi.org/10.1176/appi.ps.202000575

Paglieri, T. A., Kobek Pezzarossi, C., & Schooler, D. (2022). Social media use, acculturation, and self-esteem of deaf and hard-of-hearing adults. *JADARA, 54*(3), 2. https://nsuworks.nova.edu/jadara/vol54/iss3/2

Sanfacon, K., Leffers, A., Miller, C., Stabbe, O., DeWindt, L., Wagner, K., & Kushalnagar, P. (2021). Cross-sectional analysis of medical conditions in the US deaf transgender community. *Transgender Health, 6*(3), 132–138. https://doi.org/10.1089/trgh.2020.0028

Saunders, K. C. (2016). A double-edged sword: Social media as a tool of online disinhibition regarding American sign language and deaf cultural experience marginalization, and as a tool of cultural and linguistic exposure. *Social Media + Society, 2*(1). https://doi.org/10.1177/2056305115624529

Schaad, A. L. (2015). *An interview with three Deaf lesbians: Intersectionality and saliency of identity variables* (Publication No. 1442) [Doctoral dissertation, Wright State University]. CORE Scholar. https://corescholar.libraries.wright.edu/etd_all/1442

Schmitz, J. (2021). Deaf-queer signing in process: A qualitative sociolinguistic study of "queering Deafhood", "Deafing Queerhood,"-and "queer sign language style.". *Sign Language Studies, 22*(1), 42–74. https://doi.org/10.1353/sls.2021.0014

Shipherd, J. C., Green, K. E., & Abramovitz, S. (2010). Transgender clients: Identifying and minimizing barriers to mental health treatment. *Journal of Gay and Lesbian Mental Health, 14*, 94–108. https://doi.org/10.1080/19359701003622875

Signs of Life Psychology. (2020). *Eye movement desensitisation and reprocessing therapy*. https://thesignsoflife.com.au/eye-movement-desensitisation-and-reprocessing-therapy

The Trevor Project. (2022, March 28). *Mental health of Deaf LGBTQ youth**. https://www.thetrevorproject.org/research-briefs/mental-health-of-deaf-lgbtq-youth-mar2022/

Tully, P. (2018). *Working with LGBTQ and Hard-of-Hearing clients—from the perspective of a hard-of-hearing and gay therapist.* https://www.therapyden.com/blog/working-with-lgbtqand-hard-of-hearing-clients-from-the-perspective-of-a-hard-of-hearing-and-gay-therapist

Williams, M. A., & Adams, T. R. (2021). Deafness and sexual orientation: The lived experiences of deaf LGBTQ individuals in healthcare contexts. *American Journal of Public Health, 111*(4), 693–700. https://doi.org/10.2105/AJPH.2021.306256

Wolfe, G., & Fogwell, N. (2022). DSM discrimination and the LGBT community: Using the history of diagnostic discrimination against sexual minorities to contextualize current issues in transgender and gender diverse mental healthcare. *Psychology from the Margins, 4*(1), 2.

Young, A., Espinoza, F., Dodds, C., Squires, G., Rogers, K., Chilton, H., & O'Neill, R. (2023). Introducing the READY study: DHH young people's Well-being and self-determination. *Journal of Deaf Studies and Deaf Education, 28*(3), 267–279. https://doi.org/10.1093/deafed/enad002

Yu, H., Flores, D. D., Bonett, S., & Bauermeister, J. A. (2023). LGBTQ + cultural competency training for health professionals: A systematic review. *BMC Medical Education, 23*(1), 558. https://doi.org/10.1186/s12909-023-04373-3

Yuen, S., Li, B., Tsou, Y. T., Meng, Q., Wang, L., Liang, W., & Rieffe, C. (2022). Family systems and emotional functioning in deaf or hard-of-hearing preschool children. *Journal of Deaf Studies and Deaf Education, 27*(2), 125–136. https://doi.org/10.1093/deafed/enab044

Chapter 7
Lateral Violence Within the Deaf Community

M. Natasha Kordus and Amanda G. Somdal

Cultural Echoes of Lateral Violence

The term *lateral violence* may seem like an emerging buzzword; however, it has existed for a long time under various names, including internalized oppression, horizontal violence, intra-racial conflict, and peer-to-peer aggression. Kurt Lewin (1948) used the term *intragroup conflict* to describe tensions within Jewish communities, while Frantz Fanon (1963) examined similar dynamics in the context of colonialism in Africa. In 1967, Stokely Carmichael and Charles Hamilton wrote *Internal colonialism* to describe the systemic exploitation of the Black communities that led to intragroup tensions. Paulo Freire (1970) explored these concepts in relation to Latin America, and Jean Baker Miller (1976) introduced the term *horizontal hostility* in her analysis of women's experiences.

The terms *horizontal violence* and *lateral violence* became particularly prominent within Aboriginal and other Indigenous communities. The Native Women's Association of Canada (NWAC) (2011) defines lateral violence as "a learned behavior as a result of colonialism and patriarchal methods of governing and developing a society" (p. 1). Indigenous peoples were forcibly separated from their families, sent to residential schools operated by non-Indigenous individuals unfamiliar with their cultures, and systematically stripped of their traditions, languages, and beliefs.

The nursing profession adopted the term *lateral violence* due to the widespread occurrence of lateral violence within the field (Amrein, 2012). Slowly, other marginalized and oppressed groups recognized the harmful coping strategies within their communities; a response to the pervasive oppression and discrimination the

M. Natasha Kordus (✉)
Riverside, CA, USA
e-mail: natasha@collaborativepsychgroup.com

A. G. Somdal
Montgomery, AL, USA

T. Bone (ed.), *Deaf Mental Health*, Advances in Mental Health and Addiction,
https://doi.org/10.1007/978-3-032-06274-1_7

group was experiencing by the dominant group. Paraphrasing the writings of Dr. Maria Yellow Horse Brave Heart, a Lakota psychologist and trauma expert from 1995 and 1998, she discussed lateral violence and internalized oppression, stating that "when historical trauma is not addressed, it manifests in interpersonal relationships through lateral violence, substance abuse, and self-destruction" (Brave Heart-Jordan, 1995; Brave Heart, 1998).

Characteristics and Patterns of Lateral Violence

Lateral violence is violence that we do to others within our own community—people who share the same experiences, discrimination, oppression, and barriers as we do. We feel angry, hopeless, powerless, and ashamed with our seeming inability to thrive or overcome the pervasive oppression we experience from the privileged group therefore we take out our feelings on our peers.

Some of the lateral violence behaviors observed by Indigenous people (NWAC, 2011) and the nursing profession (Taylor & Taylor, 2017; Walrafen et al., 2012) within their communities included:

- Social exclusion (preventing the targeted person from participating in social groups by ignoring them or freezing them out)
- Sarcastic responses or facial expressions
- Blaming the targeted person
- Name-calling
- Belittling targeted person's opinions
- Bullying (making fun of or embarrassing the targeted person, making snide comments and remarks, and using put-downs then telling the targeted person they are too sensitive)
- Nonverbal intimation (eyebrow quirks, eye rolling, threatening gestures)
- Handing over tasks with unrealistic expectations that ensure the targeted person will fail
- Withholding information or giving wrong information purposely

These behaviors occur incessantly and typically involve multiple actions, not just one. They accumulate over time, affecting the targeted person's daily life, mental and emotional well-being, and relationships with others. Securing support to address lateral violence is challenging, as those surrounding the targeted individual may also be experiencing victimization, may minimize or dismiss the behavior, or may feel uncertain and fearful about how to respond due to a lack of knowledge in addressing lateral violence or fear of becoming targets themselves.

Although framed differently, the concept of lateral violence shares common patterns across other marginalized communities, including the LGBTQIA+2S community, where similar behaviors highlight the nuanced ways internalized oppression and power imbalances manifest within identity groups.

The Pain of Proximity: Intragroup Harm and the Role of Intersectionality

In their research on lateral violence, Tran et al. (2023) described similar behaviors described as microaggression *within* the LGBTQIA+2S community as behaviors perpetrated by someone with higher power status over the targeted person rather than by persons of similar power status. The lateral violence concept within the scholarly materials indicates that lateral violence implies a perpetrator, and the target is of equal or similar power status. Tran et al. (2023) however gave a relevant example of how a gay White male and a gay Asian male may share a minority status as gay men, yet the gay White male may have more power and privilege than the gay Asian male due to their ethnic identity statuses. A similar dynamic has been observed within other marginalized populations, such as the Deaf community, where intersecting identities contribute to nuanced power differentials and contribute to lateral violence within the group.

Tran et al. (2023) focuses their research on intersectionality as a theoretical framework of LGBTQIA+2S ingroup micro aggression, especially in the discussions of racial microaggression. Intersectionality theory emphasizes how one's identity, statuses intertwine and influence one's experiences, including how inequality can compound from intersecting statuses. Lateral violence, thus, may not seem like the most appropriate term to utilize in the queer context due to the different social, cultural, and para-dynamic within the community. However, LGBTQIA+2S people of color often feel that they are treated as second-class citizens and/or excluded from queer spaces, such as at events, bars, in the dating scene, and even social movement organizations. Microaggression, by its nature, is more implicit and covert rather than overt. LGBTQIA+2S people of color who wish to fit in are then pressured to assimilate to the white and homonormative culture. Another common manifestation of racial microaggression is sexualization and exoticization centered around racial stereotypes. This type of microaggression attributes LGBTQIA+2S people of color with preconceived sexual characteristics, causing the target to feel objectified/fetishized and pressured to fit the stereotypes or risk rejection.

Intragroup microaggression is more painful than microaggression done by those outside of the community. The targeted persons of the community are more unlikely to confront the aggressor and are confused that they are being targeted by someone within their own community. As Vaccaro and Koob (2019) writes that intragroup microaggressions are more harmful to the target, it is also less likely to be confronted or addressed in fear of losing their sense of belonging or support from peers. These behaviors and fears about addressing lateral violence are similar to what is observed in the Deaf community.

Manifestations of Lateral Violence Within the Deaf Community

While lateral violence and power and privilege disparities are present within the LGBTQIA+2S community, similar patterns can also be observed within the Deaf community. Within the Deaf community, there are various layers of what could be considered cultural capital, including factors such as the type of school attended (e.g., residential state school versus mainstream public school), the parents' auditory status, preferred communication modalities (e.g., American Sign Language, Pidgin Sign Language, or oral methods), and the degree of connection to the broader Deaf community. A deaf individual with higher cultural capital may hold more influence with their insular community and, as a result, may be more likely to perpetuate lateral violence without consequence. This is because others may be reluctant to confront such individuals, fearing they will become the next target of aggression.

> When a powerful oppressor has directed oppression against a group for a period of time, members of the oppressed group feel powerless to fight back and they eventually turn their anger against each other.
> —Jane Middleton-Moz

As noted by Jane Middleton-Moz (1999), prolonged exposure to oppression often fosters internalized anger, which can manifest as lateral violence—where members of a marginalized group turn their frustrations inward, targeting others within their own community. This process is typically shaped by a convergence of factors, including historical oppression, scarcity of resources, cultural misrecognition, and social isolation.

Within the Deaf[1]community, systemic barriers such as audism, limited access to equitable education, and underrepresentation in policy and decision-making contribute to the internalization of negative societal messages. This internalized oppression is embedded within broader structural forces—including governmental systems, educational institutions, technological access, and prevailing social norms—but it is also rooted in early personal experiences, particularly within family systems. The quality of familial relationships and early language access plays a critical role in shaping a Deaf individual's identity development and resilience in the face of external marginalization.

[1]Deaf (uppercase D) refers to individuals who are deaf or hard of hearing, consider themselves members of the Deaf community, and share similar cultural and linguistic values. Whereas deaf (lowercase d) means those individuals who have the audiological condition of hearing loss.

Invisible Wounds: Contributing Factors to Lateral Violence in Deaf Experiences

Ninety percent of Deaf individuals are born to hearing families (CDC data, 2025; NAD.org) who typically do not have any familiarity with the needs of the Deaf child. Their first source of information is the medical industrial complex whose job it is to provide multiple healthcare-related services for a profit. As well intended as these individual providers may be, they contribute to the idea that deafness is a condition that needs to be fixed. Parents are pushed to implant their children with promises that the Cochlear Implant (CI) is a cure rather than a *tool* for providing access. When CIs are not possible or fail, parents still hold on to hearing aids and speech services leaning on the promises from professionals that this is the only way to develop language (Marks, 2020). Parents are well meaning and depend on doctors and professionals to provide the best and most accurate information possible. However, if the information provided is biased or worse, embedded in a health care system that sees Deaf people as broken, then is it truly comprehensive and accurate? Parents are not able to make the best decisions for their children if they do not have all the information needed.

Another frequent recommendation that hearing parents receive early on is that their Deaf child must receive speech and language services. These typically mean spoken language training with the hope that the child will use their residual hearing to gain access to spoken language and be able to produce spoken words. This is embedded in the assumption that language acquisition must be done through the ears (Handspeak.com). However, more and more research shows that the infant brain is designed to acquire language as a system of patterns and can be accessed through the eyes and the ears and that either way long-term intervention and support is needed (Kuhl, 2010). Still, parents are almost invariably guided to spoken language services. In the past the approach was called "oralism" where parents were told not to learn ASL as it would distract from their children focusing on speech. Now the spoken-language-only community has shifted this paradigm to Listening and Spoken Language (LSL). LSL is a pedagogical method aimed at developing listening and speaking skills in deaf children (Hearing First). It is not a language on its own like ASL, but the similar acronym undermines the emerging knowledge that new parents are trying to acquire about their [Deaf] child because of its similarity. While CIs or hearing aids and spoken language can be useful tools in acquiring language, they should not be used in place of the rich, accessible, language of ASL. Providing children access to both the hearing and Deaf worlds—through technology when available, spoken and written language, and most importantly ASL—empowers them to fully engage with and benefit from the cultural capital of both communities.

Compared to the hearing community, the Deaf population is very small. The CDC estimates that 2 to 3 out of every 1000 children are born with a detectable hearing loss (CDC, 2025). What many parents do not realize is that even though infants may pass the newborn hearing screening, illnesses and other factors can impact hearing; by age 12, 1 in 8 children in the United States (roughly 13% or 30 million) experience some degree of hearing loss. Among American adults ages 18 and over, approximately 15% report hearing loss, with age being the strongest predictor—especially among those aged 60 to 69, who experience the greatest hearing deficits (CDC, 2025). Globally, the WHO predicts that by 2050 nearly 2.5 billion people will have some degree of hearing loss (WHO, 2024).

In a largely capitalist society, being part of a relatively small community can be a significant disadvantage. The reality is that the banquet of life is set, but not everyone is invited to the table. Resources—be they educational, employment-related, or service-based—are often distributed according to the market's logic of scarcity. In essence, limited resources create a sense of urgency and value, a basic marketing technique that drives up prices and profits by emphasizing scarcity. This dynamic contributes to the systemic marginalization of Deaf individuals and other overlooked groups, who are frequently excluded from the benefits of a nation built on the premise that wealth grants access. Within this framework, access to services, jobs, and education becomes limited, fostering internal competition, resentment, and conflict within the community itself.

This scarcity is also evident in educational attainment: among people aged 25–64 in the United States, an estimated 22.7% of Deaf individuals have completed a bachelor's degree or higher, compared to 38.4% of hearing individuals. The gap is even more pronounced among minority groups within the Deaf community, with only 16.2% of African American individuals, 16.1% of Native Americans, and 19.3% of BIPOC individuals who are Deaf attaining a bachelor's degree or higher (National Deaf Center on Postsecondary Outcomes, 2022). The barriers that contribute to lower educational attainment for Deaf individuals as well as to the broader social and economic disparities later in life are substantial and intertwined. There is limited early intervention and language access (Marschark & Hauser, 2012; Mayberry, 2002); there is a shortage of qualified educators and inadequate educational resources and accommodations (Knoors & Marschark, 2014). There are also communication barriers as well as the cultural and linguistic mismatch between the Deaf and hearing worlds. For instance, even access to training that differentiates between Deaf and hearing cultures is scarce, subsequently limiting Deaf people's access to better job opportunities (Greene-Woods et al., 2020).

In the United States, among people aged 16–64, an estimated 57.1% of Deaf people are employed, compared to 73.3% of hearing people (Bloom et al., 2025). This drops to 43.3% for African Americans and 41.7% for Native Americans who are Deaf. However, Asian American Deaf individuals have an employment rate of 61% and multiracial Deaf Americans have an employment rate of 53.7% (Bloom et al., 2025). Research indicates that the gap in educational achievement between Deaf and hearing individuals significantly contributes to the differences in their employment opportunities.

Beyond educational disparities and employment outcomes, cultural identity and affiliation also play a crucial role in shaping the experiences of Deaf individuals. Varying degrees of connection to Deaf culture (e.g., those raised using ASL versus those who became Deaf later or have cochlear implants) can lead to tensions and divisions. There is a long-standing war on communication options (Levy, 2007) and whether or not there exists a culture of the Deaf. Those who exist as part of the majority culture tend to stand in judgment often using words like "subculture" or dismissing altogether that a group of individuals who share a common experience cannot come together and define their boundaries of connection. Deaf culture exists because the Deaf community says it exists. They do not need external validation to prove this fact. They share a common language of American Sign Language and sign language is fundamental to the lives that Deaf people experience. Deaf culture is rooted in a shared experience of being Deaf in a predominantly hearing world. These experiences foster a sense of solidarity and mutual understanding that creates bonds among community members. There are cultural norms within the community (e.g., maintaining eye contact during communication, using visual signals to get attention) and traditions (e.g., storytelling through ASL and sporting tournaments at Deaf schools). These are passed down through generations and a way of preserving the culture. The Deaf community takes pride in their culture citing Deaf Gain, not loss—a fundamental tenet which reframes being Deaf as an advantage and source of richness rather than a deficit. It is crucial to understand that the Deaf identity is presented here in simpler terms due to the constraints of the chapter. However, the reality is that identity is often multifaceted in that Deaf people can also be people of color, LGBTQIA+2S, gender non-conforming, or many other identities (Lawyer, 2018).

However, most Deaf people, having grown up in hearing families, are socially isolated and frequently economically dependent on their families for survival. Without overt intention, hearing families reinforce the idea of ableism. That is, that people with disabilities are less capable than typically abled individuals. Inherent to this is the idea that abilities such as walking, hearing, or seeing are superior and it manifests in systemic barriers, social attitudes, and policies that disadvantage disabled individuals. Campbell (2008, 2009) argues that the internalization of ableism is a two-pronged strategy: "the distancing of disabled people from each other (dispersal) and the adoption by disabled people of ablest norms (emulation)" (2008, p.22). What this means is that ableism often encourages the idea that being less disabled is preferable. This leads individuals to avoid identifying with communities that take pride in their disability (e.g., rejecting Deaf identity and the concept of Deaf Gain). As individuals with hearing loss distance themselves from the very community that best understands their experiences, they reinforce internalized ableism and begin to minimize their need for or use of assistive devices to fit in.

For example, they may choose flesh-colored or inconspicuous hearing aids to make them less noticeable. Additionally, they are more likely to use spoken language rather than ASL to communicate, further aligning with hearing norms. As a result, Deaf individuals are pressured to adopt a "hearing" identity at the expense of their own. In doing so, they inadvertently participate in what Campbell (2009) calls "the process of disability disavowal"—aspiring toward the norm, attempting to achieve near able-bodiedness, or at the very least, seeking to "pass." According to Leary (1999), passing occurs in response to a perceived sense of danger: "It represents a form of self-protection that nevertheless usually disables, and sometimes destroys, the self it means to safeguard." (p.85)

Cycle of Ableism and Audism in Deaf Experience

Johannsdotti et al. (2022) point out that disabled people do not absorb negative representations of disability uncritically and passively; "rather, their responses are often contradictory. Reacting to these ambiguous responses, disabled people are shamed into unwittingly performing ableism, further establishing impairment as unattractive and undesirable" (p.367). This feeds into the most destructive of all feelings—shame. Brené Brown (2007) defines shame as the painful feeling of believing you are flawed and unworthy of connection and belonging. And thus, the cycle:

It is important to point out that the authors are identifying the cycle that contributes to intergenerational trauma, the final component of lateral violence (Fig. 7.1). This cycle goes back to cultural capital as most Deaf children of hearing families do not experience the positive cultural capital of being embedded in the Deaf community. They do not grow up with the ideas of Deaf Gain or pride in their cultural wealth. Deaf people often grow up with the idea that they are damaged, that "those

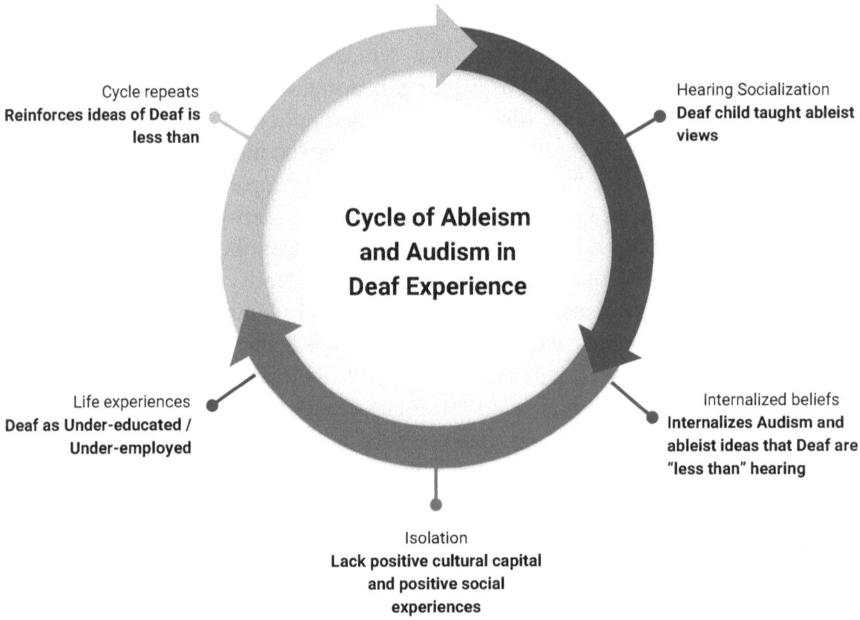

Fig. 7.1 Cycle of Ableism and Audism. Created by authors. Used with permission

who can speak are better than those who can't speak" (Hutchinson, 2024) a key factor of audism. The term "Audism" was first coined by Tom Humphries (1975) in his unpublished manuscript "The notion that one is superior based on one's ability to hear or to behave in the manner of one who hears" (p. 1). In a broader sense audism encompasses many aspects of discrimination against those who have a hearing loss. Genie Gertz (2003) further identified the following critical manifestations of audism:

- Interpersonal Audism—Prejudgment, bias, or discrimination by a hearing individual toward a Deaf or Hard of Hearing person.
- Institutional Audism—Policies, practices, procedures, and culture of an institution or system that work better for hearing people and cause harm to Deaf or Hard of Hearing, often inadvertently or unintentionally (e.g., no captioning on public TVs, no access to interpreters, hearing people that do not know ASL or look down on ASL, prioritizing mainstreaming or oral only programs, or denying access to learning ASL).
- Structural Audism—The history, culture, and current reality of audism across institutions and/or systems, when the institutional audism of multiple institutions overlaps to form a web of audism impacting people and the Deaf communities. This includes implicit and explicit social narratives about Deaf identity (e.g., "inspiring disability movies" about the Deaf suddenly being able to hear or learning to talk), such as those perpetuated by the media (e.g., YouTube videos of CIs being turned on and crying mothers).
- Internalized Audism—The internalization of the Audist stereotypes, values, images, and ideologies perpetuated by the hearing dominant society about the Deaf Community ("Deaf People can't drive, can't live independently, can't marry, can't - can't - can't").
- Internalized Audist Inferiority—The acceptance and acting out of an inferior definition of self, rooted in the historical designation of one's identity. Over many generations, this process of disempowerment and disenfranchisement is expressed in self-defeating behaviors. Some examples: discriminating against other Deaf people, isolation, protectionism, addiction, self-doubt, self-hate, rage, shame, metaphysical audism (stems from a societal belief that speech is a fundamental aspect of humanity. As a result of this perspective, people who don't speak face severe discriminatory attitudes that relegate them to "other" or "lesser"), dysconscious audism (a form of internalized audism within the Deaf community—may decide not to learn ASL or are reluctant to be involved in the Deaf community); conscious audism (individuals—both hearing and Deaf—intentionally engage in audist practices or hold audist beliefs. Although these audists are aware of their prejudice and its potential for harm, they choose to continue to discriminate).
- Internalized Audist Superiority—The acceptance and acting out of a superior definition of self, rooted in the historical designation of one's identified group. Over many generations, this process of empowerment and access is expressed as unearned privileges, access to institutional power, invisible advantages and

inflated self-image based upon hearing. Some examples: Individualism, paternalism, comfort, control, silence, intellectualization, cognitive dissonance.

Understanding audism as a manifestation of kyriocentrism[1] allows for a deeper critique of the intersections between ableism, colonialism, and linguistic oppression (Lawyer, 2018). These concepts have shaped the experiences of Deaf individuals for generations and are deeply embedded in societal structures influencing education, economic opportunities, and family relationships leading to cycles of intergenerational trauma within the Deaf community. Discrimination and exclusion from mainstream society can intensify pressure and conflict within the community. Furthermore, experiences like oralism, forced assimilation, and exclusion from their own language and culture can lead to cycles of trauma and conflict.

The Silent Harm: The Mental Health Cost of Lateral Violence

The fact is, those subjected to oppression may also be more vulnerable to experiencing traumatic life events and exhibit a limited capacity to counteract internalized oppression (Tomaszewski et al., 2025). Depression and anxiety in the Deaf community are strongly influenced by age, internalized ableism, and societal barriers. Research suggests that younger Deaf individuals are even more susceptible to depression, as they have not yet developed the coping mechanisms that older Deaf adults acquire over time. A significant 42% of young Deaf people in the UK exhibit probable or possible depression, highlighting the urgent need for mental health interventions (Young et al., 2023). Early stressful experiences, limited language access, and restricted healthcare resources further contribute to this vulnerability. Internalized ableism plays a pivotal role, as negative self-perceptions can lead to social withdrawal and isolation, exacerbating depressive symptoms.

Tomaszewski et al. (2025) found that anxiety, both state and trait, is also disproportionately high within the Deaf population due to communication barriers, social stigma, and pressures to conform to hearing societal norms. Deaf individuals who regularly interact in hearing environments experience higher levels of anxiety, as they are frequently subjected to stressful communication challenges and feelings of exclusion. Those who are more embedded in Deaf culture, tend to report lower anxiety levels due to stronger community support. However, internalized audism and linguicism can significantly increase both trait and state anxiety, as individuals internalize societal prejudices, leading to heightened vigilance and emotional distress. A staggering 64% of Deaf participants in the study by Tomaszewski et al. (2025) exhibited moderate to high trait anxiety, suggesting a lifetime of chronic stress and unresolved trauma. Compounding this issue, limited access to culturally and linguistically appropriate mental health services restricts opportunities for proper psychological care. These findings highlight the need for structural adjustments, greater accessibility in healthcare and education, and broader societal recognition of the unique mental health challenges Deaf individuals face.

Below is a figure (Fig. 7.2) that translates the interplay of discrimination within the Deaf community. Based on the lived experiences of these authors and the summary of research, we hypothesize that lateral violence within the Deaf community arises as a consequence of systemic audism, intergenerational trauma, and internalized oppression, leading to conflict and division among Deaf individuals. Rooted in historical and ongoing marginalization—such as oralism, forced integration, and exclusion from language access—this phenomenon manifests when oppression is redirected inward rather than outward toward the systems responsible for it. In the Deaf community, lateral violence often takes the form of gatekeeping, where individuals are judged on their "Deaf authenticity" based on factors such as sign fluency, cultural upbringing, Deaf social capital, or use of cochlear implants. Identity policing, exclusion based on educational background (mainstream vs. Deaf school), and the replication of hierarchical structures from the hearing world further exacerbate these divisions. These conflicts do not emerge in isolation but rather as a response to generations of discrimination, lack of access to resources, lack of access to language fluency (and therefore information), and the struggle for cultural

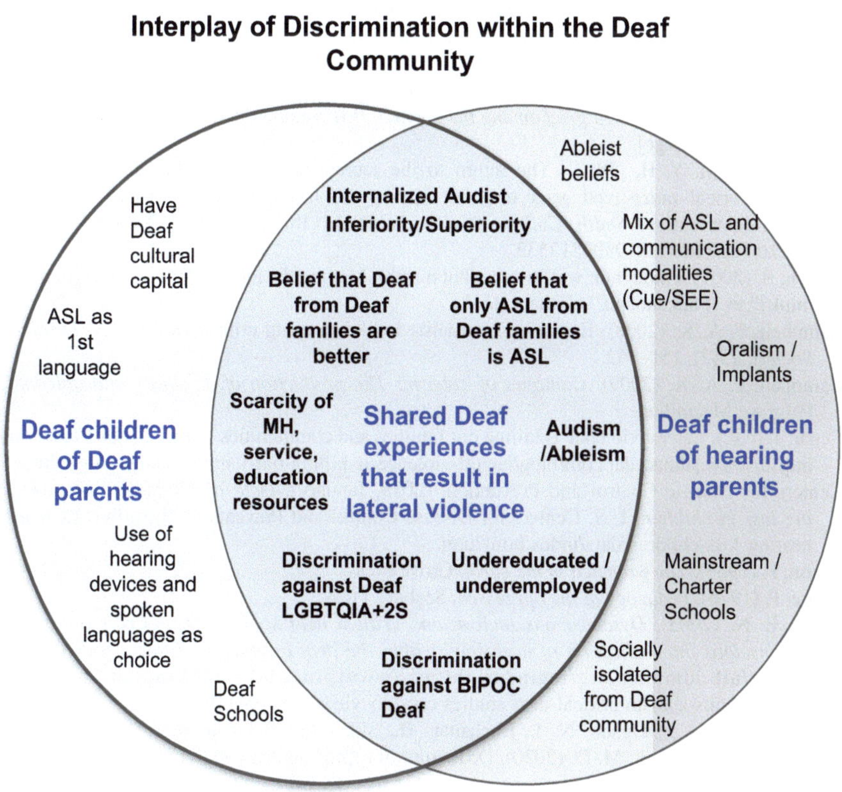

Fig. 7.2 Interplay of discrimination within Deaf Community. Developed by and used with permission of authors. Somdal—Lateral violence FIGURES

survival. Understanding lateral violence within the Deaf community requires recognizing it not as an internal flaw but as a byproduct of systemic oppression. This is, therefore, a call for collective healing, solidarity, and a dismantling of the structures that perpetuate division.

To quote Jahna Cedar, the Aboriginal and Torres Strait Islander Social Justice Commissioner, from blog article Lateral Violence is Killing our Families and Communities, "It is important to point out that lateral violence is not holding people accountable for breaching protocols or doing the wrong thing. That is in fact having the courage to call out poor behavior and show that it is not accepted, because the behavior you're willing to walk past, is the behavior you're willing to accept." (Cedar, J. (n.d.).

References

Amrein, K. R. (2012). Horizontal violence: Can anything be done? *Nursing, 42*(9), 1–2. https://doi.org/10.1097/01.NURSE.0000418620.83970.1c

Bloom, C. L, Palmer, J. L., & Winninghoff, J. (2025). Deaf Postsecondary Data from the American Community Survey [Data visualization tool]. National Deaf Center on Postsecondary Outcomes, University of Texas at Austin. www.nationaldeafcenter.org/dashboard

Brave Heart-Jordan, M. Y. H. (1995). *The return to the sacred path: Healing the historical trauma and historical unresolved grief among the lakota* (UMI Number: 9600362) [Doctoral dissertation, Smith College].

Brave Heart, M. Y. H. (1998). The return to the sacred path: Healing the historical trauma and historical unresolved grief response among the lakota through a psychoeducational group intervention. *Smith College Studies in Social Work, 68*(3), 287–305. https://doi.org/10.1080/00377319809517532

Brown, B. (2007). I thought it was just me (but it isn't): Making the journey from "what will people think?" to "I am enough." Gotham Books.

Campbell, F. A. K. (2008). Exploring internalized ableism using critical race theory. *Disability Society, 23*(2), 151–162.

Campbell, F. A. K. (2009). *Contours of ableism: The production of disability and abledness*. Palgrave Macmillan.

Cedar, J. (n.d.). Lateral violence is killing our families and communities. *Jahna Cedar Consulting*. https://www.jahnacedar.com/blog/lateral-violence-is-killing-our-families-and-communities

Centers for Disease Control and Prevention. (2025, January). *Data and statistics about hearing loss in children.* U.S. Centers for Disease Control and Prevention. https://www.cdc.gov/hearing-loss-children/data/index.html?utm.

Fanon, F. (1963). *The wretched of the earth.* Grove Press.

Freire, P. (1970). *Pedagogy of the oppressed.* Seabury Press.

Gertz, E. N. (2003). *Dysconscious audism and critical deaf studies: Deaf Crit's analysis of unconscious internalization of hegemony within the deaf community* (Order No. 3100674). https://utk.idm.oclc.org/login?url=https://www.proquest.com/dissertations-theses/dysconscious-audism-critical-deaf-studies-crits/docview/305349414/se-2.

Greene-Woods, A., Delgado, N. J., Buchanan, B., Sides, M., Behmanesh, A. A., Cheslik, B., Koo, C. K., & Clark, M. D. (2020). Deaf cultural capital and its conflict with hearing culture: Navigational successes and failures. *JADARA, 54*(1), 13–30.

Humphries, T. (1975). *In making of a word: Audism* [Unpublished manuscript].

Hutchinson, L. (2024, May 31). Striving for language equity: Early intervention is key for language acquisition in deaf children. Zero to Three. https://www.zerotothree.org/resource/resource/striving-for-language-equity-early-intervention-is-key-for-language-acquisition-in-deaf-children/?utm.

Johannsdotti, A., Haraldsdottir, F., & Elison, S. P. (2022). Implications of internalised ableism for the health and wellbeing of disabled young people. *Sociology of Health & Illness, 44*, 360–376.

Knoors, H., & Marschark, M. (2014). Teaching deaf learners: Psychological and developmental foundations. Oxford University Press.

Kordus, M. N., & Somdal, A. G. (2025). Lateral violence within the deaf community. In T. Bone (Ed.). *Deaf mental health.* Springer Nature.

Kuhl, P. K. (2010). Brain mechanisms in early language acquisition. *Neuron, 67(5), 713–727.*

Lawyer, G. L. (2018). Removing the colonizer's coat in deaf education: Exploring the curriculum of colonization and the field of deaf education. Doctoral Dissertation: University of Tennessee.

Leary, K. (1999). Passing, posing, and "keeping it real". *Constellations, 6*(1), 85–96. https://doi.org/10.1111/1467-8675.00122

Levy, N. (2007). Must publicly funded research be culturally neutral? *The Virtual Mentor, 9*(2), 140–142. https://doi.org/10.1001/virtualmentor.2007.9.2.oped1-0702

Lewin, K. (1948). *Resolving social conflicts; selected papers on group dynamics.* Harper.

Marschark, M., & Hauser, P. C. (2012). How deaf children learn: What parents and teachers need to know. OUP USA.

Marks, M. (2020). Linguistic neglect of deaf children in the United States. Ballard Brief. https://ballardbrief.byu.edu/issue-briefs/linguistic-neglect-of-deaf-children-in-the-united-states.

Mayberry, R. I. (2002). Cognitive development in deaf children: The interface of language and perception in neuropsychology. In *Handbook of neuropsychology* (Vol. 8, 2nd ed.) Part II.

Middleton-Moz, J. (1999). *Shame and guilt: Masters of disguise.* Health Communications, Inc.

Miller, J. B. (1976). *Toward a new psychology of women.* Beacon Press.

National Deaf Center on Postsecondary Outcomes. (2022). Deaf postsecondary data dashboard. The University of Texas at Austin. https://nationaldeafcenter.org/resources/research-data/dashboard/.

Native Women's Association of Canada (NWAC). (2011). *Aboriginal lateral violence.* https://www.nwac.ca/assets-knowledge-centre/2011-Aboriginal-Lateral-Violence.pdf.

Taylor, R. A., & Taylor, S. S. (2017). Enactors of horizontal violence: The pathological bully, the self-justified bully and the unprofessional co-worker. *Journal of Advanced Nursing, 73*(12), 3111–31118. https://doi.org/10.1111/jan.13382

Tomaszewski, P., Krysztofiak, P. Kowalska, J. & Hauser, P. (2025). Internalized oppression and people's mentalhealth. *Scientific Reports, 15*, 5268. https://doi.org/10.1038/s41598-025-89789-1

Tran, D., Sullivan, C. T., & Nicholas, L. (2023). Lateral violence and microaggressions in the LGBTQ+ community: A scoping review. *Journal of Homosexuality, 70(7), 1310–1324.* https://doi.org/10.1080/00918369.2021.2020543

Vaccaro, A. & Koob, R. M. (2019). A critical and intersectional model of LGBTQ microaggressions: Toward a more comprehensive understanding. *Journal of Homosexuality, 66*(10), 1317–1344. https://doi.org/10.1080/00918369.2018.1539583

Walrafen, N., Brewer, M. K., & Mulvenon, C. (2012). Sadly caught up in the moment: An exploration of horizontal violence. *Nursing Economics, 30(1), 1–13.*

World Health Organization. (2024, February 2). Deafness and hearing loss. World Health Organization. https://www.who.int/news-room/fact-sheets/detail/deafness-and-hearing-loss.

Young, A, Espinoza, F., Doods, C., Squires, G., Rogers, K., Chilton, H., & O'Neill, R. (2023). Introducing the READY study: DHH young people's well-being and self-determination. *Journal of Deaf Studies and Deaf Education, 28*(3). https://doi.org/10.1093/deafed/enad002

Chapter 8
Why Are the Complexities of Deafblind Identity Relevant to Mental Health?

Peter Simcock and Walter Wittich

> *When I was in the hospital, the psychiatrist said he had never seen anyone like me before come in; somebody with sight and hearing loss* (*Participant in* Simcock, 2020).

Introduction

Deafblindness, or combined difficulties with both vision and hearing, exists irrespective of severity, age or order of onset, or whether the condition occurred pre- or post-language development. It causes challenges with communication, access to information, mobility, and social interaction, thereby fundamentally shaping the lives of individuals living with the condition. Although some may struggle to develop or maintain a sense of personal identity, like other disabled individuals, many deafblind people have a sense of multiple or changing identities (Simcock, 2020). The complexity of deafblind identities reflects the highly heterogeneous nature of the deafblind population; a population that is at greater risk of mental health problems. In this chapter, we explore different deafblind identities and argue that in responding to mental health needs, practitioners must expect diversity in the deafblind experience and recognize the different ways of being deafblind.

P. Simcock (✉)
Birmingham City University, Birmingham, UK
e-mail: peter.simcock@bcu.ac.uk

W. Wittich
School of Optometry, University of Montreal, Montreal, QC, Canada
e-mail: walter.wittich@umontreal.ca

T. Bone (ed.), *Deaf Mental Health*, Advances in Mental Health and Addiction,
https://doi.org/10.1007/978-3-032-06274-1_8

Heterogeneity

The Nordic definition of deafblindness stipulates that an individual is considered deafblind when combined impairments of vision and hearing limit the person's ability to participate in society to such a degree that specific services, environmental adaptations, and/or assistive technologies are required to overcome access barriers (Nordic Leadership Forum on Deafblindness, 2024). This functional definition has had global impact (Danermark & Möller, 2008) and, by its very nature, covers a highly heterogeneous population that varies in severity, as well as time and order of onset of sensory difficulties, across an extensive range of diagnostic categories. Additionally, both expressive and receptive communication strategies used by deafblind people can range from oral to signed to tactile modalities, and often include a combination of multiple communication methods, some of which require the involvement of others, such as intervenors or interpreters[1] (McInnes, 1999).

In contrast to functional definitions that reflect the abilities of the person, the medical model traditionally relies on criteria that reflect the status of the sensory organs. These include visual acuity, visual field diameter, and pure-tone audiogram hearing thresholds; however, such criteria are plagued by inconsistencies across context and environment (Bright et al., 2023) because there is no agreed-upon set of indicators that are internationally shared. In line with this variability is the range of prevalence estimates that are observed. The World Federation of the Deafblind (2018) estimates that between 0.2% and 2% of the population live with some form of deafblindness, a value that has been replicated by other global estimates, and that generally increases with advancing age (Koesters et al., 2024).

The Dutch definition (Heppe et al., 2021) divides the population into three groups: those with congenital deafblindness (present before the acquisition of language), those with acquired deafblindness (impairment occurring post-language development), and those with dual sensory impairment (referring to individuals with age-related losses, such as macular degeneration and presbycusis). This categorization, however, cannot easily accommodate individuals where one impairment may be congenital while the other is age-related, highlighting that categorization based on the congenital-acquired divide is overly simplistic and inadequate (Moller, 2003; Simcock, 2020).

Further confusion is created by inconsistencies evident in terminology. While the service and rehabilitation environments often consider deafblindness as an umbrella term for all levels of combined vision and hearing difficulties, researchers often use

[1] Interpreters convert information from one spoken or signed language into another. In the context of deafblindness, this involves acting as a communication link between a deafblind person and their interlocutor, using the deafblind person's preferred language/ communication method. Deafblind interpreters may also convert written communications into the preferred communication method/language of a deafblind person, and relay any visual or nonverbal information, such as interlocutors' facial expressions. Intervenors are trained professionals who have a wider role. They accompany deafblind people as they undertake various functional activities, including communication, essentially acting as their "eyes and ears".

the term dual sensory impairment (Wittich et al., 2013). Additional heterogeneity is reflected in differences in how the term "deafblind" is spelled. Deafblind as a single term replaced the hyphenated version deaf-blind, to emphasize the uniqueness of the impairment as opposed to the simple addition of deafness plus blindness (Lagati, 1995). The choice of which letter to capitalize is used to express whether a person primarily experiences hearing loss or identifies as culturally Deaf (Deafblind), is predominantly visually impaired (deafBlind), or perceives themselves as part of both communities (DeafBlind). For some in North America, their shared identity as persons living with deafblindness centres around shared tactile language, developed by and for the deafblind community, called Protactile (Edwards, 2014). Nonetheless, the largest group of individuals living with combined vision and hearing loss are those with age-related conditions, whose identity formed before the onset of sensory impairments (Wittich et al., 2012).

Working with and for individuals living with deafblindness requires attention to the subtleties linked to identity. Roy et al. (2021) identify themes for collaboration with the deafblind community that can apply to multiple domains, including the provision of mental health services: the theme of "*Being Deafblind—it's **who** we are, not **what** we are*" directly points at the importance of recognizing deafblindness as an identity, albeit that some deafblind people, particularly those with late-life acquired impairment, do not define themselves as such. The vast range of effects that deafblindness has on the functioning of an individual is further demonstrated in the recent consultation of individuals with lived experience of the condition, that participated in the development of the Core Set for Deafblindness, rooted in the World Health Organization's International Classification of Functioning, Disability and Health (Wittich et al., 2024b). The comprehensive Core Set includes specific aspects of mental health relevant to service provision, namely, b126 Temperament and personality functions, b152 Emotional functions, and b130 Motivation (Wittich et al., 2024a).

Deafblind People at Increased Risk of Mental Health Problems

Communication challenges, unsuitable assessment tools, and limited numbers of practitioners with the requisite specialist qualification and experience all contribute to difficulties in diagnosing mental illness among deafblind people and in determining whether the deafblind population is at greater risk of mental health problems (Hersh, 2013; Wittich & Simcock, 2019). Historically, congenitally deafblind individuals were erroneously considered as intellectually impaired or emotionally disturbed, and therefore inappropriately placed in mental institutions or "asylums" (Deeming et al., 2021; Schein & Wolf-Schein, 2007). Reports of the misdiagnosis of mental illness among deafblind people remain, with such misdiagnosis being attributed to miscommunication or inaccurate interpretation of the effects of deafblindness (Hersh, 2013; Moroe et al., 2022). For example, Oleson (2012) notes that behaviours associated with deafblindness may be misinterpreted as dementia, and McDonnall et al. (2017) highlight how communication problems may be misunderstood as psychotic symptoms. Use of standardized assessment tools may also contribute to misdiagnosis. Dupuis et al. (2014) observed that 60% of people with hearing and/or sight loss failed cognitive screening when the Montreal Cognitive Assessment (MoCA) tool was used, but significantly more passed when MoCA elements relying predominantly on hearing or vision were removed from the assessment.

Notwithstanding the phenomenon of misdiagnosis, deafblind people "experience the typical mental health issues of the general population" (McDonnall et al., 2017, p. 2). Nevertheless, just as deaf and blind persons are reported as being at greater risk of mental health problems (Hardt et al., 2024), deafblind people experience higher levels of psychological distress (Wittich et al., 2022) and are at elevated risk of mental health difficulties, including serious mental illness (Mar, 1993; Wittich & Simcock, 2019). Symptoms of psychosis are common among people with congenital deafblindness (Dammeyer, 2011), and an increased risk and higher frequency of depression, including chronic depression, among deafblind people, is observed (Tiwana et al., 2016). Deafblindness is also associated with greater risk of acute confusion among those in hospital and long-term residential care (Wittich & Simcock, 2019), and Hovaldt et al. (2021) identified deafblindness as a risk factor for self-harm and suicidal ideation among older adults. Similarly, Wahlqvist et al. (2013, 2016) observed higher levels of suicidal ideation and suicide attempts, when compared to the general population, among people with Usher Syndrome, one of the most common genetic causes of acquired deafblindness. Furthermore, although mental illness is not considered an inherent feature of Usher Syndrome (Danermark & Möller, 2008), those with Usher Syndrome are more at risk of psychosis (Simcock, 2020).

While the Lancet Commission on dementia has identified both vision and hearing loss as potentially modifiable risk factors for dementia (Livingston et al., 2024), the increased risk for dementia due to combined sensory impairments remains more elusive. Nevertheless, deafblindness has been linked to an eightfold increased risk of cognitive impairment (Fuller-Thomson et al., 2022) and is observed to elevate the risk of dementia (Hwang et al., 2020). In their study of depressive symptoms in the oldest-old, Cimarolli et al. (2018) identified deafblindness as a contributory factor. Such findings should concern mental health practitioners, particularly as the prevalence of deafblindness increases with advancing age (Koesters et al., 2024). A further contemporary concern for practitioners is the inclusion of sensory impairment in the list of given reasons among those travelling to Switzerland for assisted suicide (Gauthier et al., 2015). The assisted suicide of two Deaf twins in Belgium in 2012 was widely reported in the media. The twins sought euthanasia following their diagnosis of progressive sight loss. Doctors suggested that the twins were experiencing unbearable mental suffering, particularly, according to Trott (2013), because they could not face becoming unable to communicate with each other. Mental health practitioners should also be alert to much earlier diagnoses of Usher Syndrome in children and young people, made possible by advancements in genetic testing (Johansen et al., 2024), and the consequent need for careful intervention as d/Deaf children face degenerative sight loss, described by Ingraham and Vernon (2007, p. 17) as a "severe psychological trauma".

Experiences of stress, social isolation, loneliness, identity crises, communication difficulties, and loss of functional independence are common among deafblind people (McDonnall et al., 2017; Warnicke et al., 2022). As such phenomena contribute to psychological distress and mental health problems, increased risk, and higher prevalence levels of mental illness in the deafblind population are perhaps unsurprising. Nonetheless, such risk is exacerbated by a lack of appropriate mental health services (McDonnall et al., 2017). It is therefore imperative that mental health practitioners, including social workers, psychologists, and psychiatrists, develop their knowledge of deafblindness and increase capacity and competence in the deafblind field.

Supporting Deafblind People in Mental Health Settings

The number of people living with deafblindness is expected to expand considerably, principally owing to the ageing of the population (Koesters et al., 2024). There is an increased risk of mental health problems among this group, and the psychosocial impact of the impairment can be more significant than sensory loss alone (Wittich & Simcock, 2019), Therefore, it is likely that mainstream mental health practitioners will encounter deafblind clients, and it is thus essential that they develop their understanding of deafblind people's unique needs.

An important starting point is early identification of mental health problems among the deafblind population, and there are calls for ongoing mental health screening for this group, particularly older deafblind people (Hovaldt et al., 2021). Nevertheless, we now turn to consider steps practitioners should take when working with deafblind clients, the first of which is to understand diversity in deafblind identity. Acknowledging that deafblind people have very different experiences of the condition and may accept or deny a deafblind identity (Enggrav, 2013), when a deafblind person is referred to their service, practitioners must question what is meant by "deafblind" and be prepared to explore not only how the condition impacts upon that individual's life, but also the individual's own perspective on their deafblindness (Ingraham & Vernon, 2007; Wickham, 2011). This is necessary because such matters can alert practitioners to the psychological challenges the individual may be experiencing. For example, congenitally deafblind people may struggle to develop a sense of personal identity, and the age and order of onset of deafness and blindness can result in very different adjustment difficulties among young people with acquired deafblindness (Ingraham & Vernon, 2007). Chronic stress may be present among those living with gradual progressive deafblindness, while for those who have lived their entire lives as sighted-hearing people, the impact of late-life acquired deafblindness can be overwhelming (Wittich & Simcock, 2019).

Understanding a client's perspective on their deafblindness can also inform practitioners' therapeutic approach. For example, de-pathologizing deafblindness and highlighting a client's strengths as a deafblind person are particularly appropriate when working with deafblind people who maintain a cultural identity as Deaf, notwithstanding the onset of blindness (Wickham, 2011), and with those involved in the Protactile Movement.

Effective communication is pivotal to any therapeutic intervention (Wickham, 2011), and an understanding of diverse deafblind identities is key to such communication; this is especially important as communication difficulties are associated with mental health problems among deafblind people (McDonnall et al., 2017). Numerous languages and receptive and expressive communication methods are used by deafblind people, including spoken language, signed languages, and communication methods using the tactile modality. The preferred language/methods will be informed by various factors, including age, timing, severity and order of onset of each sensory impairment, and cultural identity: the impact deafblindness has on communication manifests itself differently for different deafblind sub-groups (Deeming et al., 2021). Furthermore, choice of communication method may depend on setting, situation, and the communication partners involved, and it is important to note that use of multiple methods by deafblind people is common (Simcock, 2020). Mental health practitioners must therefore avoid making assumptions about the communicative needs and preferences of deafblind clients, made solely on the basis of the label "deafblind", and instead, ensure that they determine and record the expressive and receptive language and communication preferences of each individual.

Developing an understanding of identity differences and communicative diversity among the deafblind population supports practitioners' preparedness to work with deafblind clients. However, further considerations are required during any encounter with a deafblind individual. Longer appointment times should be allocated to deafblind clients, in recognition of both the time needed to gather a case history and the tiring and slower nature of some communication methods, particularly those using the tactile modality (Hersh, 2013). Careful attention should be paid to the environment, notably ensuring that there is adequate lighting, reducing any background noise, and agreeing the best seating position. Such environmental adaptations enhance the utility of "clear speech", considered to be the most effective and common communication method with acquired deafblind people with residual hearing and vision (Echt & Saunders, 2014). When working with deafblind clients who use signed languages (visual or tactile), practitioners without the necessary linguistic skills will need to involve interpreters and/or intervenors. Such involvement requires that practitioners be clear on the language preferences of the client and that they reflect on how the involvement of a third party may impact upon the establishment of a therapeutic relationship (Wickham, 2011).

While we support calls for mental health practitioners to enhance their understanding of deafblindness, we also acknowledge the importance of adopting a multidisciplinary approach to meeting deafblind people's mental health needs. As such, practitioners should liaise closely with specialist health and social services professionals, including those with lived experience of deafblindness, and connect with organizations of and for deafblind people, internationally, nationally, and locally. Single sensory impairment organizations are likely to be unsuitable in responding to the unique needs of deafblind people, but may be in a position to direct practitioners to local specialist deafblind provision. Engagement with such organizations enables practitioners to introduce deafblind clients to peer support groups, considered a particularly positive intervention (Ingraham & Vernon, 2007). Furthermore, recognizing that better understanding of the impairment alone is insufficient in providing support to deafblind people, seeking specialist input from such organizations enables the practitioner to spend time on understanding their clients as unique individuals (Simcock, 2020).

Conclusion

Deafblindness is a complex phenomenon. This complexity is reflected in the considerable heterogeneity of the deafblind population and diversity of deafblind identities. In mental health settings, lack of understanding of this diversity, particularly communicative diversity and the different ways in which deafblindness affects different people, can contribute to inadequate assessment and ineffective intervention. This is a particular concern in view of both the expansion of the deafblind population and heightened risk of mental health problems among deafblind people. Mental health practitioners must work alongside specialist organizations of and for deafblind people and enhance their understanding of the diversity of deafblind identities; when working with deafblind people, they must not assume anything and be ready to adapt.

References

Bright, T., Ramke, J., Zhang, J. H., Kitema, G. F., Safi, S., Mdala, S., Yoshizaki, M., Brennan-Jones, C. G., Mactaggart, I., Gordon, I., Swenor, B. K., Burton, M. J., & Evans, J. R. (2023). Prevalence and impact of combined vision and hearing (dual sensory) impairment: A scoping review. *PLOS Global Public Health, 3*(5), e0001905. https://doi.org/10.1371/journal.pgph.0001905

Cimarolli, V., Jopp, D., Boerner, K., & Minahan, J. (2018). Depressive symptoms in the oldest-old: The role of sensory impairments. *Archives of Gerontology and Geriatrics, 78*, 249–254. https://doi.org/10.1016/j.archger.2018.07.009

Dammeyer, J. (2011). Mental and behavioural disorders among people with congenital Deafblindness. *Research in Developmental Disorders, 32*(2), 571–575. https://doi.org/10.1016/j.ridd.2010.12.019

Danermark, B., & Möller, K. (2008). Deafblindness, ontological security, and social recognition. *International Journal of Audiology, 47*(S2), S119–S123. https://doi.org/10.1080/14992020802307388

Deeming, P., Gabry, K., Gasaway, M., Jordan, B., Pope, R., & Spiers, E. (2021). Deafblind people and support service providers in the 21st century. https://www.nationaldb.org/media/doc/ssp-white-paper-2021.pdf.

Dupuis, K., Pichora-Fuller, M. K., Chasteen, A. L., Marchuk, V., Singh, G., & Smith, S. L. (2014). Effects of hearing and vision impairments on the Montreal cognitive assessment. *Aging, Neuropsychology, and Cognition, 22*(4), 413–437. https://doi.org/10.1080/13825585.2014.968084

Echt, K. V., & Saunders, G. H. (2014). Accommodating dual sensory loss in everyday practice. *Perspectives on Gerontology, 19*(1), 4–16. https://pubs.asha.org. https://doi.org/10.1044/gero19.1.04

Edwards, T. (2014). From compensation to integration: Effects of the pro-tactile movement on the sublexical structure of tactile American sign language. *Journal of Pragmatics, 69*, 22–41. https://doi.org/10.1016/j.pragma.2014.05.005

Enggrav, B. (2013). The identity as deafblind—embracing or denying. National Knowledge Center for Deafblindness. https://nkcdb.se/identiteten-som-dovblind-omfamna-eller-forneka/.

Fuller-Thomson, E., Nowaczynski, A., & MacNeil, A. (2022). The association between hearing impairment, vision impairment, dual sensory impairment, and serious cognitive impairment: Findings from a population-based study of 5.4 million older adults. *Journal of Alzheimer's Disease Reports, 6*(1), 211–222. https://content.iospress.com/articles/journal-of-alzheimers-disease-reports/adr220005.

Gauthier, S., Mausbach, J., Reisch, T., & Bartsch, C. (2015). Suicide tourism: A pilot study on the Swiss phenomenon. *Journal of Medical Ethics, 41*, 611–617. https://doi.org/10.1136/medethics-2014-102091

Hardt, B., Graser, J., Heidenreich, T., & Michalak, J. (2024). A systematic review and meta-analysis of psychological interventions for persons with hearing or vision impairment: Research gaps and call to action. *Clinical Psychology: Science and Practice*. https://doi.org/10.1037/cps0000229

Heppe, E., Klomp, U., & Bak, M. (2021). The Dutch functional definition of Deafblindness—English translation. https://www.deelkracht.nl/producten/a-translation-of-the-dutch-functional-definition-of-deafblindness/.

Hersh, M. (2013). Deafblind people, communication, independence, and isolation. *Journal of Deafblind Studies and Deaf Education, 18*(4), 446–463. https://doi.org/10.1093/deafed/ent022

Hovaldt, H. B., Crowe, K., & Dammeyer, J. (2021). A cross-sectional study of prevalence and correlates of self-harm and suicidal ideation in older adults with dual sensory loss. *Disability and Health Journal, 15*(1) Article 101204. https://doi.org/10.1016/j.dhjo.2021.101204

Hwang, P. H., Longstreth, W. T., Jr., Brenowitz, W. D., Thielke, S. M., Lopez, O. L., Francis, C. E., DeKosky, S. T., & Fitzpatrick, A. L. (2020). Dual sensory impairment in older adults and risk of dementia from the GEM study. *Alzheimer's & Dementia: Diagnosis, Assessment & Disease Monitoring, 12*(1), e12054. https://doi.org/10.1002/dad2.12054

Ingraham, C., & Vernon, M. (2007). Mental health counseling with DeafBlind students: Recommendations for families and professionals. In C. L. Ingraham (Ed.), *Transition planning for students who are DeafBlind* (pp. 59–76) PEPNet-South. https://dcmp.org/learn/static-assets/566_transition-planning-for-students-who-are-deafblind.pdf.

Johansen, L., O'Hare, F. O., Shepard, E. R., Ayton, L. N., Pelentsov, L. J., Kearns, L. S., & Glavin, K. L. (2024). Exploring the support needs of Australian parents of young children with usher syndrome: A qualitative thematic analysis. *Orphanet Journal of Rare Diseases, 19*. Article Number 129, 1–14. https://doi.org/10.1186/s13023-024-03125-w

Koesters, N. B., Minhas, R., Wittich, W., McMenemy, A., & Johnson, C. (2024). Visualizing worldwide prevalence of age-related dual sensory loss. *Journal of Aging and Health*. https://doi.org/10.1177/08982643241263879

Lagati, S. (1995). "Deaf-blind" or "Deafblind"? International perspectives on terminology. *Journal of Visual Impairment & Blindness, 89*(3), 306–306. https://doi.org/10.1177/0145482X9508900320

Livingston, G., Huntley, J., Liu, K. Y., Costafreda, S. G., Selbæk, G., Alladi, S., Ames, D., Banerjee, S., Burns, A., Brayne, C., Fox, N. C., Ferri, C. P., Gitlin, L. N., Howard, R., Kales, H. C., Kivimäki, M., Larson, E. B., Nakasujja, N., Rockwood, K., et al. (2024). Dementia prevention, intervention, and care: 2024 report of the Lancet standing Commission. *The Lancet, 404*(10452), 572–628. https://doi.org/10.1016/S0140-6736(24)01296-0

Mar, H. H. (1993). Psychosocial services. In J. W. Reiman & P. A. Johnson (Eds.), *National Symposium on children and youth who are deaf-blind* (pp. 42–60). Teaching Research Publications.

McDonnall, M. C., Crudden, A., LeJeune, B. J., & Steverson, A. C. (2017). Availability of mental health services for individuals who are deaf or deaf-blind. *Journal of Social Work in Disability & Rehabilitation, 16*(1), 1–13. https://doi.org/10.1080/1536710X.2017.1260515

McInnes, J. M. (1999). Deafblindness: A unique disability. In J. M. McInnes (Ed.), *A guide to planning and support for individuals who are deafblind* (pp. 1–33). University of Toronto Press.

Moller, C. (2003). Deafblindness: Living with sensory deprivation. *The Lancet, 362*, S46–S47. https://www.thelancet.com/pdfs/journals/lancet/PIIS0140-6736(03)15074-X.pdf.

Moroe, N., Masuku, K., & Shirame, L. (2022). Rehabilitation healthcare professionals' competence and confidence in differentially diagnosing Deafblindness from autism Spectrum disorders: A cross-sectional survey in South Africa. *BMC Medical Education, 22*(194), 1–15. https://doi.org/10.1186/s12909-022-03258-1

Nordic Leadership Forum on Deafblindness. (2024). *Nordic definition on Deafblindness*. Nordic Welfare Centre. https://norden.diva-portal.org/smash/get/diva2:1920866/FULLTEXT01.pdf.

Oleson, H. H. (2012). The challenge of progressive dual sensory loss. In L. W. Wehner (Ed.), *A good senior life with dual sensory loss* (pp. 10–15). Nordic Centre for Welfare and Social Issues. https://nordicwelfare.org/wp-content/uploads/2017/10/A20Good20Senior20Life20with20Dual20Sensory20Loss.pdf.

Roy, A., McVillly, K. R., & Crisp, B. R. (2021). Working with deafblind people to develop a good practice approach. *Journal of Social Work., 21*(1), 69–87. https://doi.org/10.1177/1468017319860216

Schein, J. D., & Wolf-Schein, E. G. (2007). A brief history of services for Deafblind people in the United States. In C. L. Ingraham (Ed.), *Transition planning for students who are DeafBlind* (pp. 7–18). PEPNet-South. https://dcmp.org/learn/static-assets/566_transition-planning-for-students-who-are-deafblind.pdf.

Simcock, P. (2020). The lived experience of vulnerability among adults ageing with deafblindness: An interpretative phenomenological analysis [Unpublished doctoral dissertation]. King's College London. https://kclpure.kcl.ac.uk/portal/en/studentTheses/the-lived-experience-of-vulnerability-among-adults-ageing-with-de.

Tiwana, R., Benbow, S. M., & Kingston, P. (2016). Late life acquired dual-sensory impairment: A systematic review of its impact on everyday competence. *British Journal of Visual Impairment, 34*(3), 203–213. https://doi.org/10.1177/0264619616648727

Trott, R. (2013, January 16). Deaf Belgian Twins end lives as they start going blind. BBC News Europe. https://www.bbc.co.uk/news/av/world-europe-21039064.

Wahlqvist, M., Möller, C., Möller, K., & Danermark, B. (2013). Physical and psychological health in persons with Deafblindness that is due to usher syndrome type II. *Journal of Visual Impairment & Blindness, 107*(3), 207–220. https://doi.org/10.1177/0145482X1310700305

Wahlqvist, M., Möller, K., Möller, C., & Danermark, B. (2016). Physical and psychological health, social trust, and financial situation for persons with usher syndrome type I. *British Journal of Visual Impairment, 34*(1), 15–25. https://doi.org/10.1177/0264619615610158

Warnicke, C., Wahlqvist, M., Anderzén-Carlsson, A., & Sundqvist, A. (2022). Interventions for adults with Deafblindness—an integrative review. *BMC Health Services Research, 22*, 1–20. Article Number 1594, https://link.springer.com. https://doi.org/10.1186/s12913-022-08958-4

Wickham, K. (2011). Depression in the deafblind community: Working from a social work perspective. *DbI Review, 46*, 56–58. https://www.deafblindinternational.org/?media_dl=4219.

Wittich, W., Dumassais, S., Jaiswal, A., Ogedengbe, T. O., Lopez, R., & Granberg, S. (2024a). The ICF Core sets for Deafblindness: Version 1. Open Science Framework. https://doi.org/10.17605/OSF.IO/A942K.

Wittich, W., Dumassais, S., Prain, M., Ogedengbe, T. O., Gravel, C., Jaiswal, A., Minhas, R., Lopez, R., & Granberg, S. (2024b). Development of Core sets for deafblindness using the international classification of functioning, disability, and health: The perspectives of individuals with lived experience. *European Journal of Physical and Rehabilitation Medicine, 20*(2), 382–390. https://doi.org/10.23736/S1973-9087.24.08500-9

Wittich, W., Nicholas, J., & Damen, S. (2022). Living with Deafblindness during Covid-19: An international webinar to facilitate global knowledge translation. *British Journal of Visual Impairment, 40*(3), 487–499. https://journals.sagepub.com. https://doi.org/10.1177/02646196211002887

Wittich, W., & Simcock, P. (2019). Aging and combined vision and hearing loss. In J. Ravenscroft (Ed.), *The Routledge handbook of visual impairment* (pp. 438–456). Routledge.

Wittich, W., Southall, K., Sikora, L., Watanabe, D. H., & Gagné, J.-P. (2013). What's in a name: Dual sensory impairment or deafblindness? *British Journal of Visual Impairment., 31*(3), 198–207. https://doi.org/10.1177/0264619613490519

Wittich, W., Watanabe, D. H., & Gagné, J. P. (2012). Sensory and demographic characteristics of deafblindness rehabilitation clients in Montreal, Canada. *Ophthalmic & Physiological Optics: The Journal of the British College of Ophthalmic Opticians (Optometrists), 32*(3), 242–251. https://doi.org/10.1111/j.1475-1313.2012.00897.x

World Federation of the Deafblind. (2018). At risk of exclusion from CRPD and SDGs implementation: Inequality and persons with deafblindness. WFDB. https://wfdb.eu/wfdb-report-2018/.

Chapter 9
Alcohol and Substance Use Among Deaf and Hard of Hearing Individuals: Addressing the Unique Needs

Deb Guthmann, Kent Schafer, Christine L. Gannon, and Makoto Ikegami

Introduction

While substance misuse is a common challenge across various cultural groups, deaf[1] individuals face unique obstacles that heighten their vulnerability to alcohol and drug dependence. Deaf individuals experience communication dynamics and cultural factors that impact their health outcomes, including substance use. In this chapter, we review existing research, the history of treatment services for the Deaf community and highlight barriers such as communication challenges and inadequate resources while proposing solutions to enhance inclusivity and effectiveness. We also include a case study that offers practical insights and recommendations for providers, emphasizing the importance of inclusive, effective approaches to help

[1] We have elected to use deaf (lower case) in an all-encompassing manner to reflect the diversity within the deaf population. We follow the examples set by the National Association for the Deaf (https://www.nad.org/), a deaf consumer organization, and the National Deaf Center on Postsecondary Outcomes (https://www.nationaldeafcenter.org/). In this proposal, "deaf" refers to individuals who self-identify as deaf or hard of hearing. The use of Deaf (upper case) refers to persons who self-identify as culturally Deaf.

D. Guthmann (✉)
National Consultant, Auburn, CA, USA

K. Schafer
Alabama Institute of Deaf and Blind, Tuscaloosa, AL, USA
e-mail: schafer.kent@aidb.org

C. L. Gannon
Public Health Program, Gallaudet University, Washington, DC, USA
e-mail: Christine.gannon@gallaudet.edu

M. Ikegami
Deaf Multicultural Counselling, Atlanta, GA, USA
e-mail: makoto@deafmulticulturalcounseling.com

T. Bone (ed.), *Deaf Mental Health*, Advances in Mental Health and Addiction,
https://doi.org/10.1007/978-3-032-06274-1_9

improve the lives of deaf individuals facing substance use issues. By understanding the interplay of communication needs, cultural nuances, and the need for specialized care, providers can ensure deaf individuals get more accessible and appropriate support when dealing with substance use.

Background

Research on alcohol and drug use among deaf individuals is limited and mixed. Existing studies suggest that the rates may be similar to or higher than the general population (Guthmann & Titus, 2016; McKee et al., 2019; Titus & Guthmann, 2010, 2013). Through a secondary analysis of the 2019 National Mental Health Services Survey (N-MHSS) with 12,472 mental health facilities and the 2019 National Survey of Substance Abuse Treatment Services (NSSATS) with 15,961 substance use treatment facilities, both administered by the Substance Abuse and Mental Health Services Administration (SAMHSA), James et al. (2022) found that binge drinking is slightly higher within deaf populations. In one study with Deaf high schoolers results indicated that lifetime substance use was high or higher than those for hearing youth (Berman et al., 2010). In contrast, some studies indicate that the overall lifetime prevalence of alcohol and drug use does not significantly differ between deaf and hearing individuals (Pinquart & Pfeiffer, 2015) except when in social settings. Higher use is seen when deaf individuals are around larger groups of other deaf people (Kushalnagar et al., 2019; Pinquart & Pfeiffer, 2015). When they do use, they may use more (Anderson et al., 2018; Kushalnagar et al., 2019; McKee et al., 2019; Pinquart & Pfeiffer, 2015). As a result, they could experience increased substance use disorders (McKee et al., 2019) yet may seek treatment less due to perceived barriers (Aldalur et al., 2024). Certain populations within the Deaf community may be more likely to use alcohol in higher amounts including those who are young, male, educated, and retired (Kushalnagar et al., 2019).

Similar to using alcohol more, Anderson et al. (2018) showed that when deaf people used cannabis, they did so more regularly. Crowe (2022) found that deaf people use cannabis more but use other substances less. Noll et al. (2024) identified critical gaps in existing research on alcohol, cannabis, and opioid use among deaf individuals, with no available research addressing substance use among deaf youth under 18.

Factors such as social isolation, communication barriers, and cultural differences contribute to an increased risk of substance use among deaf individuals. When deaf and hard of hearing youth experience a high rate of isolation growing up and a lack of social experiences, this may impact their need for belonging and alcohol use can serve as a social lubricant (Gannon et al., 2024). Adverse communication experiences further elevate the risk of mental health challenges and substance use (Kushalnagar et al., 2020; Titus & Guthmann, 2010; Titus & Guthmann, 2013) and using alcohol to cope can increase alcohol-related consequences (Baschnagel & Bell, 2023; Gannon et al., 2024). Although prevalence rates vary, substance use among deaf individuals remains a significant concern that warrants further research and intervention.

A Brief History of Substance Treatment Services for the Deaf

To better understand the challenges deaf people face when seeking and receiving treatment, it is important to look at the history of these services. One of the earliest documented interventions with a deaf individual in recovery occurred in the early 1970s and was featured in an Alcoholics Anonymous (AA) Newsletter (Boros, 1980). Soon after, the first treatment center catering specifically to deaf alcoholics was established in San Francisco, utilizing sign language interpreters to ensure communication access for clients. By the mid-1970s, St. Paul, Minnesota, began providing hospital-based services for deaf individuals and Cleveland launched the *Addiction Intervention for the Deaf (AID)* program. Other centers, such as the Hurley Medical Center in Flint, Michigan, began incorporating interpreters into therapy sessions (Boros, 1980). The Stephen Miller House in Pocasset, Massachusetts, and the Minnesota Chemical Dependency Program for Deaf and Hard of Hearing Individuals (the Minnesota Program) emerged in the late 1980s and were among the first to incorporate sign language-fluent staff and provide culturally tailored services, demonstrating the effectiveness of specialized care (Guthmann, 2011; Guthmann & Sandberg, 2019; Guthmann & Sternfeld, 2013). While the Minnesota Program achieved some national recognition and laid the foundation for future efforts, such initiatives remained isolated and failed to form part of a larger, cohesive network of services for deaf individuals. Many of these centers eventually closed, changed their model of service due to census or funding, or went through programmatic changes, resulting in treatment programs for deaf individuals with substance use disorders remaining limited.

Challenges in Treatment: Language Barriers and Access to Services

One of the largest barriers in providing accessible services to deaf individuals is interpreting. The high financial cost of hiring certified interpreters and limited availability of qualified interpreters can place a significant burden on treatment centers, further limiting their ability to deliver sustainable services. James et al. (2022) found that 59% of substance use treatment centers reported not providing interpreters, and 37.2% of deaf individuals were denied an interpreter when seeking medical care. Wheatley (2021) found that deaf individuals experience barriers to effective communication in healthcare settings, leading to delays in care and inadequate treatment outcomes. If attending an in-person Alcoholics Anonymous (AA) meeting, advanced notice is often required to arrange for interpreters, which can lead to difficulty in seeking support (James et al., 2022).

Interpreters are often not covered by insurance or treatment centers, making it a voluntary and sometimes unaffordable service for deaf individuals. This leaves individuals without the support they need for meaningful participation in recovery programs, especially when treatment providers lack staff fluent in American Sign Language (ASL). This lack of access to competent communication leads to significant challenges in care, contributing to the worsening of substance use disorders within the Deaf community (McKee et al., 2019).

The negative stigma around substance use and recovery within the Deaf community, which has historically hindered many individuals from seeking help, appears to have lessened, particularly in the wake of the COVID-19 pandemic. Online platforms have provided new opportunities for deaf individuals to connect with others in recovery, participate in group meetings, as well as share experiences, often in ASL or with the support of qualified interpreters, making these options more accessible. There are now accessible 12-step meetings available online 7 days a week (DeafAA.org, n.d.) with broader geographic access and real-time communication, ensuring that participants can engage with others in their native language, which may not always be the case in traditional in-person settings (Wilkins et al., 2024).

Despite these positive changes, a concerning trend is the continued decrease in accessible treatment options for deaf individuals in many areas. Online meetings do not replace the need for comprehensive, in-person treatment services that are culturally competent and linguistically accessible. The expansion of virtual recovery options has not translated into increased availability of fluent signing staff within treatment programs, which remains a significant barrier for deaf individuals seeking substance use disorder treatment services (Guthmann, 2011; James et al., 2022). This dual challenge, expanded access to virtual recovery spaces coupled with limited in-person treatment options, underscores the need for a more inclusive approach to substance use treatment for deaf individuals.

There is an urgent need for systemic investment in the training of culturally competent providers and the expansion of accessible treatment centers to ensure that deaf individuals receive the full spectrum of care needed for long-term recovery. The Minnesota Program has provided services in ASL and incorporated visual and non-written clinical approaches, such as role-playing and drawings, to better engage deaf individuals in treatment and aftercare planning (Guthmann & Sandberg, 2019; Guthmann & Sternfeld, 2013). The Signs of Safety, a Deaf-accessible toolkit available in ASL, is designed to support trauma and addiction recovery in deaf clients (Anderson et al., 2021). Both programs represent promising advancements in the field of deaf substance use and trauma treatment that can be expanded and replicated on a national scale.

Addressing Substance Use and Misuse in the Deaf Community

In order to address substance use and misuse, multiple strategies are needed. One component of this is prevention. Education for deaf youth at younger ages is one strategy to address alcohol misuse (James et al., 2022; Kushalnagar et al., 2019; Pinquart & Pfeiffer, 2015) but also needs to include healthy coping strategies to help them counter negative experiences (Baschnagel & Bell, 2023). There needs to be additional drug and alcohol prevention materials that are accessible and available for deaf individuals (Cowgill et al., 2020; Guthmann & Titus, 2016; Titus & Guthmann, 2010, 2013) and then support to evaluate their effectiveness. In addition, schools serving deaf students need to offer drug and alcohol prevention education and begin in elementary school as part of the health curriculum.

On the college level, comprehensive strategies are necessary to address substance use and misuse. There is a wide range of intervention strategies designed for hearing students (National Institute on Alcohol Abuse and Alcoholism, 2019) and these can serve as a resource for developing education for deaf students (Gannon, 2023). Programs, such as motivational interviewing require language access, but when it exists, allows for an individualized approach. The ECheckUptoGo (2024) program has added some ASL to their personalized feedback program and is another potential tool. As a way to identify substance misuse issues early, medical and mental health providers can screen deaf clients. In order to increase accessibility of standardized instruments for deaf individuals, Wright State University validated drug, alcohol, and mental health screeners in ASL (Guthmann et al., 2017). Professionals can access these materials through a web-based portal, the ASL-STAR (Sardi Program, 2024).

Access to equitable care for deaf individuals in treatment is significantly influenced by understanding their rights under the Americans with Disabilities Act (ADA, 1990). A lack of awareness by deaf individuals of their rights and a shortage of available resources results in barriers when trying to obtain necessary accommodations (Whaley & Williamson, 2023) and limits the ability to advocate for themselves within treatment settings. Enhancing education about ADA protections within the Deaf community and among service providers is critical to ensuring deaf individuals can fully engage in treatment and achieve better health outcomes.

The challenges and solutions related to substance use in the Deaf community are complex. As an example, see the case of Joe and how his experiences with communication barriers, cultural misunderstandings, and limited access to treatment options impact his substance use and recovery.

Case Study

Joe is a 40-year-old deaf man. Growing up in a hearing family with limited ASL skills, Joe often felt disconnected and misunderstood, which contributed to feelings of isolation. He was surrounded by hearing individuals in school and work who did not sign. This lack of communication access led to a profound feeling of social isolation. Joe coped with his loneliness and anxiety by using alcohol and cannabis. In his 30s, Joe's substance use led to job losses, health problems, and an arrest for driving under the influence. Despite trying to get help on several occasions, Joe found himself unable to find services specific to a deaf person.

Joe's addiction was closely tied to his untreated mental health challenges. He battled depression and anxiety for many years. Joe experienced chronic sadness and frequent anxiety episodes which had a significant impact on his life. Unfortunately, Joe's symptoms were often mistaken for general stress or attributed to his personality.

Joe faced significant communication challenges in therapy sessions and treatment programs. Many facilities either did not provide communication access or relied on unqualified interpreters unfamiliar with mental health terminology. This often led to significant misunderstandings and ineffective care. Joe had to rely on written communication which lacked the emotional nuances needed for effective treatment, leaving him feeling frustrated and misunderstood. When Joe attended Alcoholics Anonymous (AA) meetings, interpreters were seldom available.

Joe faced financial challenges when trying to access culturally appropriate care due to low-paying jobs which often did not provide health care benefits. Many programs with ASL-fluent staff require out-of-pocket payments and publicly funded programs rarely cater to deaf individuals.

In order to effectively address Joe's needs, a comprehensive treatment plan should include culturally competent care from ASL-fluent professionals who understand Deaf culture. To address his substance misuse, this plan should combine therapy, appropriate medication, and accessible 12-step meetings, both online with ASL support and in person. Integrating mental health services will help Joe manage his underlying anxiety and depression. Additionally, peer support networks composed of deaf individuals in recovery, available in person or virtually, can provide crucial encouragement for his long-term recovery.

Another important part of the recovery process that may benefit Joe is to have a sponsor. A sponsor provides support to a person who is new to sobriety and recovery and to individuals who are in long-term recovery. Sponsors help to answer questions, work on the 12-steps, and offer accountability. To be a sponsor, a person does not have to go through treatment, but the individual should have a reasonable amount of time in sobriety, an understanding of the 12 steps and a desire to help others. Although it may be challenging to find a deaf sponsor, it is preferable for a number of reasons. First of all, there can be direct communication between the deaf sponsor and sponsee, which helps to ensure clear understanding and the ability to foster a connection. A deaf sponsor may be able to better understand the cultural nuances and provide support. Additionally, a Deaf sponsor has lived through the challenges of substance use addiction and recovery, and this shared experience allows for a deeper level of empathy and understanding. Lastly, a deaf sponsor can serve as a role model, demonstrating that recovery is possible for deaf individuals and can inspire hope and motivate their sponsee to stay on the path to sobriety.

Moving Forward: Solutions and Recommendations

Despite the progress made in recent decades, deaf individuals with alcohol and substance use disorders remain underserved. We have seen treatment programs downsize and close, leaving significant gaps in services. In order for more treatment options to be available for this underserved population, a regional or national network of specialized program options should be established.

Policymakers should also invest in training programs to help more therapists and interpreters learn ASL and specialize in substance use treatment. We can develop more strategies that encourage deaf high school graduates to consider becoming social workers, therapists, substance use counselors, psychologists, health educators, and public health workers. If educators introduce high school students to deaf professionals in these fields, it helps them see successful deaf individuals in these careers which can inspire and motivate them. High schools can also create mentorship programs where they pair deaf students with deaf professionals which can provide guidance, support, and a deeper understanding of specific career paths. Additionally, high schools that serve deaf students can host career fairs that feature professionals in these and other career fields. This will not only benefit the Deaf community but also contribute to a more diverse and culturally competent workforce in these essential fields.

Educators should also work with leaders from the Deaf community to create accessible prevention materials in ASL that accommodate their cultural needs. Healthcare providers can team up with organizations like DeafAA.org to include their services in larger treatment networks. Additionally, encouraging treatment programs to use accessible technology and hire staff who know ASL will help improve care for everyone.

There is a necessity to incentivize healthcare providers to adopt culturally competent practices. One way to do this is to form community partnerships with local, state, and national agencies well versed in working with deaf individuals. Healthcare providers can apply for grants to support cultural competency initiatives. On a more systematic level, entities can offer potential incentives to providers. These incentives may include tax credits or deductions. Another consideration might also be to have national accrediting bodies give public recognition by creating awards or certifications for facilities that excel in providing deaf-accessible services. Additionally, we recommend that insurance reimbursement policies be adjusted to consider the disability framework. This would allow providers to offer higher rates for services rendered by culturally competent centers. Treatment programs should also ensure that staff are equipped with the tools necessary to understand and navigate the unique needs of deaf clients. This involves not only language fluency but also an understanding of deaf culture, the social stigma surrounding alcoholism and substance use, and the specific communication strategies that facilitate effective therapy. Increasing the availability of qualified interpreters, developing culturally relevant educational materials, and creating more programs that are accessible to deaf individuals are also critical steps in improving outcomes for this population.

In response to these barriers, Certified Deaf Interpreters (CDIs) are a solution to bridge the communication gap (Forestal, 2014). CDIs are interpreters who are deaf themselves and are specially trained to provide interpreting services in a variety of settings, including medical, legal, educational, and mental health environments. CDIs are already used in complex or high-stakes legal (Feldman et al., 2023) and mental health (Glickman et al., 2020) situations where standard interpreters—who may not have the same cultural or linguistic insight—might struggle to convey nuanced or culturally specific information. CDIs can bridge communication gaps and improve treatment outcomes.

Research efforts must be expanded to better understand the prevalence and impact of alcohol and substance use within the Deaf community. More data is needed on substance use patterns, factors contributing to misuse, the role of isolation and communication barriers, and treatment outcomes within this population. Current studies often fail to consider how to create inclusion for deaf individuals in a culturally competent manner, which affects the accuracy and applicability of their findings. Deaf individuals often face communication barriers when participating in studies, and many are reluctant to engage with research led by hearing researchers who may lack cultural competence (Kushalnagar et al., 2023). This distrust can lead to underrepresentation of deaf individuals in studies. To ensure that findings are truly reflective of the experiences and needs of the deaf community, research must be conducted in a culturally sensitive and inclusive manner, prioritizing deaf researchers and interpreters in study design and implementation.

Conclusion

In summary, deaf individuals face unique challenges related to substance use and misuse. They often deal with feelings of social isolation, struggle with communication barriers, interpreter scarcity, and difficulty finding culturally appropriate services. These issues increase the risk of substance misuse among deaf individuals and make it harder for them to find effective prevention and treatment options. We need to create programs that are culturally appropriate and ASL accessible. These services must consider how deaf individuals communicate and their cultural backgrounds. We need to provide ongoing education and training to healthcare providers, so they are aware of the importance of having accessible programs for deaf individuals. Addressing these issues requires immediate action from local, state, and national groups. Policymakers must provide funding and support to develop prevention programs and treatment centers for the Deaf community. Researchers must conduct more studies on substance use among deaf individuals and include their perspectives and experiences. Healthcare providers must receive training in Deaf culture and ASL to better serve this population. By taking these steps together, we can create meaningful changes, break down barriers, and ensure that deaf individuals receive the care and support they need for long-lasting recovery.

References

Aldalur, A., Dillon, K. M., Rotoli, J. M., Stecker, T., & Conner, K. R. (2024). Deaf perceptions about treatment for alcohol use and mental health. *Journal of Substance Use and Addiction Treatment, 158*, 209–233. https://doi.org/10.1016/j.josat.2023.209233

Americans with Disabilities Act of 1990, H.R. 2273, 101st Congress. (1990). https://www.congress.gov/bill/101st-congress/house-bill/2273/text.

Anderson, M. L., Chang, B., & Kini, N. (2018). Alcohol and drug use among deaf and hard-of-hearing individuals: A secondary analysis of NHANES 2013-2014. *Substance Abuse, 39*(3), 390–397. https://doi.org/10.1080/08897077.2018.1442383

Anderson, M. L., Glickman, N. S., Wolf Craig, K. S., Sortwell Crane, A. K., Wilkins, A. M., & Najavits, L. M. (2021). Developing signs of safety: A deaf-accessible counselling toolkit for trauma and addiction. *Clinical Psychology & Psychotherapy, 28*(6), 1562–1573.

Baschnagel, J. S., & Bell, J. S. (2023). Drinking to cope and coping strategies in deaf/hard of hearing college students. *Addictive Behaviors, 136.*, Article 107485. https://doi.org/10.1016/j.addbeh.2022.107485

Berman, B. A., Streja, L., & Guthmann, D. (2010). Alcohol and other substance use among deaf and hard of hearing youth. *Journal of Drug Education, 40*(2), 99–124. https://doi.org/10.2190/DE.40.2.a.

Boros, A. (1980). Alcoholism intervention for the deaf, winter special issue: The multi disabled. *Alcohol Health and Research World, 5*(2), 28–32.

Cowgill, B., Herrmann, A., Richardson, J., Guthmann, D, McKee, M. Malzkuhn, M., & Berman, B. (2020). Understanding e-cigarette knowledge and use among d/Deaf and hard of hearing students and the need for tailored prevention programming: A qualitative study. *American Annals of the Deaf, 165*(3):335–352. https://dx-doi-org.uml.idm.oclc.org. https://doi.org/10.1353/aad.2020.0022.

Crowe, T. (2022). Negative life experiences, substance use, well-being, and resilience: A comparison of deaf and hearing adults. *International Journal on Social and Education Sciences, 4*(3), 391–407. https://doi.org/10.46328/ijonses.416

DeafAA.org. (n.d.). *Deaf AA meetings and ASL interpreted meetings in the USA/Canada.* https://sites.google.com/view/deafaa/home.

ECheckup to go. (2024). Online evidence-based interventions for behavior change. https://echeckuptogo.com/.

Feldman, D. M., Silvasi, P. M., Rotshtyn, D., & Covell, C. (2023). Understanding deaf culture, the deaf community, and American Sign Language in a criminal justice and legal context. In *Intersections of the legal system and the Deaf community: From law enforcement to incarceration* (pp. 1–16). Springer.

Forestal, E. (2014). Deaf interpreters: The dynamics of their interpreting process. In R. Adam, C. Stone, S. Collins, & M. Metzger (Eds.), *Deaf interpreters at work* (pp. 29–50). Gallaudet University Press.

Gannon, C. L. (2023). Deaf and hard of hearing students' experiences with alcohol and related consequences. (317). Walden University ProQuest Dissertations. https://scholarworks.waldenu.edu/dissertations/14697/.

Gannon, C. L., Gibble, T. H., & Evans, R. (2024). Alcohol use and deaf and hard of hearing college students. *American Journal of Qualitative Research*, 161–187. https://doi.org/10.29333/ajqr/14565

Glickman, N. S., Crump, C., & Hamerdinger, S. (2020). Language deprivation is a game changer for the clinical specialty of deaf mental health. *JADARA, 54*(1), 54.

Guthmann, D., & Sandberg, K. (2019). Evaluating alcohol and other drug use problems with deaf and hard of hearing persons. *JADARA, 31*(1). Retrieved from https://nsuworks.nova.edu/jadara/vol31/iss1/5.

Guthmann, D., Titus, J., Embree, J., & Wilson, J. (2017). Translation and validation of an online suite of assessments in American Sign Language. *JADARA, 51*(1):12–20. https://nsuworks.nova.edu/jadara/vol51/iss1/5.

Guthmann, D., & Titus, J. (2016). Substance abuse. In G. Gertz & P. Boudreault (Eds.), *The SAGE deaf studies encyclopedia* (pp. 932–935). SAGE Publications.

Guthmann, D., & Sternfeld, C. (2013). Substance abuse treatment and recovery: Adaptations to best practices when working with culturally Deaf persons. In N. Glickman (Ed.), *Deaf mental health care* (pp. 243–267). Taylor & Francis.

Guthmann, D. (2011). What to consider when deaf individuals have substance abuse issues. *Paradigm Magazine, 16*(1), 20–22.

James, T. G., Argenyi, M. S., Guardino, D. L., McKee, M. M., Wilson, J. A. B., Sullivan, M. K., Schwartzman, E. G., & Anderson, M. L. (2022). Communication access in mental health and substance use treatment facilities for Deaf American Sign Language users. *Health Affairs, 41*(10), 1413–1422. https://doi.org/10.1377/hlthaff.2022.00408

Kushalnagar, P., Hoglind, T., Simons, A. N., & Guthmann, D. (2019). Prevalence of alcohol use: A national survey of Deaf adults in the United States. *JADARA, 52*(2):24–33. https://nsuworks.nova.edu/jadara/vol52/iss2/3.

Kushalnagar, P., Nicolarakis, O., Mirus, G., Anderson, M., Burke, T., & Kushalnagar, R. (2023). Barriers and facilitators to the inclusion of Deaf people in clinical trials. *Clinical Trials, 20*(5), 576–580. https://doi.org/10.1177/17407745231177376

Kushalnagar, P., Ryan, C., Paludneviciene, R., Spellun, A., & Gulati, S. (2020). Adverse childhood communication experiences associated with an increased risk of chronic diseases in adults who are Deaf. *American Journal of Preventive Medicine, 59*(4), 548–554. https://doi.org/10.1016/j.amepre.2020.04.016

McKee, M. M., Meade, M. A., Zazove, P., Stewart, H. J., Jannausch, M. L., & Ilgen, M. A. (2019). The relationship between hearing loss and substance use disorders among adults in the U.S. *American Journal of Preventive Medicine, 56*(4):586–590. https://doi.org/10.1016/j.amepre.2018.10.026

National Institute on Alcohol Abuse and Alcoholism. (2019). College alcohol intervention matrix. https://www.collegedrinkingprevention.gov/CollegeAIM/Resources/NIAAA_College_Matrix_Booklet.pdf.

Noll, J., Sneed, Z., & Steward, D. (2024). A scoping review of substance use prevalence rates amongst subgroups of people living with deafness. *Alcoholism Treatment Quarterly, 43*(2), 306–312. https://doi.org/10.1080/07347324.2024.2429407

Pinquart, M., & Pfeiffer, J. P. (2015). Alcohol use among students with and without hearing loss. *Journal of Deaf Studies and Deaf Education, 20*(1), 82–90.

Sardi Program. (2024). ASL star. https://www.sardiprogram.com/ASLStar/.

Titus, J., & Guthmann, D. (2013). Using evidence-based practices with people who are deaf or hard of hearing. *Counselor, 14*(3), 68–73.

Titus, J. C., & Guthmann, D. (2010). Addressing the black hole in substance abuse treatment for deaf and hard of hearing individuals: Technology to the rescue. *Journal of the American Deafness and Rehabilitation Association, 43*(2), 92–100.

Whaley, B. A., & Williamson, P. (2023). The Americans with Disabilities Act, addiction, and recovery. *Journal of Vocational Rehabilitation, 58*, 299–305. https://doi.org/10.3233/JVR-230018

Wheatley, M. (2021, November 30). Barriers faced by deaf people while accessing healthcare. European Disability Forum. https://edf-feph.org/blog/barriers-faced-by-deaf-people-while-accessing-healthcare/#.

Wilkins, A. M., Schafer, K., & Anderson, M. L. (2024). Alcohol use research in the U.S. deaf Community: 21st century advances. *Current Addiction Reports, 11*, 869–876. https://doi.org/10.1007/s40429-024-00590-y

Chapter 10
Lived Experiences

Rosemary Wanis and Rachel Zemach

My name is Rosemary. I am a Deaf adult born to hearing parents. We all immigrated to the US from Egypt. I live in California and this is my story while working as a full-time lecturer at a university in California.

It was March 2021. I was deeply hurt by something that happened between my biological child and my foster child at the time. I could not get out of my mental angst and locked myself in the guest room of our home, which had a wooden bed frame. After lying on the floor for a few hours, crying so hard my biological daughter came in and asked me what was wrong. When I tried to explain, she laughed and walked away, as a teenager, not understanding the depth of my state of mind, would do. My heart couldn't take any more hurt, so I started to hit my head very hard on the wooden frame of the bed. I wanted to split my head in half. I wanted the pain to stop. I wanted the thoughts to stop. I wanted… my life… to… STOP! I got up.

I had to teach tomorrow. I decided to call in sick. I texted the interpreter coordinator and told her, I am not coming in tomorrow, please cancel my interpreters. I emailed my boss, told him "I am staying home sick tomorrow, cancelling all classes". I texted my parents, "Mom, Dad, I need help. Please come. NOW!" My parents lived 3 hours away, and within 30 min, they had loaded up their car and drove all the way to my house. While waiting for my parents, there was someone at my front door. It was the interpreter coordinator. She asked if she could come in and stay with me while my parents were on their way. She knew from my text and my 15 years of never missing class that something was wrong. The interpreter coordinator arrived with her husband (who is Deaf), and they both stayed with me, let me cry on their shoulders, and sat with me. Cried with me. Listened. Prayed. At that moment, she was not my interpreter; she was my friend. So grateful. My parents

R. Wanis (✉)
Monterey, CA, USA

R. Zemach
Santa Rosa, CA, USA

T. Bone (ed.), *Deaf Mental Health*, Advances in Mental Health and Addiction,
https://doi.org/10.1007/978-3-032-06274-1_10

finally arrived. At this time, the interpreter coordinator and her husband left with assurances that they would follow up with me soon.

My parents stayed and prayed with me for 3 days. Mom slept next to me. Made sure I ate. They just kept an eye on me. If I wanted to sit up, they sat with me. If I wanted to watch a movie in the living room, they watched with me. If I wanted to go for a short walk outside, they walked with me. Then 3 days later, I was "okay." Stable enough to return to work. They left. Worried, but we had a plan to stay in touch.

In October 2021, we were mid-semester, and that fall was the first full semester back from COVID-19. Students and faculty were not prepared for what life in a college would be like post-COVID. Suddenly, there were 65 students in a 65-seat classroom. They didn't want to be that close to anyone. They didn't want to turn to their partner and introduce themselves. They didn't want to be there, PERIOD! The second day of class, 30 students showed up. Then, for the rest of the semester, the numbers got smaller and smaller. Then, one day, I looked up and only had three. I would teach as if I had 65. My class was usually quite engaging, 3 days a week, 50 minutes. Not that semester. There were times when there was no input or discussion at all. I started to feel very discouraged. The silence triggered my thoughts from March 2021. That is when I knew that I was still not completely whole from that season of my life. I started to cry while teaching class and No One Noticed! I went to my office to call and share my thoughts with my department chair. He told me to talk with the Dean. I emailed the Dean. She told me to talk with HR. I called HR on the videophone through an ASL Interpreter. I explained the situation and asked if I could have mental health time leave. HR replied with "No." I asked if I could move my class online and teach virtually so that I did not have to look my students in the eye, as my mental health could not take the silence. No, they said. I asked HR, "okay, what can you do for me"? Their response: "Would you like a notetaker for your classes?" My jaw dropped! What did you ask me? A notetaker? You realize I am a faculty member and not a student. "Um, yeah. Would you like a notetaker"? How does that help me?!?! "I don't know how to help you". We have never had this type of situation come up with a Deaf faculty member. There it was. The dirty word. Deaf. I hung up in despair and desperation. The HR office was supposed to be the very people I was forced to call after no support from my chair or from my dean, and they could not help me. I called Faculty Affairs (the administrative office on campus that addresses all matters relating to academic personnel, including appointment, tenure, promotion, leaves, grievances, etc.). I was in tears and Faculty Affairs said they could not help me. I called my doctor at Kaiser Permanente, he said that the only thing I could do was go to the ER, and there was nothing he could do. I emailed, I called, I tried, I failed, then…

I collapsed.

Right there, on the floor of my office, I texted my designated interpreter, and she came as soon as she could.

I was on the floor and could not get up.

I kept signing over and over, "I can't continue… I can't continue… I can't continue..."

She asked me what she could do. I told her, I can't be alone right now, I just need you by my side. She stayed by my side. Cried with me. Prayed with me. Our interpreters are humans too. In that moment, and for many moments, she was not just my interpreter. She was my friend. So grateful.

I finally was physically strong enough to drive home. I didn't care. I took the rest of the week off to just decide what to do. Gave my classes online work and went home.

That afternoon, I packed a bag. I called the County Behavioral Health for inpatient crisis services through my videophone with an ASL interpreter. The crisis services allow a person to either voluntarily or involuntarily check themselves in for a 72-hour hold while being observed and treated to de-escalate a mental health episode. I told the County Behavioral Health that I am Deaf, and I am voluntarily checking myself in because I am suicidal. They said that they don't know how to work with me because I am Deaf. I almost hung up, then I thought to myself, No! It is your job to take care of me just like any other resident of this county. I am showing up tomorrow and you figure it out.

My daughter came home from high school. She saw my bag. I was sitting at the dining table. I told her, "momma is going away for a few days. I don't know when I will come back. I just want you to know that when you come home from school tomorrow, if I am not here, you call grandma and grandpa and tell them that you are coming to their house to stay with them for a while until momma comes back home". My daughter is smart. She figured out what was happening and begged me not to go anywhere. She sat and watched a movie with me. She ate with me. We played card games at the dining table. She lifted my spirits. She stayed by my side the whole night. I never went to the inpatient crisis program.

I decided to "fire" my doctor and go see another doctor. I arrived at the doctor's office, our first time meeting. Told her what was happening with me. She could tell from my body language and the paleness of my face that something was wrong. I cried, I told her the whole story through the ASL interpreter on the rolling iPad in the patient room. She listened. She stayed. She said that I was depressed. I asked her to give me a note to excuse me from work. She gave me 3 days off. She prescribed medication and referred me to immediate therapy with Kaiser Mental Health. I accepted, as I knew I needed the support and needed it now.

My dean followed up with me once. My department chair never did. I went back to work and just taught class with no expectations of follow-up. I was transparent with my students. Told them, your instructor is not well, but here I am, showing up. Many students shared their own mental health struggles to say "I am not alone".

When I shared my struggles with faculty, they would say things like "it's because of COVID, a lot of people are struggling." That was not helpful. My issues were not about COVID. My issues were about the lack of support and were exacerbated by turning to those who were supposed to support me and getting absolutely nothing, nada, zilch, zip! I stayed two more years, then I couldn't stay any longer. After 17 years of being invisible and dismissed, I left.

Then I started to think, how many other Deaf people have been in my shoes? How many have tried unsuccessfully to get mental health support but faced numerous barriers that made it impossible? How many Deaf people who don't have employment services and who don't have health insurance that includes mental health and needed that type of intensive support and actually received it? Where do they go? Who helps them? I had to do something, so I reached out to the state Department of Social Services (which has oversight for services for Deaf, hard of hearing, DeafBlind, and DeafDisabled people in California) and informed them of my situation. I begged them to please do something to improve mental health. We are still working on that. I reached out to the state association of the Deaf, and while they agreed that mental health is an important topic, they were not ready to discuss suicide as they were afraid that the discussion itself would encourage people to unalive themselves. Ummm....

How do we continue to survive, find support, when there are walls all around us, from within and from without? Hence in this chapter, I am sharing with you, that the needs of Deaf, hard of hearing, DeafBlind, and DeafDisabled individuals for services are no different than anyone else's. We need ASL interpreters. We need access to outpatient individual and group opportunities, and we need access to inpatient intensive care as well. My issues had nothing to do with me being Deaf (as is often wrongly assumed by mental health and medical providers). It had to do with me being a mother, foster mother, daughter, teacher, friend, and being human. Who will help me? Who will see me? Who will stay by my side and listen? Will it be you?

Another sector that has a tremendous impact on the mental health of Deaf, hard of hearing, DeafBlind, and DeafDisabled individuals is the education system; specifically, K-12th grade mainstream settings where children are often learning in isolation, separately from their peers, and/or in schools where their cultural identity is not recognized, valued, or celebrated. One Deaf friend of mine, Rachel Zemach, taught in mainstream schools in northern California for 10 years. Rachel shares her story, along with those of her students, in her memoir, "The Butterfly Cage," with snippets included here for inclusion in this chapter on lived experiences.

Deaf Students in Hearing Schools: The Perfect Storm by Rachel Zemach

I became Deaf suddenly at age 10. From age 10–18, I attended seven different schools while I missed out on close to 100% of the instruction and classroom dialogue. Things that stand out in memory: my Deafness mistaken for my being "retarded" by a boy I liked. A driver's education class where the teacher paced, impossible to lipread, and there was no other way I could pass the class but to cheat. I could not support my intellectual curiosity, so my coping mechanisms included sketching, cutting classes, and dabbling in substance use. The decision to skip prom and graduation took all of 2 seconds, because I did not feel like a true member of the school.

When I tried to get help from teachers or other staff, I did not fare much better. As a teen, I didn't know how to fight for my rights. I discovered dance classes where I could shine. But overall, I felt detached, lonely, hopeless, and disengaged from school. Not despite of but *because of* my intellectual longing to learn and participate.

How does the mental health of a person in this position thrive?

Our schools are breeding grounds for depression, and unnecessarily so. The majority of our Deaf and hard of hearing students attend public schools with a majority of hearing peers. This is referred to as mainstreamed education. Despite current laws from the Americans with Disabilities Act and Individuals with Disabilities Education Act, discrimination—both systemic and social—continues. Students (and most parents) are ill-equipped to advocate for their needs. Deaf and hard of hearing students must create coping skills in an oftentimes hostile and unwelcoming environment. Linguistic, communicative, social, identity, and educational issues all come into play daily during those critical school years. The risk of self-harm, or at least thoughts of it, in such environments is high.

Many years later, I became a teacher myself.

I taught Deaf students in a mainstream school, and in my second year there, an amazing seven-year-old, who I'll call "Lazlo," was placed in my class. He had a voracious appetite for learning language, and the year was positively dreamy. In a memoir I wrote about my career, I described him this way: "It was as if he had brought a magic carpet with him. He simply elevated us all."

However, he fell into a depression when his teacher, the next year, took a prolonged absence, during which time none of the substitute teachers signed.

Years later, I was thrilled to finally see him again, on a field trip my class and his high school class attended, to see a play at a local School for the Deaf. But when I asked how he felt at his school, he told me he felt disconnected from both ASL and the Deaf community.

The following year, this tall, handsome, brilliant, kind 16-year-old boy jumped in front of a train, ending his life, and taking his next-level intelligence and desire to make films with him.

I found he had been bullied for his "different" speech, had developed a crush on a girl who was also Deaf, and had often sat alone at lunchtime, playing video games on the floor in the hall.

I found he had gotten counseling from a therapist at the school who did NOT know signs or anything about Deaf culture. And his interpreter there, rather than being a neutral outsider, which would have given him appropriate privacy to speak freely, was the same interpreter he had in all his classes.

For sure, his suicide was complicated and there was a multi-layered and intricate confluence of causes. However, I believe there were many ways the school could have done things differently. They could have found a signing therapist or one knowledgeable in Deaf/hard of hearing issues, or provided an interpreter who was not his classroom interpreter.

He would have had many more potential friends to choose from. And if he was encouraged and allowed to look into the school for the Deaf as an alternative school environment, perhaps the change would have been life-altering, feeding his natural curiosity and thirst for language. His intellect would have been inspired by the intelligent, high-powered dialogue at the school about Deaf history and access issues, while in the sophisticated film-making department there, he would have found adult mentors and embarked on advanced projects.

After his devastating death, I reached out to another former student of mine who was still in that school district. "Daniella" was in middle school when we texted. I sensed something was off with her. "Do you have friends? Are there any other Deaf students there?" I asked about the huge mainstream middle school she was attending. "I was told there is one Deaf girl, and I keep trying to meet her, but no one will tell me where she is," Daniella responded.

Later that year, she expressed suicidal ideation and was swiftly transferred to the School for the Deaf (which she had asked to attend a couple of years earlier, and was turned down.) There, she thrived, winning awards and making many close new friends rapidly.

Mainstream schools are so often places of dysfunction and mental health challenges for Deaf and hard of hearing students. The convergence of a child or teen's needs, the invisibility of their issues, and the ignorance of the staff and hearing students all contribute to a difficult and dangerous path for a young person. A path that will scar some, detach others from their own education and future careers, and for others, almost—or literally —cost them their lives.

Some will eventually find the Deaf world, later in life, while others, with grit, creativity, luck, and endurance, will find a way to thrive in an environment not designed for them. Two of my former students are now "doing well," as young adults; one is in college for art, and one an athletic star at a high school. But these same two students had the intellectual smarts, as kids, to potentially become doctors, professors, or lawyers. Just like me, re-focusing my energy towards dance and drawing as a coping strategy, these searingly bright young people found more visual, physical careers where they could excel, instead. For them, too, a school for the Deaf could have provided an antidote to the barriers they encountered and provided the intellectual stimulation they needed to soar; perhaps in different directions.

Our futures are strongly impacted by our educational years.

In school, powerlessness, surviving, trying to fit in, or finding ways to cope should not be the focus. Instead, learning, conversing, and sensing the abundance of an unlimited future should be.

And *could be.*

For Professionals: Be the Change!

From Rachel: Most students will have no idea that they can ask for accommodations such as an interpreter or CART. Unless they are from a Deaf family, most won't know their legal rights, or anything about disability rights and laws, or agencies. I went to college for 3 years before someone happened to mention that Vocational

Rehabilitation (now called DOR) could pay for my tuition and books. As a professional, you have a vital role in educating families and students about their rights. Do your research BEFORE a student needs it; find interpreting agencies, CART providers, Deaf agencies that have advocates, and services, and post the information widely; in hallways, offices, and distribute to students, staff, and families.

Make SURE that students understand their rights, what they can request, that you are willing to accommodate, and how to request those services. Show students how to stand up for themselves politely but firmly, when needed. I used to do role play with my students, and they loved it. At one point in a job, I got accommodations only when a union lawyer asked me if I had requested them, and offered to help. She assured me that I would not be fired for requesting them. K-12 students will have their own ignorance and mental blocks. Encourage them to go to local Deaf events. Be the person who opens the gateway for them to better access, equity, and mental health.

The list below includes some powerful videos and books for students and their families to read. Most middle schoolers and high schoolers are focused on trying to blend in and not call attention to themselves. Requesting or using accommodations is counter to that, as is a sense of identity or pride in one's disability. But when teens learn about the history and fierceness of Deaf and disabled people fighting for their rights—and winning— it can provoke an awakening of important qualities they will need in their lives; an attitude that's the opposite of hiding and denying authentic identity. It can be powerful and positive, and at the very least, unforgettable. They will not learn these valuable life lessons anywhere else while attending mainstream schools. Bring to them the beauty of fighting for change and asking unapologetically for what they need to thrive in school.

From Rosemary: Working with Deaf, hard of hearing, DeafBlind, and DeafDisabled children, youth, and adults requires first, a heart and mindset of openness and cultural humility. Recognize that you may be working with a population with which you have little to no exposure and/or experience. Yet, recognize that we are whole beings and deserving of quality care with warmth, empathy, and respect for our lived experiences. As you learn, grow, and work alongside us, consider the following resources for your orientation and/or review as you embrace a new culture, language, and communities.

When working with Deaf, hard of hearing, DeafBlind, and DeafDisabled children, youth, and adults, we ask you to consider the following five actions.

1. **Recognize us as whole beings with multiple identities**. For example, one of the authors of this chapter, Rosemary, is Deaf and she is also an Egyptian Christian Female. If you work with someone like Rosemary, recognize her intersectionality. Therefore, she interacts with multiple systems and experiences multiple impacts from within those systems based on her identities.
2. **Challenge the dominant perspective.** Identify inequities that have been experienced and are a potential cause, trigger, or dynamic in the current presenting mental health incident. Challenge the dominant perspective by breaking away from the status quo. Don't accept "things have always been this way" or "we

have never provided an interpreter before" or other comments that perpetuate the lack of services made available and accessible to our communities.

3. **Commit to Social Justice.** After identifying inequities, address social change by committing to reducing and removing harm to our communities.
4. **Value Experiential Knowledge.** Value the stories that are shared with you and believe them to be real. Accept the realities of the impact on our lived experiences and use that information to inform the decisions and changes that will be made.
5. **Use an Interdisciplinary Approach.** To effect real and lasting change, involve all shareholders to engage in an active and meaningful collaboration that addresses the issues impacting the availability and accessibility of services from multiple angles and entry points into the mental health system.

References

Working with Children—Child Resilience Center at Gallaudet University. https://gallaudet.edu/deaf-hard-hearing-child-resilience-center/deaf-and-hard-of-hearing-child-resilience-resources/.

Emergency Crisis Support in ASL—DeafLEAD—https://deaflead.org/services/crisis-intervention/disaster-distress-helpline/. 988 Suicide & Crisis Lifeline. 988 supports callers in suicidal crisis or emotional distress. Chat, Text, Call or Videophone 988.

"Audible" on Netflix—trailer: https://www.youtube.com/watch?v=G5htMIBhdGk. Synopsis: Football player Amaree McKenstry-Hall and his Maryland School for the Deaf teammates attempt to defend their winning streak while coming to terms with the tragic loss of a close friend. The graduating students face mounting pressures of entering the hearing world while tackling adversity and demanding to be heard in this moving coming-of-age story.

I'll Tell You Later: Deaf Survivors of Dinner Table Syndrome—a book by Raymond Luczak (Editor), available through Barnes and Noble. https://www.barnesandnoble.com/w/ill-tell-you-later-raymond-luczak/1146590431.

On The Fence—a book By Mark Drolsbuagh. https://www.barnesandnoble.com/w/on-the-fence-mark-drolsbaugh/1125438717?ean=9780965746052.

"Through Deaf Eyes"—A PBS Documentary. https://www.youtube.com/watch?v=PL5d8kyZUQk. Synopsis: Through Deaf Eyes explores almost 200 years of Deaf life in America and presents a broad range of perspectives on what it means to be deaf. The film is propelled by the stories of people, both eminent and ordinary, and sheds light on events that have shaped Deaf lives.

"I'll Scream Later"—a memoir by Marlee Matlin (includes mental health, substance abuse, domestic violence, and more). https://www.barnesandnoble.com/w/ill-scream-later-marlee-matlin/1100364423?ean=9781439171516.

"Show Me a Sign"—a book by Ann Clare LeZotte for younger audiences. https://www.ala.org/winner/show-me-sign.

Part III
A Deaf-centric Approach to Practice and Why It Matters

Chapter 11
Supporting Recovery and Community Integration of Deaf and Hard of Hearing Adults with Serious Mental Illness

Teresa Crowe

Introduction

Deaf and Hard of Hearing (DHH) adults with serious mental illness (SMI) face unique and multifaceted challenges that require tailored approaches to treatment, rehabilitation, community integration, and recovery of mental health symptoms. As a group that sits at the intersection of disability and mental health care systems, especially those for whom American Sign Language (ASL) is the native language, DHH individuals with SMI are underrepresented in research and underserved in clinical practice. Despite significant advancements in mental health care and rehabilitation models, the needs of this population are often unmet due to systemic barriers, a lack of cultural and linguistic competency, and limited accessibility to specialized services. This chapter provides an examination of the complexities involved in supporting recovery and community integration for DHH adults with SMI, offering insights and strategies for mental health professionals and community stakeholders.

Understanding Serious Mental Illness

According to the Diagnostic and Statistical Manual of Mental Disorders (DSM-5TR), serious mental illness encompasses a subset of psychiatric diagnoses, including schizophrenia spectrum and other psychotic disorders, bipolar and related disorders, depressive disorders, anxiety disorders, obsessive-compulsive and related disorders, trauma- and stressor-related disorders, dissociative disorders, and others

T. Crowe (✉)
Master of Social Work Program, Gallaudet University, Washington, DC, USA
e-mail: Teresa.crowe@gallaudet.edu

T. Bone (ed.), *Deaf Mental Health*, Advances in Mental Health and Addiction,
https://doi.org/10.1007/978-3-032-06274-1_11

(APA, 2022). In addition to specific criteria for specific disorders, another hallmark of serious mental illness is that the symptoms must be severe enough to significantly impair daily functioning and quality of life. When clinicians use the term "serious mental illness," they typically mean diagnoses that include schizophrenia spectrum disorders, bipolar disorders, major depressive disorders, and anxiety disorders. These conditions involve chronic and severe symptoms, such as psychosis, mood instability, and profound difficulties in managing daily responsibilities.

Individuals with SMI often face poor physical health outcomes, including higher risks of cardiovascular disease (Polcwiartek et al., 2024), cancer (Tuschick et al., 2024), suicide (Trott et al., 2024), and increased risk for physical illnesses (Bergman et al., 2024). Comorbidities and complex trauma are common among individuals with SMI, especially DHH individuals. Many DHH adults have experienced childhood adversities, such as neglect, abuse, or systemic discrimination, which can exacerbate mental health challenges (Crowe, 2019; Rogers et al., 2024). For DHH individuals, mental health challenges are compounded by communication differences, cultural influences, and a lack of accessible mental health resources, making early identification, accurate diagnosis, and effective treatment particularly challenging.

Symptom manifestation of SMI can have unique features in DHH adults (Moreno et al., 2023). For example, some DHH individuals with SMI report auditory hallucinations despite being deaf, while others may report tactile or visual hallucinations with or without ASL. Paranoia may be influenced by misinterpretations of visual cues, such as ambiguous facial expressions or gestures when people around them are not using sign language. The experience of mental illness is shaped by the social, linguistic, and cultural contexts and experiences (Moreno et al., 2023). Those who grew up with limited access to ASL or language development (i.e., language deprivation) may struggle to express their experiences of mental health symptoms (At, 2024). The lack of linguistic tools, such as a lack of provider and/or DHH client language fluency, can result in underreporting symptoms, miscommunication, misdiagnosis, and ineffective treatment plans (Gwaltney, 2022).

Social factors, including lack of accessibility, distrust in healthcare providers, and negative cultural attitudes toward mental health, influence exacerbation of symptoms and help-seeking behaviors among DHH individuals with SMI (Crowe, 2021; Rogers et al., 2024; Terry & Robins-Talbot, 2024). Many DHH consumers face challenges finding mental health providers who are fluent in American Sign Language (ASL) or trained in culturally competent care, leading to delays or avoidance in seeking treatment. Miscommunication and a lack of understanding of Deaf-specific needs can result in misdiagnosis or inadequate care, perpetuating the cycle of unmet needs. Understanding SMI in the context of DHH communities requires a holistic perspective considering the interplay of individual, familial, and community dynamics. By addressing the gaps in service delivery, enhancing cultural and linguistic competency, and recognizing the unique experiences of DHH individuals with SMI, mental health professionals can develop more effective strategies to support recovery and social integration.

Case Example: Jonah

Jonah is a 28-year-old Deaf male who communicates with American Sign Language (ASL). He was referred to a community mental health agency for evaluation and treatment. He was diagnosed by a psychiatrist, using a mental health trained, certified interpreter, as having schizoaffective disorder, bipolar type.

Presenting concerns: *Jonah has experienced severe psychosis episodes over the past 8 years, including auditory and visual hallucinations, delusions of persecution, and periods of mania followed by severe depression. His most recent psychiatric hospitalization followed a suicide attempt. Language deprivation in early childhood resulted in limited ASL proficiency and limited English skills in reading and writing. Jonah lives with his mother, a retired teacher who does not use ASL and struggles with her own health issues and stress from caring for Jonah.*

Background: *Jonah attended a mainstream high school with an interpreter but often felt isolated, which led to early signs of depression in adolescence. His first psychotic episode occurred at age 20 while he was attending a job training program. Since then, his mental health has significantly declined, resulting in multiple hospitalizations, fractured relationships, and loss of independence. Jonah struggles with medication adherence, partly due to side effects and partly due to difficulty understanding written information about his treatment. He is ambivalent about therapy, citing prior frustration with hearing therapists who could not sign well. Jonah now sees a Deaf therapist who is fluent in ASL.*

Understanding Jonah's Mental Illness

Symptoms: *Jonah's schizoaffective disorder manifests differently from hearing clients. He experiences visual hallucinations in the form of shadowy figures and ASL "messages" that he believes are warnings from ghosts. Though Jonah's audiogram reveals that he is profoundly deaf, he "hears" these ghosts moaning loudly, which interferes with his ability to focus on what is happening around him. His depressive phase includes periods of sadness, emptiness, and worthlessness. During the manic phases of his illness, he sleeps very little, is irritable, and will often have altercations with strangers.*

Language and communication: *Jonah relies on ASL for communication but struggles because of early childhood language deprivation. His current therapist is fluent in ASL and can adjust her signing style and speed to facilitate effective communication.*

Impact on psychosocial functioning: *Jonah's illness severely impacts his ability to engage in daily activities, maintain interpersonal relationships, and pursue education or employment, which contributes to his feelings of hopelessness.*

Rehabilitation and Recovery

Recovery-oriented mental health care is a guiding framework for addressing the needs of individuals with SMI. The recovery model for treatment of individuals with SMI emphasizes personal growth, empowerment, self-determination, and community inclusion, even when mental health symptoms are persistent (Jambrina et al., 2024; Jordan et al., 2024). This model shifts the focus of treatment from simply reducing symptoms to enabling individuals to lead meaningful lives. The key components of the recovery model of SMI treatment are:

- **Person-Centered Care:** The recovery model prioritizes an individual's personal goals and values while promoting empowerment and self-determination.
- **Holistic Approach:** The model encompasses clinical, functional, social, and spiritual recovery, recognizing the multifaceted nature of mental health recovery.
- **Self-Directed Recovery:** Self-directed recovery allows individuals to explore their needs and challenges without predetermined goals set by the clinician.
- **Empowerment:** Clients are given the tools and resources to make informed decisions about their care.
- **Peer Support:** Connections with others who share lived experiences foster mutual understanding, encouragement, and learning.
- **Respect and Dignity:** Recovery-oriented care emphasizes the inherent worth of every individual, promoting cultural competence and inclusion.

The rehabilitation and recovery model of SMI treatment offers an evidence-based framework to support individuals with SMI in achieving their highest potential and integrating into their communities. For DHH individuals with SMI, these models must be adapted to address the unique intersection of mental health, cultural identity, and communication needs. This can be accomplished in several ways.

Communication is the cornerstone of effective mental health care, yet DHH individuals often encounter significant barriers in accessing linguistically and culturally appropriate services. Rehabilitation and recovery approaches emphasize the importance of client-centered care, which requires accessible communication methods to meet the needs of DHH clients (Rogers et al., 2024; Terry & Robins-Talbot, 2024). Providing ASL-fluent providers with training in mental health allows for direct communication, building trust, and fostering a deeper therapeutic alliance. Educational resources, such as videos in ASL, visual aids, and plain language materials, help ensure that DHH individuals can fully understand their diagnoses and treatment plans. Technology integration, such as video relay services and telehealth platforms with ASL accessibility, can provide DHH clients with immediate access to care, especially in crisis situations.

Culturally competent mental health care recognizes that DHH cultural identity is pivotal. Deaf-centered program services ensure that services are aligned with cultural norms and communication preferences (Bonany et al., 2024). Peer support from DHH role models provides clients with relatable role models who share their lived experiences. Hearing mental health providers, especially with Deaf services embedded in their agency structure, should receive training on Deaf culture, the sociolinguistic aspects of ASL, and the systemic barriers faced by many DHH individuals. Recovery plans must incorporate the intersectionality of identities, such as race, gender, and socioeconomic status, which impact their mental health experiences.

Rehabilitation and recovery emphasize the importance of community integration as a cornerstone of recovery. For DHH individuals with SMI, community connections are a protective factor and a source of empowerment. Deaf-led mental health support groups provide a safe space for DHH clients to share experiences, build connections, and learn from one another (Bonany et al., 2024). Encouraging and assisting DHH clients to engage in Deaf-related activities, such as ASL events, Deaf-organized events, or sports leagues, fosters a sense of belonging and strengthens social networks. Collaborating with Deaf organizations ensures that mental health programs are aligned with the community's needs and values. Inclusive vocational training and placement specifically for DHH individuals help them achieve economic independence and integrate into the workforce.

Families and caregivers play critical roles in supporting DHH individuals with SMI, yet they often face unique challenges, including communication barriers and caregiver burnout. The recovery model recognizes the importance of involving families in treatment while promoting healthy boundaries and self-care (Terry & Robins-Talbot, 2024). Family support strategies can include family psychoeducation, teaching families about mental illness, treatment options, and communication strategies that help them better support their loved ones. Caregiver support groups can help Deaf and hearing family members share experiences and coping strategies. For hearing family members, learning ASL enhances communication and fosters stronger relationships with their DHH loved ones. Supporting families improves the client's recovery outcomes and strengthens the entire support system.

Case Example: Jonah

After Jonah's most recent hospitalization following a suicide attempt, his inpatient team referred him to an Assertive Community Treatment (ACT) program offering wraparound services. This program provides individualized, holistic care, ensuring Jonah receives the support he needs to achieve recovery while addressing his unique needs as a Deaf individual with a serious mental illness.

Admission to a community ACT program: *Jonah was initially hesitant about joining the program, expressing mistrust due to past experiences with inaccessible care. To build trust and facilitate treatment, Jonah was admitted to the Deaf program, which provided accessibility to ASL and services culturally aligned with Jonah's needs. The community treatment program offered several services tailored to Jonah's needs:*

- *Psychiatric care: Jonah saw a psychiatrist who used a certified interpreter and a certified deaf interpreter (CDI) for their meetings. This allowed the psychiatrist to better understand the nuances of Jonah's symptoms and treatment. During the sessions, the psychiatrist provided psychoeducation about medications and explained Jonah's diagnoses, using visual aids to clarify concepts like the impact of mood cycles and early psychosis warnings. Jonah was prescribed a new medication with fewer side effects, making adherence more manageable.*

- *Individual and group therapy: Jonah attended weekly individual therapy sessions with a Deaf therapist using ASL. Therapy sessions focused on cognitive-behavioral strategies to challenge Jonah's paranoid thoughts and delusions. He also joined a peer-led Deaf support group, where he connected with others who shared similar experiences. This gave Jonah a safe space to share his story, learn from others, and feel less isolated.*
- *Vocational rehabilitation: Jonah met with a VR counselor in the agency to create an individualized employment plan. When Jonah expressed a desire to learn photography, the counselor connected him with a nonprofit organization that offered workshops. The agency scheduled an interpreter to accompany Jonah to the workshops to ensure the content was accessible.*
- *Life skills training: Jonah attended Deaf day program classes at the agency designed to teach skills in budgeting, meal planning, medication organization, and self-advocacy. The Deaf teachers in the program helped ensure Jonah understood the content and practice skills in the classroom.*
- *Residential services: Jonah was evaluated and admitted to the agency's residential program services. Jonah moved in with two other Deaf members in a home supervised 24/7 by Deaf staff. This allowed Jonah to develop independence skills and improve his relationship with his mother.*

The ACT program's wraparound services played a critical role in Jonah's recovery by:

- ***Promoting empowerment*** *because Jonah felt respected and understood, motivating him to actively engage in his treatment.*
- ***Fostering independence*** *by developing skills, finding meaningful work, and moving into his own home, helping Jonah regain a sense of purpose and autonomy.*
- ***Building social connections*** *through formal and informal social and recreational activities, helping Jonah strengthen relationships within the Deaf community.*
- ***Preventing relapse*** *with early intervention strategies and improved medication adherence significantly reducing the severity and frequency of Jonah's psychotic and cyclic mood episodes.*

Challenges in Managing Serious Mental Illness

Clinicians addressing the unique needs of DHH individuals with SMI must consider additional barriers to mental health care. These challenges are deeply rooted in systemic inequities, communication barriers, cultural misunderstandings and mistrust, and stigma, which collectively hinder access to effective treatment and recovery for DHH clients. Addressing these issues requires a comprehensive understanding of the interplay between mental health and Deaf identity.

One of the most significant challenges is pervasive communication barriers created by inaccessible communication between providers and clients. Many mental health professionals lack ASL proficiency or do not know what proficient interpreter services are (Bonany et al., 2024). While interpreters can facilitate communication, inadequate mental health training and proficiency can slow the therapeutic process, limit nuanced conversations, and create feelings of discomfort or mistrust. Additionally, mental health information, such as written instructions or spoken explanations, is often inaccessible or ineffective for DHH clients with SMI. Written materials may not align with the reading levels or linguistic understanding of DHH individuals whose primary language is ASL rather than English. The lack of accessible communication can contribute to misunderstanding diagnoses and treatment plans, nonadherence to medication, and feelings of exclusion from the decision-making process (Terry & Robins-Talbot, 2024).

The stigma around mental illness and social isolation are significant challenges for DHH individuals with SMI (Bonany et al., 2024). Many DHH individuals with SMI worry about the consequences of their diagnoses becoming known within the community, which can lead to social withdrawal and reluctance to seek help. Stigma can exacerbate social isolation caused by systemic barriers, such as the lack of accessible social and recreational opportunities for DHH individuals, and by the symptoms of SMI, which may interfere with clients' ability to form and maintain satisfying interpersonal relationships.

Case Example: Jonah

Jonah's case highlights the multidimensional needs of Deaf individuals with serious mental illness. Complex and multifaceted challenges stem from systemic barriers, cultural differences, communication issues, and stigma in both the hearing and Deaf communities. Addressing these barriers requires an intersectional recovery approach that considers the unique needs of Deaf clients while also addressing broader challenges in mental health care. Some of the barriers Jonah previously faced when engaging mental health care were:

- ***Previously inaccessible providers:*** *Before referral to the agency, Jonah had frequently encountered hearing clinicians and psychiatrists with either limited or no proficiency in ASL. Agency personnel were unfamiliar with the different types of interpreters, and when they hired them, the interpreters were insufficiently skilled to provide adequate communication. This interrupted the flow of conversation, hindered rapport-building, and limited Jonah's ability to fully understand and express himself in nuanced ways. Jonah reported feeling misunderstood and dismissed, leading to mistrust and resistance to obtaining treatment.*

- ***Cultural barriers:*** *Jonah expressed frustration that many mental health programs lacked staff who understood Deaf culture or provided services tailored for Deaf individuals with SMI. For example, past providers didn't realize the importance of including Deaf role models or peers in Jonah's treatment.*
- ***Stigma:*** *Mental illness carries stigma in both hearing and Deaf communities, but Jonah reported that the small size of the Deaf community intensified his feelings of shame. He worried about being judged by his peers as "not smart enough" and for needing psychiatric care.*
- ***Limited access to services:*** *Jonah had limited access to ASL-fluent mental health providers and competent interpreters with mental health training. During crises, Jonah was often admitted to hospitals where interpreters were unavailable or untrained in psychiatric care. This left him unable to communicate about his symptoms, leading to inadequate assessments and interventions.*
- ***Lack of accessible information:*** *Jonah had difficulty adhering to his medication regimen because most of the materials explaining them were in English, which Jonah found difficult to understand. When Jonah experienced side effects, he felt his concerns were dismissed by providers who couldn't fully explain alternative options in ASL. This created distrust and contributed to his reluctance to continue treatment.*

Supporting Recovery and Community Integration

Supporting recovery and community integration for DHH individuals with SMI requires a holistic and culturally competent approach that empowers clients to rebuild their lives while addressing their unique challenges. Recovery-oriented care emphasizes fostering independence, building social connections, and promoting access to meaningful opportunities within both the DHH and broader communities. Peer support, vocational rehabilitation, residential, and in-person or telemental health programs support service access and promote recovery (Terry & Robins-Talbot, 2024). Family engagement and education are also important, equipping caregivers with tools to provide support while maintaining healthy boundaries (Kara et al., 2024). Accessible crisis prevention and intervention systems, such as ASL-friendly hotlines and telehealth services, ensure that clients feel supported and safe during times of need. By integrating these strategies, recovery and community integration efforts help DHH individuals with SMI manage their symptoms and lead fulfilling lives.

Case Example: Jonah

Supporting recovery and community integration for Jonah focused on building his strengths, fostering independence, and helping him reconnect with both the Deaf and broader communities. The goal for Jonah's recovery is to ensure that he manages his mental illness but also thrives as a valued and contributing member of society. His recovery journey is guided by culturally competent, recovery-oriented principles, emphasizing self-determination and empowerment.

Jonah's recovery goals are:

1. ***Improve symptom management*** *by equipping Jonah with the tools to recognize and manage symptoms of schizoaffective disorder.*
2. ***Enhance independence*** *by helping Jonah rebuild skills to live independently and pursue meaningful life goals.*
3. ***Rebuild social connections*** *by fostering relationships within the Deaf community and building a sense of belonging.*
4. ***Develop vocational skills*** *by offering support, training, and job coaching to achieve stable, meaningful employment in a job he enjoys.*
5. ***Promoting holistic well-being*** *by addressing Jonah's physical, emotional, and social health through comprehensive support by linguistically and culturally competent professionals.*

Jonah's case demonstrates the importance of tailored, holistic approaches to supporting DHH individuals with serious mental illness. By addressing communication barriers, fostering independence, and promoting community integration, Jonah's treatment team helps him achieve recovery and build a meaningful life. His story highlights the potential for empowerment and growth when clients are supported in ways that honor their unique identities and needs.

Summary

This chapter explored the unique challenges and opportunities in supporting DHH individuals with SMI using a rehabilitation and recovery model. Understanding mental illness and the intersection with Deaf identity is crucial for providers. Communication barriers, cultural misunderstandings, and systemic inequities impact diagnosis, treatment, and recovery outcomes. The principles of the recovery model emphasize self-direction, empowerment, and holistic care, combined with Deaf-centric programming, and can be tailored to meet the mental health, linguistic, and cultural needs of DHH clients. Key strategies include addressing communication barriers, integrating culturally competent practices, fostering peer support, and promoting community and vocational engagement. Recovery-oriented approaches have a transformative potential for empowering DHH individuals with SMI to achieve independence, build meaningful connections, and fully integrate into their communities. By adopting these strategies, mental health professionals and systems can provide equitable, effective, and culturally aligned care, ensuring that every DHH person with SMI has an opportunity for recovery.

References

American Psychiatric Association (APA). (2022). *Diagnostic and statistical manual of mental disorders* (5th ed., text rev.). https://doi.org/10.1176/appi.books.9780890425787

At, G. (2024). The effect of delayed language acquisition on criminal behavior of deaf individuals involved in the criminal justice system. *Open Access Journal of Criminology Investigation & Justice, 2*(1). https://doi.org/10.23880/oajcij-16000113

Bergman, A., Chang, E., Cohen, A., Hovsepian, S., Oberman, R., Vinzon, M., & Young, A. (2024). Patient experiences with primary care medical home tailored for people with serious mental illness. *Families, Systems & Health, 42*(2), 214. https://doi.org/10.1037/fsh0000853

Bonany, M., De Iturbe Catania, G., Navia, R., Merlos, T., Diez, M., Martinez, P., Seoane, R., Martinez, G., & Hernandez, G. (2024). Bipolar disorder, deafness, and culturality in psychiatric home hospitalization: A clinical case. *European Psychiatry, 67*(S1), S435. https://doi.org/10.1192/j.eurpsy.2024.901

Crowe, T. (2019). Deaf adult consumers of public behavioral health services in Maryland: January 1, 2016—January 1, 2018. *JADARA, 53*(1), 22–35. https://repository.wcsuedu/jadara/vol53/iss1/3.

Crowe, T. (2021). Factors associated with help-seeking and self-efficacy among a sample of deaf adults. *Journal of Developmental and Physical Disabilities, 33*(1), 51–63. https://doi.org/10.1007/s10882-020-09739-9

Gwaltney, I. (2022). Improving communication among providers serving D/deaf populations in mental health settings. *Columbia Social Work Review, 20*(1), 57–75. https://doi.org/10.52214/cswr.v20i1.9642

Jambrina, J., Fernandez, L., Garcia, A., Gonzalez, C., Martinez, C., Llorca, A., Diaz, R., Ortola, F., & Guzman, N. (2024). The recovery concept in assertive community treatment: Truth or fake? *European Psychiatry, 67*(S1), S715–S716. https://doi.org/10.1192/j.eurpsy.2024.1488

Jordan, G., Bassetto, S., DeLuca, J., Dobbs, M., Florence, A., Allemang, B., O'Keeffe, D., Basile, M., Funaro, M., Davidson, L., Ben-David, S., & Shah, J. (2024). Personal recovery among people at risk for developing serious mental health problems: A qualitative systematic review. *Psychiatric Services*, appips20230133. Advance online publication. https://doi.org/10.1176/appi.ps.20230133

Kara, H., Cogen, T., & Telci, F. (2024). Family resilience in primary caregivers of children who are deaf and hard of hearing. *American Journal of Audiology, 33*(3), 1–13. https://doi.org/10.1044/2024_AJA-23-00173

Moreno, C., Ramalheira, F., & Bartolo, C. (2023). Seeing voices? The importance of raising awareness on deaf mental health. *European Psychiatry, 66*, S904–S904. https://doi.org/10.1192/j.eurpsy.2023.1914

Polcwiartek, C., O'Gallagher, K., Friedman, D., Correll, C., Solmi, M., Jensen, S., & Nielsen, R. (2024). Severe mental illness: Cardiovascular risk assessment and management. *European Heart Journal, 45*, 987–997. https://doi.org/10.1093/eurheartj/ehae054

Rogers, K., Rowlandson, A., Harkness, J., Shields, G., & Young, A. (2024). Health outcomes in Deaf signing populations: A systematic review. *PLoS One, 19*(4):e0298479. https://doi.org/10.1371/journal.pone.0298479.

Terry, J., & Robins-Talbot, C. (2024). Mental health first aid for deaf communities: Responses to a lack of national deaf mental health service provision. *Journal of Public Mental Health, 23*(2), 107–116. https://doi.org/10.1108/jpmh-12-2023-0107

Trott, M., Suetani, S., Arnautovska, U., Kisley, S., Kar Ray, M., Theodoros, T., et al. (2024). Suicide methods and severe mental illness: A systematic review and meta-analysis. *Acta Psychiatrica Scandinavica*, 1–18. https://doi.org/10.1111/acps.13759

Tuschick, E., Barker, J., Giles, E., Jones, S., Hogg, J., Kanmodi, K., et al. (2024). Barriers and facilitators for people with severe mental illness accessing cancer screening: A systematic review. *Psycho-Oncology, 33*(1), e6274. https://doi.org/10.1002/pon.6274

Chapter 12
The D.R.E.A.M. Program Staff: A Human Rights Approach to Facilitate Access

Tracey Bone, Richard Claeys, Aaron Montney, and Elaine Newhook

Introduction

This chapter is based on interviews conducted by Tracey Bone, Ph.D., with three staff from the D.R.E.A.M. program. The aim was two-fold: first, to explore what factors make this program unique, innovative, and accessible for individuals with intellectual disabilities who are also members of the deaf or hard of hearing communities, and second, to explore best practices that could be adopted by professionals in a variety of professional fields interested in or beginning to work with deaf and/or hard of hearing clients. A note of clarification: the interviews with the Direct Support Workers (DSW) were conducted through an American Sign Language (ASL)-English Interpreter, as both DSWers are members of the Deaf or hard of hearing communities and use American Sign Language as their first language. Any comments presented in this chapter as reported from the two DSWs are therefore the English interpretation of their comments as shared through the ASL interpreter.[1] The comments will, however, be enclosed by quotation marks to indicate their specific comments.

T. Bone (✉)
Faculty of Social Work, University of Manitoba, Winnipeg, MB, Canada
e-mail: Tracey.bone@umanitoba.ca

R. Claeys · A. Montney · E. Newhook
New Directions D.R.E.A.M. Program, Winnipeg, MB, Canada

T. Bone (ed.), *Deaf Mental Health*, Advances in Mental Health and Addiction,
https://doi.org/10.1007/978-3-032-06274-1_12

New Directions for Children, Youth, Adults, andFamilies

The roots of this community-based, non-profit organization date back to 1885, with services and supports provided first under the original name, Children's Home of Winnipeg. The program has since evolved in scope and size. In 1996, the organization changed its name to New Directions for Children, Youth, Adults and Families. It currently provides a variety of services, supports, and programs to over 3000 individuals across their many programs (New Directions, 2025).

D.R.E.A.M. Program

The Diversity, Respect, Empowerment, Achievement, and More (D.R.E.A.M.) program is one of the six Adult Day services offered by New Directions for Children, Youth, Adults & Families, a community-based, non-profit organization based in Winnipeg, Manitoba, Canada. As reported by the Program Supervisor, Richard Claeys, the program operates Monday to Friday during regular business hours, excluding holidays, and offers supports to individuals with intellectual disabilities who are also deaf or hard of hearing. Based on data from the Canadian Survey on Disability 2017 to 2022, approximately 0.2% of the Canadian population has a developmental disability and is Deaf, hard of hearing, or uses non-traditional methods of communication (Statistics Canada, 2023). The individuals in the program have varying degrees of sign language or English communication skills, including some individuals who are non-verbal. Some individuals in the program are New Directions clients, while others are referred from separate programs in the city of Winnipeg. The two primary referral sources for individuals in the D.R.E.A.M. program are the Manitoba School for the Deaf and Community Living disABILITY Services (CLDS). As noted by the Direct Client Service Workers, they use ASL, signs, gestures, or other strategies as necessary to meet the communication needs of the individuals with whom they work. The two Direct Client Support Workers noted, "If there isn't any vocabulary or any way of (verbally) expressing themselves, we show them pictures. And we try very hard to make sure that they're being understood and they're understanding us". Claeys noted that while their focus is not specific to mental health issues, they support the general mental and physical health of all individuals in the program in a variety of ways.

The D.R.E.A.M. program offers recreational, educational, and other skill-building exposure and opportunities in both the hearing and the Deaf community to an average of 22 adults a day who[1] attend the day program. Individuals currently in

[1]The role of the Sign Language (ASL)–English Interpreter is to provide both hearing and Deaf Sign Language users with equal access to information and interactions. It is to effectively facilitate communication between two different languages, English, and in North America, American Sign Language (ASL), French Sign Language (LSQ), or Indigenous Sign Languages (ISL). The ASL-

the program range in age from 18 to 79. The program is unique in a variety of ways, though the most significant focus of this program is that it provides a Deaf-centric environment that employs a full-time ASL-English interpreter.

As reported, "There are not a lot of (support) programs, we're the only ASL environment. We're the only one that has ASL immersion. The other ones don't have signing… You often see deaf people isolated in these hearing programs, or non-deaf programs, and it makes it worse (for them). Here, we're a program where we provide American Sign Language as the language in our environment, and we support these individuals who don't have a daily life of work. These programs are to keep them busy during the day—doing many different things." (Direct Case Worker—A. Montney)

The "many different things" referred to above include teaching basic life and social skills, general literacy, and supporting general sensory classes. There is also an important recreational component, which includes access to a variety of outings in the community. As Montney reported, "If they stay home, they're isolated, they don't get to do those things necessarily. Some are in Group Homes and, if in Group Homes, maybe there is only that one deaf person in a group home along with other (hearing) people. If they're a deaf person or hard of hearing person, they often have no one in the home who can converse with them. So, when they come here to this program, that's what we do, we keep them busy, we encourage them." In addition to these, there are a variety of work experiences available. Opportunities vary but have included custodial-related work at the Canadian Human Rights Museum, The Forks Market, and other locations in Winnipeg, Manitoba. All work experiences provide some opportunity for individuals to gain skills while also earning income, two factors which help improve self-esteem. Most importantly, access to these opportunities is through an ASL-signing environment.

The program also provides an important social environment. As one Direct Support Worker noted, "You know, (all) individuals need friends. And when they're isolated and by themselves, they don't necessarily have friends. So, their staff, us, are supporting them, you know (offering) friendship. Supporting them on a daily basis, making sure that they're doing OK while they're in the program. And if a person comes and has a problem at home, for example, they're able to talk with us about it. They feel that they can trust us as a staff person, so that they can tell us what's going on. And then if we need to talk to CLDS about it or their case manager we can be in contact in order to support them."

It was reported that some individuals have been involved with the D.R.E.A.M. program for "such a long time" (Direct Support Worker). It was noted that "If somebody gets bored, for example, and they want to transfer out and go somewhere else that's fine, that's their decision. Often what happens if they go to another program,

English Interpreter must have a high level of fluency in both languages, though also the necessary cultural knowledge, experience, and specialized knowledge and vocabulary to work effectively in the setting(s) in which they work. A Deaf Interpreter (DI) is a Deaf or hard of hearing person who has native fluency in ASL and its culture, who provides specialized interpreting services to support Deaf and hearing people across a variety of settings (National Deaf Center, 2025).

recognize, wait a minute, these programs are lacking all these things; the main thing they're lacking is communication, so they often come back (to the D.R.E.A.M. program)." Their return highlights the communication environment as one strength of the D.R.E.A.M. program.

Individuals involved in residential services available through New Directions receive additional support from an assigned Case Manager. If the individual lives with a family or is referred from an agency outside New Directions, they may not have that additional support from a Case Manager. Case Managers assist individuals with their daily needs and general program involvement. It was reported, at the time of the interviews for this chapter, that only one Case Manager with any of the Day Programs at New Directions is Deaf and a native Sign Language user (That person has since left their Case Manager position). A second Case Manager is hearing, though familiar with ASL. Given their expertise with ASL and Deaf culture, these two staff offer an additional layer of support to the Deaf and hard of hearing individuals on their caseloads.

Supporting a Deaf-Centric Approach to Service Delivery

At New Directions, all staff who work in any of the programs, including the D.R.E.A.M. program, and the sister program, The Transition Program, are required to attend and complete the first level of ASL (ASL 101). Staff pay for the course up front and are then reimbursed upon successful completion of the course. Those in management and other instructional positions are encouraged to complete additional levels of ASL training. All staff at New Directions are also required to complete a half-day Deaf Culture course within their first year of employment with the organization as part of their onboarding process. As noted by one Direct Support Worker, "We have a lot of hearing people that don't know anything about deafness and Deaf culture, so it's primarily for them."

As noted, the D.R.E.A.M. program is a Deaf-centric environment, with a full-time ASL-English Interpreter providing communication between the Deaf/hard of hearing signing staff and non-Deaf staff. As the Deaf/hard of hearing staff are native ASL users, the ASL interpreter also assists these staff with grammar, vocabulary, and/or writing consistent with written English in the completion of Incident and other regular reports, as English is the second language for these staff members. The ASL-English Interpreter is also available to assist in unique circumstances, such as making emergency calls, as necessary to support the well-being of participants in the program.

Supporting Deaf and Hard of Hearing Individuals in the Home Environment

Many of the individuals in the program live in a group home or home-share setting. The agency (New Directions) aims to support a communication-appropriate environment for the deaf and hard of hearing individuals in their home environment. While attempts are made to recruit home share parents with fluency in ASL, it was reported that few such home environments are available. As a result, Deaf and hard of hearing individuals often find themselves in communication-deficient environments, which reinforces the value of the D.R.E.A.M program for these individuals.

Home Share Providers are required to complete three courses prior to approval as a provider, including the Deaf Culture course. The focus of the course is about "exposure." The course includes information necessary to support a Deaf or hard of hearing through topics such as Deaf history, booking interpreters, additional communication methods including the use of video relay services (VRS), and others. One Direct Service Worker noted that there is a range of communication abilities amongst the Home Share Providers. For that reason, a Deaf culture course, which includes communication strategies by and with Deaf Sign Language users, and access to weekly ASL courses are necessary. As noted, "With ASL, when people are learning sign language and if they don't use it, they lose it" (Montney).

One Direct Service Worker was clear, "Hearing people (professionals or students working with Deaf clients) should learn about deaf culture for sure, get involved. If they're interested in getting immersed, (for example, take the one-week ASL Immersion course) or they can learn ASL, even basic sign language (through ASL courses). They should also learn about interpreters (ASL-English and Deaf Interpreters), and what deaf culture is all about… if they're not interested though it's going to be really hard (to work with Deaf and hard of hearing clients)" (Newhook). Newhook added, "Deaf culture is very in-depth and there are so many nuances like classifiers, signs, vocabulary, language terms that we use, socializing, comfort. You know conversations that are different than hearing people." Based on comments from the staff interviewed, New Directions aims to provide a respectful environment for all the individuals it serves.

As reported in Chap. 2 of this text, early language deprivation has an impact on the child's developing brain and acquisition of communication skills (see also Statewide Outreach Center Videos, [Hall] 2023). It was acknowledged in the interviews for this chapter that a communication-starved environment impacts mental health. One Direct Support Worker noted, "You know, I'm thinking of hearing home care providers that have deaf individuals, I think about mental health. I think about (mental health) and that it might get worse if individuals are isolated at home without communication. If there's no one there to communicate with them I think mental health would be an issue. That's why it's so important to have staff that can communicate with them. If not, how do you know what they want?"

Supporting Staff Development

One theme that emerged during the interviews for this chapter was the acknowledgement that access to staff training and/or professional development for Deaf or hard of hearing staff requires additional consideration and financial accommodation to ensure access. While training available through New Directions itself may include ASL interpretation, organizations unrelated to New Directions do not automatically provide ASL Interpretation, rendering the educational information inaccessible to Deaf ASL users. It has been the experience of some individuals interviewed for this chapter that organizations both external to New Directions and New Direction itself, have cite lack of funding for ASL interpretation, or unfamiliarity with the Interpreter booking process, or unavailability of ASL interpreters as reasons for not providing ASL interpretation.

Recommendations for Non-Deaf Professionals and Students Working with Deaf Individuals/Clients

- *Deaf culture*: Engage in a course from a Deaf-centric organization, with a Deaf facilitator to learn about Deaf culture.
- *ASL*: Active participation in and completion of, at minimum, a Level 1 ASL course to familiarize oneself with, and gain at least an introductory level of skill in Sign Language. Though competency is not required, gaining basic greeting and simple communication skills demonstrates respect for the individuals'/ client's communication and culture. It was recommended that if a non-Deaf staff member is not clear on what is being communicated, it is culturally respectful to seek clarification. It is important that a non-Deaf person not falsely nod in acknowledgment if one does not truly understand the communication.
- New learners of ASL must understand that ASL and English are two distinct languages with their own grammar, syntax, and word order/use. A new ASL learner must also appreciate that English is a second language for most Deaf or hard of hearing individuals. For that reason communication in written English may be more difficult for them. By way of example, written communication may include word order that is more consistent with ASL than with English. If their written English is not consistent with the grammatical structure of English, it is important to remember that such is not a reflection of intelligence but rather use of a language which is not their first.
- Patience with the communication process is fundamental to facilitate equal access to communication.
- *ASL Interpreters*: Familiarize oneself with the ASL-English Interpreter booking process in your area, including interpreter availability and costs. In Canada, interpreters should be registered with the Canadian Association of Visual Language Interpreters to ensure quality interpretation as per a formal code of

ethics (CASLI, n.d.). Each country will have its own registering or licensing body, and expectations regarding training, skill, and booking processes. Use of family members as interpreters is strongly discouraged as there is no guarantee of their skill level, or if they possess the necessary specialized skill set or terminology to interpret in a particular field, such as the field of disability. There is also no guarantee family members will be non-biased during the interpretation process. Even if the family member is a certified ASL Interpreter, use of family member as an interpreter could also breach client confidentiality, so should be avoided. The use of a certified ASL English Interpreter is always recommended.

- *Timing and Space for meetings*: When planning a meeting with an individual/client whose first language is ASL, it will be important to consider that the meeting will require additional time to accommodate communication through an ASL-English Interpreter and possibly also that offered by a Deaf Interpreter. An individual/client may also request a support person be present in the meeting to offer additional support and information, which could require additional time to ensure full access to communication.
- The inclusion of additional individuals in the meeting will require additional seating and larger meeting space. Finally, the space itself should be conducive to signed communication, with careful consideration for appropriate lighting, seating placement, and reducing visual noise. (See Chap. 13, this text; and Bone [2019]).

Conclusion

The D.R.E.A.M. Day program supports individuals with intellectual disabilities who are also Deaf or hard of hearing. The latest Canadian Survey on Disability, 2017–2022, reports that the number of individuals who live at the intersection of intellectual disability and sensory (sound) disability is small, at approximately 0.2%. The needs of this small group of Canadians are unique. The D.R.E.A.M. program is the only ASL-immersion program environment across Manitoba to provide supports for this population. Staff from this specialized program have provided important information for non-Deaf professionals to consider when engaging with Deaf and/or hard of hearing individuals who also live with intellectual disability. This chapter acknowledges that communication is a two-way process that can and does have an impact on mental health. Non-Deaf professionals are encouraged to gain at least a fundamental understanding of Deaf culture, including signed communication if considering working with Deaf or hard of hearing signing clients. To fail to do so is not only disrespectful to that Deaf or hard of hearing client and could also significantly impact the therapeutic or working relationship.

Acknowledgement The authors of this chapter wish to acknowledge the ASL-English Interpreter who served as the conduit between two languages, spoken English and American Sign Language, during the interviews with the Direct Support Workers. An active member of the Canadian Association of Sign Language Interpreters (CASLI), this interpreter is an invaluable member of the D.R.E.A.M. team, possessing cultural knowledge, skills, and experience "to support accurate and appropriate interpretation" (CASLI, n.d.).

References

Bone, T. (2019). Deaf mental health: Enhancing linguistically and culturally appropriate clinical practice. In M. Zangeneh & A. Al-Krenawi (Eds.), *Culture, diversity, and mental health: Enhancing clinical practice* (pp. 61–80). Springer Nature Switzerland.

Canadian Association of Sign Language Interpreters (CASLI). (n.d.). *Home.* https://www.casli.ca/.

New Directions for Children, Youth, Adults & Families. (2025). *About us.* https://newdirections.mb.ca/about-us/.

Statewide Outreach Center Videos. (2023 Oct. 18). *Dr. Wyatte hall—language deprivation* [Video]. https://www.youtube.com/watch?v=Hg3DTt-SSHs.

Statistics Canada. (2023). *Canadian survey on disability, 2017 to 2022.* Ottawa, ON: Statistics Canada. https://www150.statcan.gc.ca/n1/daily-quotidien/231201/dq231201b-eng.htm.

Chapter 13
Working in the field of Deaf Mental Health: What Clinicians Need to Know

Megan Kaluba, William Schmidt, Michal Morgan, Tim Likely, and Michael Dawthorne

Introduction

This chapter introduces essential concepts for providing psychotherapy to d/Deaf,[1] Deafblind, and deafened clients. The need for skilled practitioners is particularly pressing due to a significant shortage of Deaf clinicians, especially those from underrepresented groups such as Indigenous, racialized, and 2SLGBTQ+ communities (Goghari, 2022; MacDougall, 2022). While we continue to advocate for more Deaf clinicians, hearing mental health professionals in Canada frequently find themselves working with d/Deaf clients in therapy.

Not only do d/Deaf individuals experience higher rates of mental health difficulties or challenges than their hearing counterparts, but they overall typically receive less (and less skilled) support from hearing mental health professionals (Todd, 2022).[2] This happens when (hearing) clinicians believe that adding interpreters is the only step needed to provide culturally and linguistically accessible

The original version of the chapter has been revised. A correction to this chapter can be found at https://doi.org/10.1007/978-3-032-06274-1_15

[1] In this chapter, "deaf" (with a lowercase 'd') refers to the audiological experience of not being able to hear sound; "Deaf" (with an uppercase 'D') refers to individuals who share a signed language (such as American Sign Language) and a culture, despite any feelings of marginalization they may experience from that culture.

[2] People who are Deaf have higher rates of posttraumatic stress disorder (PTSD), substance use disorder (SUD) and interpersonal trauma compared to the general hearing population (Pollard et al., 2014; Anderson et al., 2011; Porter & Williams, 2011).

M. Kaluba (✉) · W. Schmidt · M. Morgan · T. Likely · M. Dawthorne
Canadian Hearing Services, Toronto, ON, Canada
e-mail: mkaluba@chs.ca; Wschmidt@chs.ca; Mmorgan@chs.ca; Tlikely@chs.ca; Mdawthorne@chs.ca

T. Bone (ed.), *Deaf Mental Health*, Advances in Mental Health and Addiction,
https://doi.org/10.1007/978-3-032-06274-1_13

psychotherapy (for more on the "illusion of inclusion" see Caselli et al., 2020).[3,4] Most psychotherapists are familiar with Adverse Childhood Events (ACE), but are perhaps less aware of how predominant comorbid Adverse Childhood Communication Experiences (ACCEs)[5] are for d/Deaf individuals.

The five cases[6] in this chapter highlight the challenges that emerge from differing levels of clinician familiarity with Deaf culture and clients' varied language abilities, underscoring the need to address the effects of communication neglect on mental health and the value of culturally affirmative approaches in treating comorbid conditions. Peoples (2002) emphasizes that the pool of expertise in Deaf mental health is small, while the scope of need is substantial, creating an ethical dilemma between "giving it a try" and doing nothing. Deaf clients often present with higher levels of care than are typically seen in community mental health, yet there are inadequate resources to refer them to culturally appropriate services.

The field of Deaf mental health has benefitted significantly from diverse therapeutic approaches. Narrative therapy, particularly, aligns well with Deaf storytelling traditions (Freedman, 1994; Isenberg, 1996; Munro et al., 2008) while systemic therapies (Harvey, 2003), psychoanalytic (Cohen, 2004), and third-wave CBT (Glickman & Gulati, 2003, Glickman, 2009, Glickman, 2017) as well as DBT (O'Hearn et al., 2010), have also made valuable contributions. This chapter will also add to the above modalities fourth-wave approaches like compassion-focused virtual therapy, which prioritize overall well-being. We will also highlight trauma-informed treatments aligned with social constructionist, strengths-based perspectives on Deafness (Ouellette & Wood, 1998), such as Internal Family Systems, sensorimotor psychotherapy, and Brainspotting. This eclectic approach offers a comprehensive framework for supporting Deaf, Deafblind, and deafened clients.[7]

Case 1: Katy, a 29-year-old Black, gay, culturally Deaf business owner whose business was thriving despite challenges such as ADHD-C, depression, and increasing marijuana use—working with a white, hearing clinician who identifies as a queer woman with little Deaf culture experience.

---

[3] Deaf people have the right to ASL, Langue des Signes Quebecois (LSQ), or Indigenous Sign Languages (ISL) for their mental health treatment (for more on the Supreme Court of Canada's Eldridge decision, see Canada.ca, Eldridge v. British Columbia, 1997 CanLII 327 (SCC), [1997]3SCR).

[4] Receiving mental health therapy via an ASL interpreter is not considered equal access according to a US Federal Court rule (Leigh et al., 1996). See also Harvey (2003) for variables that can occur when a hearing (majority) culture is treating a member of a (minority) culture.

[5] Due to lack of accessible linguistic input (Lillo-Martin & Henner, 2021). See how ACCEs (Kushalnagar et al., 2020) are associated with increased risk of chronic diseases.

[6] The vignettes use fictional names and details, representing composite versions of cases and demographics for teaching purposes.

[7] This is based on our clinical experience; however further research is needed on these modalities and their effective use with Deaf clients.

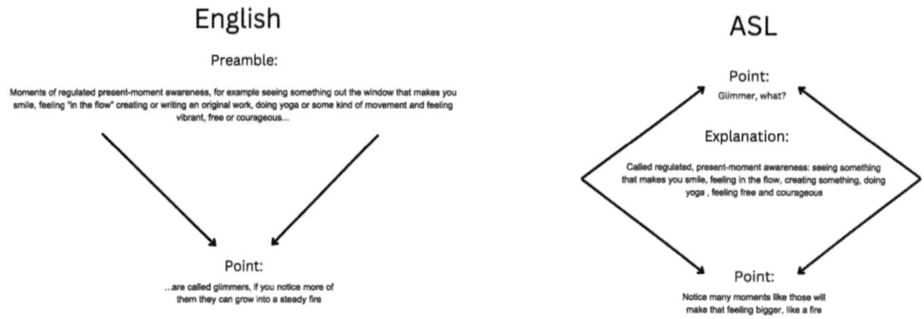

Fig. 13.1 Triangle (English) vs. Diamond (ASL): structure of speech

The clinician used Video Relay Service (VRS) to arrange the appointment. Upon arriving for her first therapy session, Katy entered and burst into laughter, greeting her American Sign Language (ASL) interpreter with a warm hug,[8] which initially raised slight confusion for the clinician who soon learned that such expressions are culturally appropriate within Deaf culture.

During the 1.5-hour intake session, Katy expressed a clear preference for somatic,[9] attachment-based therapy over Cognitive Behavioural Therapy (CBT). When the clinician inquired about Katy's partner, Katy clarified a misunderstanding from the referral that had mentioned a boyfriend.[10] Katy interpreted the clinician's occasional note taking as disinterest,[11] assertively addressing the error.[12]

After the session, the clinician gathered feedback from the interpreter, who suggested a more direct approach in interactions rather than prolonged preambles. The clinician later learned that ASL has a diamond conversational structure, contrary to the inverted triangle form common in English discourse (Ashton et al., 2013). (See Fig. 13.1 – Triangle (English) vs. Diamond (ASL): Structure of Speech). Clinicians

[8]The ASL interpreter was a surprise to Katy, but this should never be the case. It's important to ask the Deaf client who their preferred interpreter is for therapy sessions, and check with the client if a switch must be made. Many clients have deep bonds with interpreters who have seen them through the births of their children, cancer, divorce etc., and they have the right to determine who should be privy to any sensitive information about their past they want to share.

[9]Prosody (patterns of rhythm, tone, frequency in the voice) has equivalencies in signed language but requires working closely with an interpreter, and the clinician must pay careful attention to what the face, eyes, tone, speed of signing, moments of playfulness are conveying (Dana, 2020).

[10]ASL does not have gendered pronouns, and the referring case worker must have made a heteronormative assumption. See Miller and Clark (2019) for more on how Deaf 2SLBTQIA+ identities are minoritized and oppressed.

[11]Note taking during an intake may detract from the Deaf person feeling seen, whereas increased eye contact and head nodding can show active listening.

[12]Cultural incompetence on the part of the clinician, transference reactions to hearing (majority) therapist, as well as Katy's ambivalent attachment style (being hypervigilant to perceived rejection) all intermingle to form distress that can be worked through. Hamerdinger and Karlin (2003) argue the therapy work will never be same between a monolingual therapist and Deaf client via an

are not required to adopt a diamond structure in their speech; however, it is valuable to understand how their statements may be interpreted. Typically, this style involves making a point, elaborating on it, and then reiterating the initial point. This approach can be particularly effective when paired with visuals and written headings.

Deaf clients have the same conceptual thinking skills and heterogeneity of preferences for certain therapeutic modalities as their hearing counterparts, and MacDougall (2022) emphasizes the harm caused by psychology's misguided notion in the twentieth century that d/Deaf people were limited in their capacity for abstract thought.[13] For instance, Katy demonstrated insight into how her obstructed communication with her hearing parents directed her focus towards potential signs of abandonment, rather than being able to take in her girlfriend's caring behaviours.

In Katy's case, having a preferred interpreter with whom she shared a strong bond seemed to transfer positive feelings towards the therapist.[14] Clinicians may initially find it intimidating to build rapport with a client through a third party already possessing a deep connection. Sometimes it's necessary to experiment with chair placements and interpreter lag to allow for shared moments of eye gaze between the therapist and client.[15]

Therapists must embody unconditional positive regard, conveying that being Deaf is not a problem while emphasizing Deafhood as a source of pride and belonging.[16] Hearing loss can be integrated into one's identity rather than perceived as a detriment to self-worth (Cohen, 2003). In his TEDxGallaudet talk, Peter Hauser[17]

interpreter but can present interesting transference and countertransference opportunities that don't exist in Deaf-Deaf pairings. In our experience working from a People-Centred care perspective, most Deaf clients typically prioritize Deaf-Deaf communication while some value the anonymity provided by a hearing clinician who is not part of the broader Deaf community.

[13] Promising therapeutic modalities, such as Adlerian play therapy (Ashori & Shamsi, 2023), show deaf students continue to gain insight into their emotional language and take responsibility for creating greater social connection.

[14] In our experience, this "halo effect" happens far more commonly than dyads/coalition forming against the third party (therapeutic triangle-client, therapist, interpreter) as per Levinger (2020) although it is useful to be aware of these unconscious processes that could be taking place especially during the initial rapport-building phase.

[15] This therapist-clinician rapport is even more challenging virtually if clients are joining on iPhone, etc. and only have screen space to view the interpreter. If possible, we recommend meeting in-person for a first appointment to avoid the therapist becoming enmeshed with the personhood of the interpreter (especially for clients with **language deprivation** who may need more detailed explanation of the different roles of each professional). Emailing a photo of the therapist beforehand can help, as well as technical expertise in coaching Deaf clients how to spotlight or pin the interpreters in platforms like Zoom for full communication access.

[16] Crowe (2017) summarizes how Deaf individuals will be quick to pick up on any deficit-oriented (or disability-focused) lens of the therapist.

[17] Effects of Linguisticism and Audism on the Developing Deaf Person (March 6, 2015). TEDxGallaudet.

highlights the pervasive nature of audism[18] and linguisticism within hearing society, which perpetuates prejudice against Deaf individuals and directly affects their psychological resilience. It is crucial for therapists to avoid replicating societal oppressions within the therapeutic settings. If they inadvertently do, self-reflection and repair are essential.

Interventions can require more setup at the front end of exercises, especially when looking at future or past timelines. Katy expressed a desire to address her ambivalent relationship with her parents. Once sufficient rapport was established with Katy, therapy questions—such as the attachment-based query, "What would have happened if your mom and dad had had really good support from medical professionals, language instruction, and Deaf mentors early on in your life?"—elicited a flat, "but that didn't happen". This required deconstruction so the clinician could provide a richer introduction to the imaginal nature of the conditional clause, encouraging the desired response. The clinician explained, "How we internalize our stories often lacks the full picture of what actually occurred. Negative experiences tend to linger more than positive ones". The clinician then suggested an exercise that could help: envisioning a "fake" past where her parents received necessary support and asking Katy to slow down and then reflect on her interactions with them. This prompted Katy to separate her parents' grief, anger, and confusion from her own experiences, allowing her to rediscover blocked memories of connection and exclaim, "They *really* loved me!"

Treatments that place cultural values at centre stage result in improved outcomes (Rathod et al., 2019; Barrera & Castro, 2006; Domenech-Rodríquez & Wieling, 2005). The question of *how* to respectfully prioritize Deaf cultural values has not received a lot of attention in the literature.[19]At CHS, the onboarding process of becoming anti-audist and journeying towards Deaf cultural competence includes the following practices: going through an audiology appointment, listening to the "unfair" hearing test, conducting "mock" sessions with Deaf counsellors, learning ASL from a Deaf instructor, Deaf culture training, listening to colleagues' experiences in Deaf and mainstream schools, meeting with mental health interpreters to understand their role, and building awareness of positive Deaf role models in the community. Hearing clinicians must be vigilant to not exoticize Deaf individuals to the detriment of missing critical presenting problems.

The tendency for new clinicians to overlook a potential mental health concern as being part of someone's Deaf culture/Deafhood can be addressed with increased exposure to the Deaf community and the many Deaf individuals who are thriving in life. In Katy's situation, the clinician initially misinterpreted Katy's rapid signing as typical for a young Black Deaf person, only to later recognize it as a sign of racing thoughts and anxiety after seeing other young Black Deaf signers. Feedback from

[18] For more on audism, see Bauman (2004).

[19] See Crowe (2017) for summary on how unconscious bias of hearing therapists may impair therapy.

interpreters familiar with signing speed and normative linguistic differences[20] can be valuable in this context, improving the clinician's understanding without touching upon diagnosis.

Clinicians must also learn to relinquish some control when working with interpreters, embracing a form of "unlearning" that challenges the values of traditional Western, hearing, non-directive, insight-oriented therapy. Clinicians may also feel a pull away from their primary therapeutic role in order to respond to Deaf client needs such as fund of knowledge deficits, advocacy, class action lawsuits, and case management. Being aware of these demands and incorporating a broader team of teachers, caseworkers, lawyers, family, etc., can help preserve the clinician role.

Onboarding also needs to include an expertise in navigating various technologies to ensure communication access for d/Deaf and Hard of Hearing clients:

Case 2: Cassie, a white 44-year-old deafened female, presented with sudden sensorineural hearing loss (SSHL) and worked with a white hearing counsellor. Cassie was recently diagnosed with Meniere's disease and feared vertigo attacks would continue to progress. Her excellent speech led people to assume she could hear more than she actually could, resulting in frustration during daily interactions with strangers.

When discussing Cassie's communication needs, a range of options were presented, such as an FM system, a pocket talker, captioning tools CART (Communication Access Real-time Translation), or written aids enabling typed communication between the client and therapist.[21]

In terms of her counselling objectives, Cassie expressed a desire to explore both the advantages and disadvantages of cochlear implant (CI) surgery. She sought support for grief and anxiety concerning her hearing loss worsening over time, as well as fears that possible vertigo attacks might limit her ability to go outside.[22] It is important to note that while depression rates tend to be higher among postlingually deafened individuals (Du Feu et al., 2014), post-traumatic growth is possible[23] (see, for example, Kobosko et al., 2021).

[20] Clinicians must be aware and not pathologize dialects in signed languages (Black ASL (BASL), ChicanX ASL) as well as regional differences based on the history of segregation at Deaf residential schools, etc. (Glickman et al., 2020).

[21] While text therapy can be just as effective as speech, we do recommend in-person or virtual videoconferencing options to add body language, eye contact and interpersonal connectedness.

[22] See Harvey and Miller (1998) on stages of grieving acquired hearing loss and construction of meaning inspired by the work of psychiatrist Victor Frankl.

[23] Kobosko et al. (2021) discuss CI surgery but also includes the concept of Deaf-Gain.

Cassie joined a psychotherapy group specifically designed to address the experiences of acquired hearing loss, which significantly enhanced her individual therapy. These groups focus on regulating the nervous system, managing anxiety and depression (using mindfulness, CBT, DBT approaches), and providing support so that clients feel less alone. These virtual groups (with captioning) provide a culturally resonant supportive environment that normalize the frustrations related to communication barriers, help individuals feel understood, and instil hope. Cassie reported an increased sense of well-being, reduced feelings of loneliness, going out more despite vertigo attacks, and greater acceptance of the uncertainty surrounding her condition.

Case 3: Dave, a 51-year-old Indigenous, oral Deaf residential school survivor, worked with a culturally Deaf, white male clinician. Following a period of rehabilitation for alcohol use disorder, which resulted in increased suicidality and an inpatient hospital stay, Dave sought community mental health services. He had been sober for over a month and lived with his hearing, non-Indigenous ex-partner, who complained about his lack of household help.

Prior to the intake session, Dave's communication preferences were assessed. Although fluent in ASL, Dave reported he preferred spoken English[24] so ASL interpretation was arranged as the clinician's primary language is ASL. During the intake, Dave was able to speak freely due to full access to communication. As often happens when a Deaf person has a rare moment of full access, information poured out of Dave, requiring several intake meetings.[25]

At the rehabilitation facility, Dave reported that staff had lacked experience in booking interpreters, leaving him without one for many daytime activities. After a week with no language support, the centre finally provided an interpreter, but only for group sessions. This left Dave unable to communicate during meals, meditation, and evening events. Dave began to suspect others were talking about him, and when he tried to engage others in conversations, such as about the weather, they seemed to disengage quickly. These experiences heightened his belief that others were

[24] **Language dysfluency** can sometimes create imbalance where someone is stronger with receptive (understanding others') communication than expressive (their own signing) or vice-versa (in this case, Dave's receptive skills are stronger than his expressive skills in ASL). Dave also appreciated the double feedback of receptively seeing the Deaf clinician's ASL then hearing the spoken English interpretation. Dave's preference was to have a Deaf clinician (See Williams & Crump, 2019 for more on norm-referenced communication assessments).

[25] It is often essential to interrupt cascading information to ensure informed consent including the potential benefits and risks of treatment. This usually includes basic psychoeducation on what to expect in counselling, roles, how it differs from advice-giving, limits of confidentiality, etc. In the Deaf community, confidentiality is extremely important and needs to be emphasized as part of one's regulatory responsibilities.

speaking negatively about him. Eventually, Dave expressed suicidal thoughts to his therapist[26] and was transferred to a hospital.

At the hospital, Dave initially tried to communicate verbally, and through writing, but then requested ASL interpreters after meeting with his doctor who had a strong accent. This "change" was met with annoyance by staff. Video Relay Interpreting (VRI) was introduced using an iPad, but without a stand, forcing Dave to hold it and sign one-handed, complicating communication. Nurses frequently entered for brief check-ins without bringing the iPad and discussed medical matters in front of him without inclusion. When he sought explanations, they seemed irritated and left him with unanswered questions. Dave would have preferred in-person interpreters, but VRI was the only option the hospital offered. While VRI provides human interpreters, the emergence of agentic AI highlights the urgent need to determine who will decide what constitutes "communication access" in Deaf mental health care.[27]

Dave's presentation necessitated ongoing suicide risk assessment and a culturally appropriate understanding of institutional violence against both Deaf and Indigenous people and intergenerational trauma. The clinician inquired into Dave's suicidal ideation using the terms "suicide" and "killing yourself", and noticed the rapport felt more strained based on Dave's annoyed facial expression and constant leg movement.

The clinician asked for a 5-minute eye break during this virtual session, privately chatting with the interpreter to stay and setting up a waiting room for a mid-session debrief. It was revealed that the interpreter found the terms "suicide" and "killing myself" uncomfortable, opting instead for "death". The clinician had been focused on Dave and didn't realize the interpreter had changed the language. This likely made Dave feel dismissed, as altering his words demonstrated a lack of empathy and acknowledgment of his thoughts.

The clinician helped process the interpreter's discomfort,[28] and the interpreter agreed not to repeat the mistake. The clinician could then resume normalizing Dave's suicidal thoughts, attenuating shame, and gathering information on plans

[26] In our work we often see paranoid or suspicious thinking increase in correlation with higher incidence of being left out of communication, daily injustices in lack of access or barriers, and real instances of financial, emotional, and even physical abuse in Deaf people's environments. Isolation breeds further suspicious thinking. By the time people reach out for help they may present with clinical levels of paranoia or psychotic breaks. It's important to look holistically at the person's sociocultural and linguistic history and work collaboratively with psychiatric professionals as language alterations can sometimes be due to thought disorders versus **language deprivation** (Thylur et al., 2020).

[27] In some Canadian hospitals who have contracts with US-based mental health interpreting agencies, regional variations in signs are sometimes not well-understood by Deaf patients.

[28] Interpreters have external access to support and case consultations thus counsellors should not feel the post-debrief needs to include "therapy" for the interpreter. Although post-debriefs are not required by either party (or their respective professional bodies), they are a best practice to improve interprofessional collaboration and can increase good teamwork and smooth communication.

and methods using the gentle assumption method[29] of Assessing and Managing Suicide Risk (AMSR). Together, the counsellor and Dave identified that communication frustrations, particularly in social situations, often triggered feelings of hopelessness and suicidal ideation. Using strength-based questions helped Dave recognize areas of resilience and apply that to self-advocacy. Dave's risk state was lower than during his initial hospital stay when he had active suicidal thoughts and risk status was similar to other Deaf clients that the clinician saw with substance use disorders, language deprivation, and trauma. The clinician co-constructed a basic visual safety plan[30] he could use until their next appointment and continued in subsequent sessions to determine risk and protective factors and assess Dave's use of the safety plan.

After several intake sessions,[31] the counsellor determined that language deprivation played a significant role in Dave's challenges.[32] Dave lost his hearing at age 2.5 from unknown causes.[33] Though he used spoken English (oral method), his vocabulary was limited, and he tended to express concrete rather than abstract concepts. While Dave claimed to understand a lot, further conversation showed simplified answers, limited grasp of cause-effect, and frequent shifts between ASL and SEE (Signed Exact English). He often needed questions rephrased for clarity and typically gave one-word answers lacking context, such as when he mentioned talking about baseball with a friend without offering details beyond naming the team, the Toronto Blue Jays.

It was assessed that Dave had experienced lifelong isolation, leaving him with a restricted social circle. He distrusted the Deaf community, having faced criticism for using oral communication instead of sign language. Dave had hearing friends, yet their interactions were limited, becoming more challenging in groups, which

[29] Such as, "What other methods have you thought of for killing yourself?" (N.B. ask interpreter not to use imagery or examples of other suicide methods).

[30] Outlining, for example: warning signs, internal coping strategies, people to ask for help (professionals/friends), places to go for distraction, and making the environment safe.

[31] A hearing clinician might judge an inordinate amount of time was spent debriefing lack of communication access; however, Dave's suicidal thoughts were directly related to limited communicate access and the perceived shift in attitude he experienced from the staff when he tried to advocate for his right to having ASL interpreters.

[32] Experienced clinicians will be able to detect signs of language deprivation such as lack of time markers or theory of mind deficits (Gulati, 2019). A formal communication assessment, such as the Communication Skills Assessment (Williams & Crump, 2019), Sign Language Proficiency Interview (SLPI), or ASL-DT (Discrimination Test) were not used. For more on language deprivation, see Glickman & Hall (2018). In a study of 107 Deaf adults seeking substance abuse treatment, Embree et al. (2017) found that the more significant the language acquisition delay, the higher the incidence of co-occurring mental illness and past suicidal behaviours.

[33] Prelingual vs. postlingual Deafness can be important in perception of thought processes and diagnosing (see Thylur et al., 2020); Dave's Deafness occurred right in the middle of language acquisition. It's helpful to know the timing but also the cause of hearing loss (for example, hearing loss due to Waardenburg syndrome type III can co-occur with intellectual disabilities).

required he put extra effort into maintaining the conversation. Regarding his Indigenous tribe, Dave struggled with access due to a lack of interpreters during tribal meetings. His hearing family did include him in rituals and ceremonies, but he expressed often not understanding their purpose.

Feelings of isolation from various communities contributed to Dave's dependence on alcohol as a coping mechanism for social anxiety. The counsellor collaborated with Dave to identify triggers[34] for his stress and anxiety. Initially, Dave struggled with introspective questions, likely due to his language deprivation. The clinician worked to first build a sighted vocabulary for a range of feeling states, connecting them with concrete stressors in Dave's day-to-day life and somatic states. Higher awareness of physiological signals is linked to greater resilience (Haase et al., 2015), and the clinician helped Dave build interoception by breaking down information into shorter, simpler questions and giving a menu of options after teaching feeling states ("Does that thought of "I don't have support" in the hospital and the tightness in your neck feel like disappointment, anger, sadness, or fear?")

During sessions, Dave often asked, "tell me what to do about my ex-partner". This tendency towards helplessness or decision-making anxiety likely stemmed from his lack of access to information growing up and having others dictate his choices. While it can be tempting for a counsellor to provide answers, it was crucial to support Dave in developing decision-making skills and taking ownership of his choices.

For instance, when exploring Dave's frustration with his ex-partner's nagging about household chores, he became overwhelmed by simple questions. The counsellor helped him gain perspective by asking possible reasons for his ex-partner's frustration, prompting Dave to make appropriate guesses. This approach shifted Dave's focus from the nagging itself to considering the underlying reasons. The counsellor aimed to help him break the thought cycle centred on nagging. Building theory of mind for language-deprived clients takes time and requires the clinician to take a more active role in providing possible suppositions, role-playing, or feeding questions to deepen curiosity.

The clinician eventually pieced together that Dave hears "vibration sounds in his home", which Dave thought were created by his neighbour or ex-partner to disturb him. Dave reported that these sounds hindered his ability to do chores, such as cleaning or cooking. When the counsellor tried to learn more about the vibrations, Dave became defensive, insisting he was not crazy. Despite the counsellor's efforts to build rapport, Dave remained resistant to considering the possibility that the vibrations might be auditory perceptions rather than external sounds.

Eventually, Dave agreed to see an audiologist. After testing his hearing and examining his hearing aids, the audiologist found them to be in perfect working order, with Dave showing no signs of tinnitus. This conclusion was based on Dave's

[34] See Anderson et al. (2016) regarding pre-therapy work of empowerment, trust & skill building for comorbid PTSD and SUD and their adaptations of *Seeking Safety* (Najavits, 2002) and *Addictions and Trauma Recovery Integration Model* (Miller & Guidry, 2001).

report that he only hears the vibrations at home, not while food shopping or visiting family. Following this assessment, Dave felt validated, believing it provided proof that the vibrations he heard were real.

Shortly after, the counsellor met with Dave virtually. Being at home allowed the counsellor to request an ASL interpreter to "listen" for any ambient sounds during the session. The interpreter confirmed that the home was quiet, and she heard no sounds.

Dave eventually agreed to be assessed by a psychiatrist, who prescribed a low-dose antipsychotic, but only after the counsellor provided psychoeducation about the fact that Deaf individuals can and do experience auditory hallucinations. Dave eventually agreed to consider medications to manage the hallucinations; however, later refused to take the medications once it was prescribed because the label on the bottle indicated the medications should be taken "as needed".[35]

The clinician recognized the need to consult further with the psychiatrist to help Dave understand why medication may have been appropriate, considering his other medical conditions. Further psychoeducation on the potential benefits of medication for his well-being was also necessary. Unfortunately, Dave continued to resist the idea of the medication and experienced bothersome vibrations. The clinician also considered including Dave's ex-partner in a future session, with Dave's consent, in order to gather more comprehensive history and foster understanding of his needs, helping to set realistic expectations about his contributions at home without absolving him of responsibility.

Throughout this process, the clinician navigated ongoing role confusion, often feeling compelled to advocate for Dave beyond traditional therapeutic boundaries. This dynamic underscores the complexity of providing mental health support to language-deprived Deaf clients, where advocacy and understanding are vital to the therapeutic relationship.

For Dave, the intervention process required scaffolding priorities: first, establishing rapport and trust; then addressing suicidality and expanding the client's feelings and somatic vocabulary. Following this, the focus shifted to identifying triggers, supporting the client's abstinence goals, and providing psychoeducation on the relapse-abstinence cycle.[36] Techniques were employed to counteract traditional shutdown and collapse responses through relational mindfulness (Ogden & Fisher, 2015). Additionally, the process normalized communication access barriers and role-modelled overcoming them to foster collaborative movement towards well-being goals that continued to evolve as the clinician learned more about Dave's

[35] It is difficult to totally rule out subjective tinnitus and auditory hallucinations, although antipsychotic medication could be used as a diagnostic tool confirming the latter if helpful. In Dave's case, given his sobriety, alcohol-induced psychosis (hallucinosis) was ruled out (see Felhofer et al., 2022 for case study of Deaf patient with complications due to alcohol use disorder).

[36] See Fisher (2000).

Table 13.1 Key information to share pre- and post-session with interpreters

Pre-debrief	Post-debrief
• Names and sign names of key players, such as significant friends or partners • Outline the agenda/goals for the meeting • Review any documents to be shared (ideally emailed to interpreters prior to sessions) • Establish a protocol for handling interruptions, particularly if the client tends to be verbose or detail-oriented • Decide who will provide examples if any concepts are not fully understood by the client • Exercise caution when sharing sensitive details with interpreters, especially if they are not familiar with the client—always confirm with the client before disclosing personal history, such as experiences of trauma or sexual assault • For clinicians without full fluency who use both a ASL and Deaf Interpreter (DI), request the ASL interpreter to voice what they see the DI conveying to give a better sense of how information is further broken down or presenting symptomology or thought patterns	• Assess any tones from the session that may have gone unnoticed during the meeting • Conduct a post-mortem analysis of any communication breakdowns that occurred • Note any atypical language patterns or uses that the clinician may have missed • Discuss changes in signing style, speed, or size that might have influenced communication effectiveness[a] • Review any modifications made to the interpreting process, explaining why changes were necessary—for instance, switching from simultaneous interpreting to consecutive to better chunk complex information that may have been confusing or disjointed *N.B.* Other examples may apply depending on the situation/interpreter[b]

[a]Interpreters can comment on language skills and patterns but not speak diagnostically
[b]See Bone (2019) for more practical strategies when working with signed interpreters during formal assessments

subjective tinnitus/auditory hallucinations. Dave's case also highlights the ongoing need for pre- and post-debriefing with interpreters.[37]

See the chart below (Table 13.1) for examples of key information to share pre- and post-session with sign language interpreters.[38]

Case 4: Marianna, a 34-year-old, first-generation Canadian, prelingually Deaf woman with work stress and a history of anger issues—working with a hearing male clinician with limited ASL-fluency.

Born into a hearing (non-signing) family and moving to Canada at age 11, Mariana was taught both Mexican Sign Language (LMS) and ASL. Mariana

[37] If a Deaf person answers a question off-topic or a problem in rapport is noted, the clinician should take responsibility to check if there has been a communication breakdown. It is not the interpreter's responsibility to report all of client's non-verbal communication; for example, a Deaf client may look off to the side subtly and unless the clinician is paying close attention, they may miss the client's visual hallucination.

[38] Virtual waiting rooms can be used for prep and debrief in virtual psychotherapy. Also see Taylor (2002) for more on ethical considerations that can arise during these debriefs and how it can be used to deconstruct interpreter filters that might be at play.

presented as detail-oriented, leaving little time for turn-taking in conversation. Clarifications from the clinician were met with a sigh, "you don't understand", and shifting to another topic. Mariana expressed how her family had inadequate sign language to communicate anything even slightly complex. When her hearing family members struggled to articulate difficult ideas in sign language, they either provided only fragmented information or dismissed the topic altogether. This pattern of limited communication restricted Mariana's ability to develop essential problem-solving skills over time. Her family then didn't know how to handle her upset feelings and would further push her to the side in an attempt to avoid her emotions. It appeared her family framed her anger as Mariana attempting to get control and would only talk about her "anger problems" instead of communication issues. Mariana's anger with her family grew over her teenage years and she recalled prolonged episodes of intense "out-of-control" rage. In these episodes she would destroy property and harm herself. Her family's view of her as being unruly was then internalized, leading her to believe that there was something fundamentally wrong with her.

As Mariana grew, she noticed she became fixated on how she was perceived by others. She continued to feel intense anger when she felt others were withholding information from her, but this anger was pushed down with intense internal messages of shame. She believed if anyone saw her become angry, they would dismiss her as "another angry Deaf woman" or having too much "Latina fire". In her relationships, she developed strong avoidance tendencies and would freeze when she started to become angry which then strained relationships and prevented her from getting desired information.

Mariana recalled a distressing workplace incident where the anger-shame cycle appeared. An important meeting was rescheduled to a time when she had booked time off. Her colleagues provided only vague answers when she tried to understand why the change was made. She started to feel like management didn't care about her time off, that she would have to cancel plans or that they were deliberately excluding her from the meeting where important decisions were to be made. She believed she was the only person who was excluded and felt a deep sense of alienation. Noticing rising feelings of rage, she went to the restroom where she felt a strong impulse to destroy property. She then became paralysed by fear that others would hear her and think she was out-of-control again which would only confirm what she believed was their current assumption of her. Frozen in this place of anger and shame she was unable to focus at work for the next couple of days.

Understanding that Mariana carried trauma from poor communication and lack of access to information, it was beneficial to explore any transference that arose when things were not clear in session.[39] As a therapist with limited ASL and with

[39] In the US and Canada, the increase in families that use a foreign language in the home has led to more Deaf people who are "linguistic minorities within linguistic minorities" (Glickman et al., 2020). The challenges of interpreting dysfluent language have resulted in specific interpreter trainings such as Alabama's Mental Health Interpreter Training programme and the Centre for Atypical Language Interpreting at Northeastern University (Glickman & Hall, 2018).

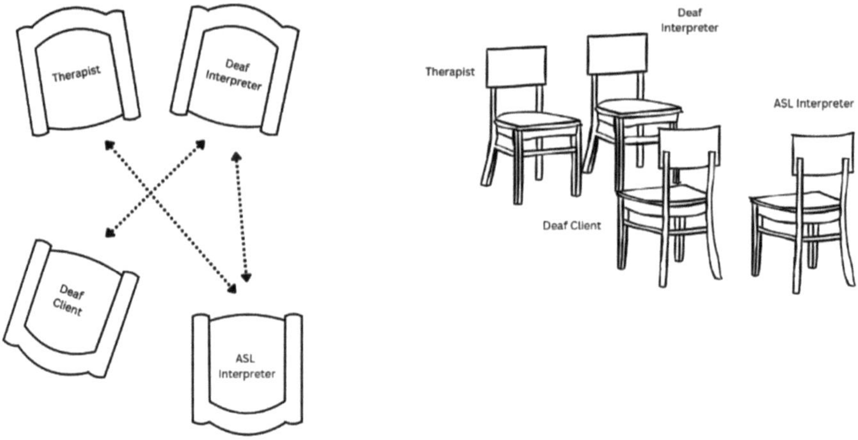

Fig. 13.2 Therapist–DI–ASL–Client Set-up

ASL being a second or third language for Mariana,[40] miscommunications may echo early experiences where her family failed to "get" her.[41] This could have led to feelings of disappointment, frustration, and emotional overwhelm in session.

After consulting with Mariana, it was beneficial to bring in the support of a Deaf Interpreter (DI) who reduced the likelihood of miscommunication.[42] Additionally, DIs help balance the Deaf-hearing ratio and mitigate transference-related frustrations. They can be used either as an addition to the train of communication (Speaker to ASL interpreter to DI to client, and the reverse) or function as observers who step in only when clarification or expansion are needed.[43] (See Fig. 13.2 Therapist–DI–ASL–Client Set-up).

[40] For late-language Deaf migrant adult learners, not having a solid first language (L1) foundation can make acquiring a second language (L2) such as written English difficult and necessitates first filling in the L1 foundation (Dugan, 2023; Mayberry, 2010; Williams & Crump, 2019). This issue is further compounded when adult Deaf migrants have a different L1 and L2 than is being taught in the Canadian classroom, and Deaf migrants have often faced "dual displacement"—first within their hearing families, and then through experiences of war, violence, and human rights violations (McAuliff, 2021).

[41] Multidisciplinary study of sign language errors is just emerging but can provide etiology clues—for example, time sequencing errors might indicate language deprivation, not using "I" might suggest Autism Spectrum Disorder, clanging (repetition of handshapes that aren't meaningful semantically) may indicate psychosis, or other language errors might indicate a stroke (Williams & Crump, 2019).

[42] Fluency is often not enough when language is dysfluent due to mental health, language, or learning challenges. Having someone else in the room focusing on communication can free up clinicians to allow their sole focus to be clinical and intervention-focused versus split between communication and clinical issues.

[43] When DIs are used in conjunction with ASL interpreters for non-fluent hearing clinicians, clients may sometimes need instruction and patience to wait for information to flow through both profes-

In situations where clinicians use both ASL and Deaf interpreters without complete fluency, they can request that the ASL interpreter voice what they observe the Deaf interpreter signing. This practice helps in two ways:

- **Enhancing Communication Clarity:** By voicing what the DI is interpreting, hearing clinicians gain insight into how information is being conveyed, which helps them better respond to and engage with the Deaf client.
- **Feedback Loop:** This method creates an opportunity for dynamic feedback during the session, allowing the clinician to confirm understanding and make adjustments in real time.

The presence of a DI can be likened to the difference between watching a television programme in black and white versus in full colour. In particular, DIs enhance the clarity of abstract therapeutic concepts. In the next paragraph we discuss Internal Family System's exercise of "unblending" from emotions, wherein a DI helped bring these ideas to life in a way that was more accessible and meaningful for Mariana.

Certain therapeutic modalities, like Internal Family Systems (IFS), which focus on externalizing problems, align naturally with the structure of sign language (Schwartz & Sweezy, 2019). In ASL, the physical act of signing about a problem or an internal part inherently places the concept outside of the self, reinforcing psychological separation (Freedman, 1994). As Mariana was guided through the process of "unblending" from her feelings of anger and shame, this linguistic dynamic became especially valuable. When Mariana, her therapist, and the interpreters all signed about the part of her that felt anger about being denied access to information in the shared space outside of Mariana,[44] it became easier to see that it was the part's anger rather than Mariana's.

When Mariana was asked to "unblend" from this part, she noticed that it was trying to protect her from being devalued in important relationships. The part believed that if others devalued her, she wouldn't be safe, so it lashed out in anger to try and hold onto her value. Knowing that the part was trying to protect her, she was able to give it compassion and understanding, which helped decrease its intensity. When the part recognized that it wouldn't be ignored or suppressed by shame, it was then given the new job of finding creative ways to ensure she was included and valued.

---

sionals. When done virtually, clients may prefer the ASL interpreter to have their camera off (where ASL and DI have a separate video connection).

[44] This is also true of externalization in narrative modalities. Paul Freedman (1994) discusses how ASL promotes externalization by reinforcing the problem as outside the client making it easier to see the problem as less inherent and fixed and instead develop a relationship with it that is protest-oriented.

One important factor for Mariana was the cumulative impact of being denied access to important information over a lifetime. Growing up in a family without a shared language can mean a child loses out on complex information and is less likely to receive modelling on how to regulate or understand emotions as well as how to evaluate and make decisions. Gaps in understanding problems and building desired futures can be addressed by using White's (2007) maps of problems or states of identity hierarchy for scaffolding conversations. For example, Mariana named the problem, "*go ahead with meeting without me* (ASL gloss);" outlined the consequences, "couldn't concentrate for days;" evaluated, "I don't want this to happen anymore;" realized intentions, "work's important to me;" and formed a plan, "I will talk to my supervisor about what I need to be my most productive". At each step, clinicians can build understanding of the known and familiar patterns to increase a client's knowledge bank with new possibilities and skills of living. Similarly, using simple reminders such as DBT's problem-solving matrices can help remind clients they have choices and empower them to pursue these. Explaining different options or offering choices could have frequently been too difficult for the families with limited sign language. These families may have more often chosen to either do things for their deaf children or tell them what they should do without offering alternatives, limiting their problem-solving skills over time. By systematically introducing decision-making strategies, Mariana begins to recognize her choices and assert her agency in both personal and professional contexts rather than feeling powerless.

Case 5: Angela, a white 31-year-old congenitally Deafblind client,[45] worked with a sign-fluent white female clinician who wore a plain black shirt (for contrast) to address goals of moving out from her parents and rumination related to the loss of a valued **intervenor (IV).**[46]

The counsellor checked in to understand Angela's field of vision and whether she wanted to include an intervenor. Angela declined saying she wanted privacy and could understand the clinician just fine. Angela had a mild intellectual disability and was deemed capable of understanding the risks and benefits of treatment and providing informed consent.

[45] There is heterogeneity of the Deafblind population, which can be affected by etiology (hereditary or chromosomal syndromes, congenital and non-congenital complications, and symptoms linked to prematurity), differing amounts of sight and hearing, mobility issues, types of communication (e.g. sign language, tactile sign, spoken English, etc.), and preferences (De Feu and Chovaz, 2014; Leigh, 1999; The Ohio Centre for Deafblind Education). Deafblind people can have complex problems and risk having reduced access to services (De Feu and Chovaz, 2014).

[46] Intervenors become the eyes and ears of the Deafblind person, providing necessary auditory and visual information via ASL, two-handed manual, braille, etc.

At the commencement of treatment, Angela expressed concern about being considered "mentally retarded" by receiving counselling or receiving a mental health diagnosis. It seemed that receiving counselling was reinforcing her negative self-view. The clinician took the time to address this concern by explaining which professionals are eligible to diagnose in Ontario (family physicians, psychiatrists, and psychologists) and emphasized that mental health support is accessible to the general population, thereby helping to normalize seeking help and reducing associated stigma.

A main focus of therapy was Angela's desire for increased independence from her parents. Throughout her life, Angela's parents took a primary role; for example, making her meals, transporting her, providing feedback for important decisions, etc. It is not uncommon for Deafblind individuals to have extra support due to the many barriers to access in society and in her case a mild intellectual disability. That said, Angela felt ready to start navigating life with less parental input. Assertiveness training using a DBT approach (Linehan, 1993, Linehan, 2015) helped Angela establish boundaries with her parents, while involving them in some sessions promoted shared goals. After hearing her parents' concerns but also support for her to become more independent, Angela expressed some panic that her goals would somehow be blocked. The clinician taught Angela some self-compassion exercises and diaphragmatic breathing.

Using a biofeedback device that monitored her heart rate variability, Angela was asked to direct her attention to the screen displaying a colourful hot air balloon. She was instructed to use her breath to lift the balloon from the ground and send it soaring into the sky. As Angela achieved greater coherence in her heart rate, she observed the balloon gliding across the horizon and her feelings of panic subsided. Angela appreciated the real-time feedback and the structured, game-like nature of biofeedback, which contributed to her confidence in being able to regulate her stress. Confronting internalized stereotypes, such as "Deafblind people can't live alone", was part of the clinician's role while helping Angela set realistic expectations based on her abilities.

Another issue addressed in therapy included Angela's struggle to accept the cessation of services from a highly valued intervenor (IV). It is important to note the bond between a Deafblind individual and IV can be strong due to the type of personal and intimate information shared, even if it may be one-sided. The sense of personal loss she felt was apparent in sessions. Angela described missing her IV and having difficulty trusting new IVs.

Through the application of Worden's grief approach, the loss of the strong bond with her intervenor was acknowledged (Worden, 2002). Biofeedback and breathing exercises were again used to help Angela process her grief (Graham, 2024). Angela identified forming a new bond with her online "boyfriend".

As soon as Angela brought up the subject of her boyfriend asking for money in session, this topic became the focus of several sessions. Angela reported meeting her boyfriend on a free dating website but had never met him in-person. Angela disclosed she was concerned about her boyfriend because he told her his family was taking his money, and he did not have enough money for food and other essentials.

She described ruminating about this issue constantly to the point that her intrusive thoughts disrupted her sleep cycle and daily functioning. When her boyfriend asked her for money, she felt she had *no choice* but to send him money to help him. Over a period of approximately one year, she reported sending him thousands of dollars. She explained feeling constantly tired, anxious, and angry. Her thoughts circulated around his safety, housing, whereabouts, and feelings of anger towards his family for taking his money.

While not typical in psychotherapy, a more directive psychoeducational approach was used to discuss the pitfalls of continued monetary support and with Angela's consent; the police were involved and provided education and support about financial and romantic scams. Despite feeling ambivalent, Angela stopped sending him money and agreed to an interim collaborative financial trusteeship with her father. Angela began ruminating on the ex-boyfriend's betrayal. The issue of loneliness and Angela's desire for socialization and dating opportunities were addressed by sharing a list of local Deaf events; however, access barriers (distance, personal preference) persisted.

To address Angela's lingering feelings of anger and shock related to her ex-boyfriend as well as the loss of a longtime intervenor, Brainspotting was introduced. Brainspotting is a next-wave iteration of EMDR developed by harnessing the client's visual field to heal unresolved emotional trauma (Grand, 2013). The clinician observes certain eye wobbles/blinking along specific locations on the x, y, or z axis (typically via a pointer held by the clinician) and assists clients to process their feelings in a particular spot via bottom-up unrestricted stream of consciousness processing. This can be largely non-verbal/non-signing in nature and is typically assisted via biolateral stimulation, either with tapping on knees/shoulders, via biolateral music on headphones, or thera-tappers (under the feet or under the knees can allow Deaf clients to continue to sign). Deaf clients with varying degrees of language dysfluency can find Brainspotting accessible because, like EMDR,[47] it does not necessitate the client be able to articulate the full extent of the concern or trauma.

After working on a brain and body scan and finding some resources spots, Angela was able to find an activation spot associated with the recent betrayal by her ex-boyfriend, which turned out to be a trauma capsule[48] and brought up other memories of being bullied and feeling behind in school. The clinician encouraged Angela to just notice fluidity of the internal sensations and emotions, reassured her that it was part of her processing, and see what she was noticing now in her brain and body. Once all memories were processed to Subjective Units of Distress (SUDS) of zero, Angela felt more in control, and she was brought back to her adult-self coping skills.

[47] See Doornkate (2015) regarding EMDR work with Deaf family members.

[48] As per Scaer (2014), a trauma capsule describes a specific neural network, in this case holding Angela's traumatic memories, within the brain and may be activated by finding specific eye positions (brainspots) that correlate with the encapsulated memories. The Brainspotting process facilitates the release and processing of the trapped emotions and memories to allow for healing and integration.

At the conclusion of treatment, Angela had successfully moved to a supported residence and reported feeling more comfortable in her new surroundings with staff and other residents. She also expressed satisfaction with her parents' involvement in her life and that she was involved in personal activities, volunteering, and community events. That being said, she continued to find changes in her IV schedule and new routines difficult. Ongoing feelings of loneliness and a request to continue treatment created an ethical dilemma about appropriate treatment termination.

In summary, Deafblind clients can present to counselling with a variety of issues and goals. It is recommended to research conditions linked to your client's Deafblindness; for example, syndromes have distinct symptoms that can be progressive (i.e. Ushers syndrome, retinitis pigmentosa) and unpredictable (neurofibromatosis type 2) (De Feu & Chovaz, 2014). De Feu and Chovaz (2014) and Hallgren (1959) mentioned psychosis may present in a small number of individuals with Usher's syndrome. Conditions and their prognosis impact an individual's physical, cognitive, emotional and relational experiences and can lead them or their caregivers to seek out support.

Depending on the client's counselling goals, wrap-around services may include other professionals and organizations. In cases where a client has an intellectual disability, assisting the client to connect with adult developmental services can help them gain access to funding for increased socialization opportunities. Other supports include involving residential staff, general case management support, trusted intervenors (if applicable), family members, and others. Working with Deafblind clients provides unique insights and can be incredibly professionally fulfilling.

Conclusion

We hope this chapter encourages readers to cultivate increased care in this fulfilling work and a more socially responsive profession led by Deaf mental health clinicians in the future. Case examples have shown the importance of hearing professionals working cross-culturally to exercise caution and "the right attitude" of respect, humility, and receptivity of Deaf ways of thinking and being in the world (Anderson et al., 2016, p. 4), scaffolding assessment and treatment based on comorbidities and abuse histories. Working with interpreters requires more, not less, involvement with both the process and content of intervention delivery. Additionally, meeting Deaf clients' needs—which may include addressing knowledge gaps, advocating for their rights, navigating legal processes (e.g., class action lawsuits), and providing case management—can shift clinicians away from their traditional therapeutic roles. Acknowledging these expanded demands and integrating a broader support network, encompassing educators, social workers, legal counsel, and family members, is crucial for maintaining the integrity and effectiveness of the clinician's therapeutic function. Deaf people have a higher suicide risk than hearing people (Fox et al., 2020),[49] and incorporating AMSR alongside visual safety planning has been effectively used in our work to respond to this need.

In conclusion, clinicians need to continue to practise self-reflexivity of their privilege, ignorance, and audism prior to, and while working in this field. Being anti-audist includes a commitment to understanding how our hearing society that does not prioritize accessibility leads to cumulative fatigue. While allyship to ensure accessibility (i.e. communication access) in the therapeutic field is inviolable, it is merely a first step of cultural competence. More research is needed to validate the use of third-, fourth-, and trauma-treatments for this population as well as the best use of developmental and attachment theories to redress d/Deaf children's missed stages due to ACCEs. We wish to move beyond the oral-manualism debate and prioritize deaf children having full access to *all* possible languages (signed and spoken) as often and early as possible to avoid missing critical developmental stages. Co-design of mental health services that includes Deaf Canadians with lived and living experience, mentorship and scholarship for aspiring Deaf clinicians, as well as community-based participatory research are future directions for this field.[50]

Glossary

Audism Prejudice against individuals who cannot hear (Crowe, 2017); a belief in the superiority of those who can hear over those who cannot (Humphries, 1977).

(Certified) Deaf Interpreter has native language abilities, is culturally Deaf themselves, and provides interpreting, translation, and transliteration services (trained in multiple communication strategies)

Intervenor become the eyes and ears of the Deafblind person, providing necessary auditory and visual information via ASL, two-hand manual, braille, etc.

Language deprivation failure to provide access and effective exposure to a language during early development (Humphries et al., 2016). Without auditory access to hearing parents or proficient Deaf signers, these children lack a foundation in any language. This lack of exposure results in having no language or becoming a-lingual, with no fluency in either spoken, written, or signed languages (such as BSL, ASL, LSQ, for example). Exists on a continuum, people who are language-less tend to be from rural, isolated parts of North America or from third-world countries.

Language dysfluency lack of proficiency in any particular language, due to deprivation of language exposure during 0–5 years of age (Crowe, 2022)

---

[49] Canadian statistics unknown. Fox et al. (2020) found higher rates of suicide ideation and attempts amongst college-aged Deaf and Hard of Hearing students in the US using sample size N=12, 056.

[50] See Chovaz et al. (2022) for more on lived experience of Deaf Canadians and self-described barriers to their well-being.

Appendix A: Recommended Resources

Aranda, B. E., & Sleeboom-van Raaij, I. (Eds.). (2015). *Mental health services for deaf people: Treatment advances, opportunities, and challenges.* Gallaudet University Press.

Pollard, R. Q., & Dimeff, L. (Executive Producers). (2006). *Opposite action: An adaptation from the Deaf perspective* [Motion picture]. Behavioral Tech, LLC.

Pollard, R. Q., & Dimeff, L. (Executive Producers). (2007). *Practicing radical acceptance: An adaptation from the Deaf perspective* [Motion picture]. Behavioral Tech, LLC.

Spradley, T.S., Spradley, J.P. (1985). *Deaf like Me.* Washington: Gallaudet University Press.

Zemach, R. (2023). *The Butterfly Cage: Joy, heartache, and corruption: Teaching while Deaf in a California public school. Unruly Voices.*

Books

Harvey, M. (2004). *Odyssey of hearing loss: Tales of triumph.* DawnSign Press.

Journal Articles

Admire, A., & Ramirez, B. (2021). Violence and disability: Experiences and perceptions of victimization among deaf people. *Journal of Interpersonal Violence, 36*(1-2), NP1-NP25. https://doi.org/10.1177/0886260517730564

Andersen, M. L., & Pezzarossi, C. M. (2012). Is it abuse? Deaf female undergraduates' labeling of partner violence. *Journal of Deaf Studies and Deaf Education, 17*(2), 273–286.

Anderson, M. L., Glickman, N. S., Wolf Craig, K. S., Sortwell Crane, A. K., Wilkins, A. M., & Najavits, L. M. (2021). Developing *signs of safety*: A deaf-accessible counselling toolkit for trauma and addiction. *Clinical Psychology & Psychotherapy, 28*(6), 1562–1573. https://doi.org/10.1002/cpp.2596

Anglemyer, E., & Crespi, C. (2018). Misinterpretation of psychiatric illness in deaf patients: two case reports. *Case Reports in Psychiatry, 2018*, 3285153. https://doi.org/10.1155/2018/3285153

Ball, J., & Sankin, L. (2024). Case study in deaf mental health care: Integration of therapeutic attunement and skills-training. *JADARA, 56*(2), 1–28. Retrieved from https://nsuworks.nova.edu/jadara/vol56/iss2/3

Egbert, J. (2024). Adverse childhood experiences among deaf and hard-of-hearing adults. *Disability and Health Journal.* Advance online publication. https://doi.org/10.1016/j.dhjo.2024.101711

Elgar, F. (1997). *A Comparative study of native residential schools and the residential schools for the deaf in Canada* (Doctoral dissertation). Carleton University.

Fellinger, M., Holzinger, D., Fogler, J., & Fellinger, J. (2023). Exploring spirituality and quality of life in individuals who are deaf and have intellectual disabilities. *Social Psychiatry and Psychiatric Epidemiology: The International Journal for Research in Social and Genetic Epidemiology and Mental Health Services, 58*(11), 1709–1718. https://doi.org/10.1007/s00127-023-02451-x

Ladd, P. (2003). *Understanding deaf culture: In search of deafhood.* Multilingual Matters.

The Ohio Center for Deafblind Education. (2025, January 17). *Syndromes and causes of Deafblindness.* https://www.ohiodeafblind.com/what-is-deafblindness/syndromes-and-causes-of-deafblindness/

Trumm, A., Lau, E. J. S., Farthing, S., & Breen, K. (2023). The use of video remote interpreting (VRI) in a medium secure psychiatric setting during the COVID-19 lockdown. *Journal of Forensic Practice, 25*(3), 263–275. https://doi.org/10.1108/JFP-12-2022-0065

References

Anderson, M., Leigh, I., Samar, V. (2011). Intimate partner violence against Deaf women: A review. *Aggression and Violent Behavior, 16*(3), 200-206, ISSN 1359–1789 https://doi.org/10.1016/j.avb.2011.02.006

Anderson, M. L., Glickman, N. S., Mistler, L. A., & Gonzalez, M. (2016). Working therapeutically with deaf people recovering from trauma and addiction. *Psychiatric Rehabilitation Journal, 39*(1), 27–32. https://doi.org/10.1037/prj0000146

Ashori, M., & Shamsi, A. (2023). The effect of Adlerian play therapy on the alexithymia and social isolation of deaf students. *International Journal of Play Therapy, 32*(1), 10–21. https://doi.org/10.1037/pla0000192

Ashton, G., Cagle, K., Kurtz, K., Newell, W., Peterson, R., & Zinza, J. (2013). Standards for Learning American Sign Language: A Project of the American Sign Language Teachers Association. http://www.interpretereducation.org/wp-content/uploads/2013/06/National_ASL_Standards_approved.pdf

Barrera, M., & Castro, F. G. (2006). A heuristic framework for the cultural adaptation of interventions. *Clinical Psychology: Science and Practice, 13*(4), 311–316. https://doi.org/10.1111/j.1468-2850.2006.00043.x

Bauman, H. D. (2004). Audism: Exploring the metaphysics of oppression. *Journal of Deaf Studies and Deaf Education, 9*(2), 239–246. https://doi.org/10.1093/deafed/enh025

Bone, T. (2019). Deaf mental health: Enhancing linguistically and culturally appropriate clinical practice. In M. Zangeneh & A. Al-Krenawi (Eds.), *Culture, diversity, and mental health: Enhancing clinical practice* (pp. 61–80). Springer Nature Switzerland.

Caselli, N. K., Hall, W. C., & Henner, J. (2020). American Sign Language interpreters in public schools: An illusion of inclusion that perpetuates language deprivation. *Maternal and Child Health Journal, 24*(11), 1323–1329. https://doi.org/10.1007/s10995-020-02975-7

Chovaz, C. J., Russell, D., & Daly, B. (2022). Lived experiences of deaf Canadians: What we want you to know! *Canadian Psychology / Psychologie canadienne, 63*(4), 651–666. https://doi.org/10.1037/cap0000313

Cohen, B. (2003). Psychotherapy with deaf and hard of hearing individuals: Perceptions of the consumer. *Journal of Social Work in Disability and Rehabilitation, 2*(2/3), 23–46.

Cohen, C. (2004). Psychotherapy with deaf and hard of hearing individuals: Perceptions of the consumer. In F. Yuen (Ed.), *International perspectives on disability services. The same but different* (pp. 22–45). Routledge.

Crowe, T. (2017). Breaking the silence: Empowering deaf and hard of hearing survivors of domestic violence. In A. J. Johnson, J. R. Nelson, & E. M. Lund (Eds.), *Religion, disability, and interpersonal violence* (pp. 131–148). Springer International Publishing/Springer Nature. https://doi.org/10.1007/978-3-319-56901-7_8

Crowe, T. (2022). Negative life experiences, substance use, well-being, and resilience: A comparison of Deaf and hearing adults. *International Journal on Social and Education Sciences, 4*(3), 391–407. https://doi.org/10.46328/ijonses.416

Dana, D. A. (2020). *Polyvagal exercises for safety and connection: 50 client-centered practices.* W. W. Norton & Company.

De Feu, M., & Chovaz, C. (2014). *Mental health and deafness*. Oxford University Press.

Domenech-Rodríguez, M., & Wieling, E. (2005). Developing culturally appropriate, evidence-based treatments for interventions with ethnic minority populations. In M. Rastogi & E. Wieling (Eds.), *Voices of color: First-person accounts of ethnic minority therapists* (pp. 313–333). Sage Publications, Inc. https://doi.org/10.4135/9781452231662.n18

Doornkate, L. (2015). EMDR work with deaf family members. *Journal of EMDR Practice and Research, 9*(2), 132–145.

Dugan, N. (2023). Deaf migrants in Swedish adult education: Language ideologies, repertoires, and translingual practices. *Stockholm University, Faculty of Humanities, Department of Linguistics*. Retrieved from https://www.su.se/nationellt-centrum-for-svenska-som-andrasprak/forskning-och-konferenser/avhandlingar-och-uppsatser/nora-duggan-deaf-migrants-in-swedish-adult-education-1.740094

Eldridge v. British Columbia (Attorney General), 1997 CanLII 327 (SCC), [1997] 3 SCR 624. Retrieved from https://canlii.ca/t/1fqx5

Embree, J. A., Kinzeler, N. R., Fraker, S., Castle, S., & Wilson, J. F. (2017). Age of language acquisition and prevalence of suicidal behavior in a deaf population with co-occurring substance use disorder. *JADARA, 51*(3), 1–24. Retrieved from https://repository.wcsu.edu/jadara/vol51/iss3/1

Felhofer, A., Crowe, T., AhnAllen, C., Mistler, L., & Suzuki, J. (2022). Assessment and treatment of a deaf patient with alcohol use disorder—limitations and special considerations. *Harvard Review of Psychiatry 30*(3), 198–206, 5/6 2022. https://doi.org/10.1097/HRP.0000000000000333

Fisher, J. (2000). *Addictions and Trauma Rec*overy. Paper presented at the International Society for the Study of Dissociation. November 13, 2000. San Antonio, Texas.

Fox, M. L., James, T. G., & Barnett, S. L. (2020). Suicide behaviors and help-seeking attitudes among deaf and hard-of-hearing college students. *Suicide and Life-Threatening Behavior, 50*(2), 387–396. https://doi.org/10.1111/sltb.12595

Freedman, P. (1994). Counselling with deaf clients: The need for culturally and linguistically sensitive interventions. *JADARA, 27*(4) Retrieved from https://nsuworks.nova.edu/jadara/vol27/iss4/7

Glickman, N. (2009). *Cognitive-behavioral therapy for Deaf and hearing persons with language and learning challenges*. Routledge.

Glickman, N. (2017). *Preparing deaf and hearing persons with language and learning challenges for CBT*. Routledge.

Glickman, N. S., Crump, C., & Hamerdinger, S. (2020). Language deprivation is a game changer for the clinical specialty of deaf mental health. *JADARA, 54*(1), 54. Retrieved from https://repository.wcsu.edu/jadara/vol54/iss1/4

Glickman, N. S., & Gulati, S. (Eds.). (2003). *Mental health care of Deaf people: A culturally affirmative approach*. Lawrence Erlbaum Associates.

Glickman, N. S., & Hall, W. C. (Eds.). (2018). *Language deprivation and deaf mental health* (1st ed.). Routledge. https://doi.org/10.4324/9781315166728

Goghari, V. M. (2022). Reimagining clinical psychology. *Canadian Psychology / Psychologie canadienne, 63*(2), 169–178. https://doi.org/10.1037/cap0000328

Graham, J. K. (2024). Effect of heart rate variability biofeedback on prolonged grief disorder in bereavement: A case series study. *Dissertation Abstracts International: Section B: The Sciences and Engineering, 85*(1-B).

Grand, D. (2013). *Brainspotting: The revolutionary new therapy for rapid and effective change.* St. Martin's Press.

Gulati, S. (2019). Language deprivation syndrome. In N. S. Glickman & W. C. Hall (Eds.), *Language deprivation and deaf mental health* (pp. 30–59). Routledge. https://doi.org/10.4324/9781315166728-2

Haase, L., Stewart, J., Yousef, B., May, A., Isakovic, S., Simmons, A., Johnson, D., Potterat, E., & Paulus, M. (2015). When the brain does not adequately feel the body: Links between low resilience and interoception. *Biological Psychology, 113*, 37–45. https://doi.org/10.1016/j.biopsycho.2015.11.004

Hallgren, B. (1959). Retinitis Pigmentosa Combined with General Deafness; with Vestibulo-Cerebellar Ataxia and Mental Abnormality in a Proportion of Cases. *Acta Psychiatricia Scandinavica 34*, Supplement 138, 1–101.

Hamerdinger, S., & Karlin, B. (2003). Therapy using interpreters: Questions on the use of interpreters in therapeutic setting for monolingual therapists. *JADARA, 36.*

Harvey, J. H., & Miller, E. D. (1998). Toward a psychology of loss. *Psychological Science, 9*(6), 429–434. https://doi.org/10.1111/1467-9280.00081. (Original work published 1998).

Harvey, M. A. (2003). *Psychotherapy with deaf and hard-of-hearing persons: A systemic model* (2nd ed.). Lawrence Erlbaum Associates.

Humphries, T. (1977). *Communicating across cultures (deaf-hearing) and language learning (Doctoral dissertation).* Union Institute and University.

Humphries, T., Kushalnagar, P., Mathur, G., Napoli, D. J., Padden, C., Rathmann, C., & Smith, S. (2016). Avoiding linguistic neglect of deaf children. *Social Service Review, 90*(4), 589–619. https://doi.org/10.1086/689543

Isenberg, G. (1996). Storytelling and the use of culturally appropriate metaphors in psychotherapy with deaf people. In N. S. Glickman & M. A. Harvey (Eds.), *Culturally affirmative psychotherapy with deaf persons* (pp. 169–183). Lawrence Erlbaum Associates Publishers.

Kobosko, J., Jedrzejczak, W. W., Porembska, D. B., Geremek-Samsonowicz, A., & Skarzynski, H. (2021). Posttraumatic growth in postlingually deaf patients with cochlear implants: The effect of stress-coping strategies, sociodemographics, and deafness-related factors. *Frontiers in Psychology, 12*, 546896. https://doi.org/10.3389/fpsyg.2021.546896

Kushalnagar, P., Ryan, C., Paludneviciene, R., Spellun, A., & Gulati, S. (2020). Adverse childhood communication experiences associated with an increased risk of chronic diseases in adults who are deaf. *American Journal of Preventive Medicine, 59*(4), 548–554. https://doi.org/10.1016/j.amepre.2020.04.016

Ladd, P. (2003). *Understanding deaf culture: In search of deafhood.* Multilingual Matters.

Leigh, I. (Ed.). (1999). *Psychotherapy with Deaf clients from diverse groups.* Gallaudet University Press.

Leigh, I. W., Corbett, C. A., Gutman, V., & Morere, D. A. (1996). Providing psychological services to deaf individuals: A response to new perceptions of diversity. *Professional Psychology: Research and Practice, 27*(4), 364–371. https://doi.org/10.1037/0735-7028.27.4.364

Levinger, M. (2020). Triad in the therapy room - the interpreter, the therapist, and the Deaf Person. *Journal of Interpretation, 28*(1) Retrieved from https://digitalcommons.unf.edu/joi/vol28/iss1/5

Lillo-Martin, D., & Henner, J. (2021). Acquisition of sign languages. *Annual Review of Linguistics, 7*(1), 395–419. https://doi.org/10.1146/annurev-linguistics-043020-092357

Linehan, M. M. (1993, 2015). *DBT skills training manual* 2nd ed Guilford Press.

MacDougall, J. C. (2022). Dialogue with the deaf: The future role of psychology. *Canadian Psychology/Psychologie canadienne, 63*(4), 637–650. https://doi.org/10.1037/cap0000341

Mayberry, R. I. (2010). Early language acquisition and adult language ability: What sign language reveals about the critical period for language. In M. Marschark & P. E. Spencer (Eds.),

The Oxford handbook of deaf studies, language, and education (Vol. 2, pp. 281–291). Oxford University Press. https://doi.org/10.1093/oxfordhb/9780195390032.013.0019

McAuliff, K. (2021). Deaf refugees: A critical review of the current literature. *CENDEP Working Paper Series*. https://doi.org/10.24384/CENDEP.WP-01-2021

Miller, C. A., & Clark, K. A. (2019). Deaf and queer at the intersections: Deaf LGBTQ people and communities. In I. W. Leigh & C. A. O'Brien (Eds.), *Deaf Identities: Exploring New Frontiers* (pp. 305–335). Oxford University Press. https://doi.org/10.1093/oso/9780190887599.003.0013

Miller, D., & Guidry, L. (2001). *Addictions and trauma recovery*. W. W. Norton & Company.

Munro, L., Knox, M., & Lowe, R. (2008). Exploring the potential of constructionist therapy: deaf clients, hearing therapists and a reflecting team. *Journal of Deaf Stud Deaf Education. Summer, 13*(3), 307–323. https://doi-org.uml.idm.oclc.org/10.1093/deafed/enn001

Najavits, L. M. (2002). *Seeking safety: A treatment manual for PTSD and substance abuse*. Guilford Press.

O'Hearn, A., Pollard, R., Jr., & Haynes, S. (2010). Dialectical behavior therapy for deaf clients: Cultural and linguistic modifications for outpatient mental health settings. In *Psychotherapy with deaf clients from diverse groups* (2nd ed., pp. 372–392). Gallaudet University Press.

Ogden, P., & Fisher, J. (2015). *Sensorimotor psychotherapy: Interventions for trauma and attachment*. Norton Professional Books.

Ouellette, J. A., & Wood, W. (1998). Habit and intention in everyday life: The multiple processes by which past behavior predicts future behavior. *Psychological Bulletin, 124*(1), 54–74. https://doi.org/10.1037/0033-2909.124.1.54

Peoples, K. (2002). *Ethical challenges in training professionals for mental health services with deaf people*. Gallaudet University Press.

Pollard, R. Q., Dean, R. K., O'Hearn, A., & Haynes, S. (2014). Adapting cognitive-behavioral therapy for deaf and hard of hearing individuals. *Cognitive and Behavioral Practice, 21*(2), 217–229. https://doi.org/10.1016/j.cbpra.2013.07.004

Porter, J., & Williams, L. M. (2011). Intimate violence among underrepresented groups on a college campus. *Journal of Interpersonal Violence, 26*(16), 3210–3224. https://doi.org/10.1177/0886260510393011

Rathod, S., Phiri, P., & Naeem, F. (2019). An evidence-based framework to culturally adapt cognitive behaviour therapy. *The Cognitive Behaviour Therapist, 12*, e10. https://doi.org/10.1017/S1754470X18000247

Scaer, R. C. (2014). *The body bears the burden: Trauma, dissociation, and disease* (3rd ed.). Routledge.

Schwartz, R. C., & Sweezy, M. (2019). *Internal family systems therapy* (2nd ed.). Guilford Press.

Taylor, L. (2002). Defining the Shadow: Recognizing the imprint of the interpreter in the mental health setting. In V. Guttman (Ed.), *Ethics in Mental Health and Deafness*. ([page numbers needed]). Gallaudet University Press.

Thylur, D. S., Singleton, J. L., & Schwartz, A. C. (2020). Assessing psychosis in a prelingually Deaf Man: Diagnostic challenges and pitfalls. *Psychosomatics, 61*(6), 830–833. https://doi.org/10.1016/j.psym.2019.12.007

Todd, S. (2022). Deafness and Trauma: A journey to equitable trauma-informed care. In P. Willmot & L. Jones (Eds.), *Trauma-informed forensic practice* (pp. 130–146). Routledge. https://doi.org/10.4324/9781003120766-10

White, M. (2007). *Maps of narrative practice*. WW Norton.

Williams, C. A., & Crump, C. (2019). Norm-referenced communication assessments for deaf individuals. *Journal of Deaf Studies and Deaf Education, 24*(2), 132–145. https://doi.org/10.1093/deafed/enn001

Worden, J. W. (2002). *Grief counselling and grief therapy* (3rd ed.). Springer Publishing Company.

Chapter 14
A Deaf Mental Health Strategy (DMHS) for Canada

Tracey A. Bone

In July 2025, Member of Legislative Assembly (MLA) Nahanni Fontaine, Minister of Families of Manitoba, and Manitoba's Accessibility Minister presented at the first annual Mino'Ayaawag Ikwewag Celebration of Indigenous Women Graduates held in Winnipeg. Leaving the stage after her speech, her comments were, unbeknownst to her, captured on a live microphone. In a conversation with her aide, she expressed disparaging remarks about sharing the stage with an American Sign Language (ASL)-English Interpreter. Minister Fontaine questioned "why" the ASL-English Interpreter was on stage, claiming the interpreter distracted her during her speech. When the aides asked if it was the "frantic hand movements," Minister Fontaine said simply, yes (Jonas, 2025). It is important to note that the ASL-English Interpreter was on stage to facilitate effective two-way communication between the speakers at the event and the Deaf graduate and her daughter, both of whom are Deaf ASL speakers. After her own speech, Minister Fontaine instructed the Interpreter to leave the stage and provide interpretation from a different location, separate from the stage and speaker. As noted by the graduate after the event, though the interpreter moved to stand in front of her table, doing so visually and physically separated the interpreter from the speaker, thereby preventing full simultaneous access to the signed and spoken content. The graduate noted that if the interpreter is separated from the speaker, it makes it difficult for the Deaf ASL user to simultaneously view both the emotions and facial expressions of the speaker and the content signed by the Interpreter. It appears Minister Fontaine was not aware that Sign Language interpreters stand alongside the speaker to reduce the distance the Deaf participant must move their eyes to simultaneously view both the speaker and the interpreter.

T. A. Bone (✉)
Faculty of Social Work, University of Manitoba, Winnipeg, MB, Canada
e-mail: Tracey.bone@umanitoba.ca

T. Bone (ed.), *Deaf Mental Health*, Advances in Mental Health and Addiction,
https://doi.org/10.1007/978-3-032-06274-1_14

Minister Fontaine later apologized for her comments and actions. In subsequent interviews and posts on her Instagram account, Fontaine reported that her comments stemmed from the design of the stage, feeling it was too small to accommodate her and the interpreter alongside the celebratory balloon display also on stage, with Fontaine feeling the interpreter blocked her view of one side of the room. Fontaine committed to attending "Deaf and Deaf culture" training and to making every future public event through her office accessible with the inclusion of an ASL-English Interpreter. She also noted she would hire a dedicated ASL interpreter to support all government departments (Jonas, 2025 July 17). Minister Fontaine did subsequently participate (d) in an 11-minute radio interview on a local radio station in Winnipeg, Manitoba, discussing her commitment to accessibility for the Deaf community. The radio interview appeared contradictory to Minister Fontaine's goal of inclusion for the Deaf community. As an update to the original incident and radio interview, Minister Fontaine has engaged with the Manitoba Deaf Association, and supported their raising of the Deaf Flag for the first time at the Manitoba Legislative Building on September 23, 2025 to celebrate International Week of the Deaf, and specifically, International Day of Sign Language. The flag raising acknowledges and celebrates Deaf culture, sign language, and indicates an initial and important commitment to accessibility and inclusion of Deaf people in all aspects of society.

Deaf Mental Health—Current Situation

The aim of this chapter is to introduce a Mental Health Strategy that addresses the needs of the Deaf and Hard of Hearing (DHH) communities; a Deaf* Mental Health Strategy (DMHS). It has been created in response to results from the author's research in the area, and findings from the Canadian Mental Health Association report, *The State of Mental Health in Canada 2024* (CMHA, 2024) that acknowledges mental health supports are "uneven across Canada" (p. 4). The report further states, "In Canada, mental health is a privilege. It should be a right" (p. 1). The strategy introduced in this chapter enhances Canada's existing, though admittedly now dated, mental health strategy (MHCC, 2025), while building on the Quality Mental Health Care Framework of 2025 (MHCC, 2025). It highlights key areas in which change is necessary and is based on the author's past and current work in and with the Deaf, Hard of Hearing, and Deafblind (DHHDB) communities, recently completed community-based research, previous employment with members of the Deaf community, findings from the literature, and personal experiences as a family member of a Deaf adult. This integrated strategy incorporates components that are culturally and linguistically respectful, appropriate, and necessary to meet the needs of the Deaf, Hard of Hearing, and Deafblind communities.

Deaf, Hard of Hearing, and Deafblind (DHHDB) individuals who use ASL are a subpopulation in the disability community. It is important to note that there is great diversity in the larger Deaf community. Many individuals, for example, who identify as culturally Deaf view their deafness as part of their identity, with their deafness denoting difference. They reject the view of themselves as disabled or as members of the disability community. It is important for professionals working with this community to acknowledge this diversity. It is also important for professionals to recognize that individuals from the Deaf community may inconsistently face systemic, attitudinal, and/or personal-level barriers to accessing quality health and mental health care, including ineffective patient-physician communication (Bone, 2018), language and cultural discordance with their health care providers (Pertz et al., 2018), audism (Crowe, 2017), and financial barriers, the latter if expected to cover the cost of ASL-English Interpreters directly. For many, access to mental health information is limited if Sign Language is their first language, and English their second, as few mental health resources or services are available in ASL, Langue des Signes Québéquoise (LSQ), or Indigenous Sign Language (ISL). This author, too, found, in her past research (Bone, 2018), and most recent though as yet unpublished community-based participatory action research study with a local community-based disability organization, that participants reported inequities in mental health assessment and service access.

The Canadian Mental Health Association's (2024) report referenced above highlighted inequities for some Canadians in accessing life-saving mental health care. The CMHA acknowledged that mental health care in Canada has been "profoundly neglected," with the provinces and territories spending approximately one-half of their allocated mental health care budget (2024, p. 7). The report further acknowledged that research in this area is inadequately funded, resulting in gaps in understanding where and how to enhance services to best meet the needs of Canadians.

The number of professionals who serve the minority Deaf, Hard of Hearing, and Deafblind population is few and, as a highly specialized area, often find little understanding in mainstream practice of the unique linguistic and cultural needs of Deaf, Hard of Hearing, or Deafblind individuals. In Canada, there is also limited mental health information easily available in Sign Language. Two exceptions exist, including the Deaf, Hard of Hearing, and Deaf-Blind Wellbeing Program in Burnaby, British Columbia (DWP, 2025), and the Canadian Hearing Services in Toronto, Ontario (CHS, 2025). The former, established in 1991 through funding from the Ministry for Children & Family Development (MCFD), provides accessible health and mental health services to Deaf, Hard of Hearing, and Deaf-Blind people throughout British Columbia (DWP, 2025). The team includes a number of professionals who are themselves members of the Deaf or Hard of Hearing community, with many services provided directly in ASL. This organization also has a series of educational health and mental health videos in ASL publicly available on their website, with videos also including closed captioning and English translation. Canadian Hearing Services (CHS) is a Canadian non-profit that has been serving and empowering Deaf and Hard of Hearing Canadians for 85 years (CHS, 2025). They provide a variety of services including counseling services, audiology services, educational programming, employment services, research funding, and communication devices. Of note, their website is fully accessible in ASL. See Chap. 13 in this text for details regarding services provided by CHS clinical staff.

Mattering

The concept of "mattering" refers to a psychological human need to feel that a person contributes both in some way to others and feels valued for that contribution. It refers to feeling valued by an individual, community, or even society at large. Reconceptualized by Rosenberg and McCullough (1981), this concept was applied in the development of this Deaf Mental Health Strategy. As cited by authors Rosenberg and McCullough, mattering refers to "the feeling that one is the object of others' attention, one is important to others, and others are dependent on us." It includes concepts of awareness, importance, reliance, the feeling of being missed, and, as originally identified, ego-extension, revised to separate from importance (Dixon, 2018). Flett (2025) identifies "mattering" as a core feeling and a core need in children. He reports that differences in children's sense of mattering in relation to their family, friends, and significant others impact that child's adaptation to the world in general. Flett further reports that a feeling that one does not matter has implications for children's feelings of depression, anxiety, aggression, and violence, with Flett also reporting that a sense of mattering or 'importance to others' is reflected in measures of resilience, adaptability, and motivation. Though not specific to deaf, hard of hearing, or deafblind children, this concept is easily translatable to the work of Kushalnagar et al. (2020), and the impact of adverse childhood communication experiences for deaf children, and its later impact on health as adults.

Deaf* Mental Health Strategy (DMHS)

The Deaf Mental Health Strategy focuses on six primary pillars. These include Deaf Awareness Training, Professional Training Opportunities, Enhanced Sign Language Interpreter services, Accessible mental health information & services, Mental Health Navigators, and Research funding. Each is discussed below. See Fig. 14.1 Deaf* mental health strategy.

1. **Deaf Awareness Training:** *Post-Secondary Students and Professionals*

   As has been discussed throughout this text, Deaf, Hard of Hearing, and Deafblind individuals are as diverse as the general population. There are often, however, individual identity factors that require accommodation in professional settings. Deaf Awareness Training for future professionals, including post-secondary students in professional programs and existing professionals with little prior knowledge or exposure to the larger Deaf community, should include topics such as understanding Deaf culture and values, the range of communication methods that may include Sign Language and a Sign Language Interpreter, Adaptive Interactive Tactual Sign Language (AITSL), types of hearing assistive devices or even speech (NC Department of Health and Human Services, n.d.). It also should include understanding that accommodation must be made during appointments such as allocating additional time if an ASL Interpreter, Deaf

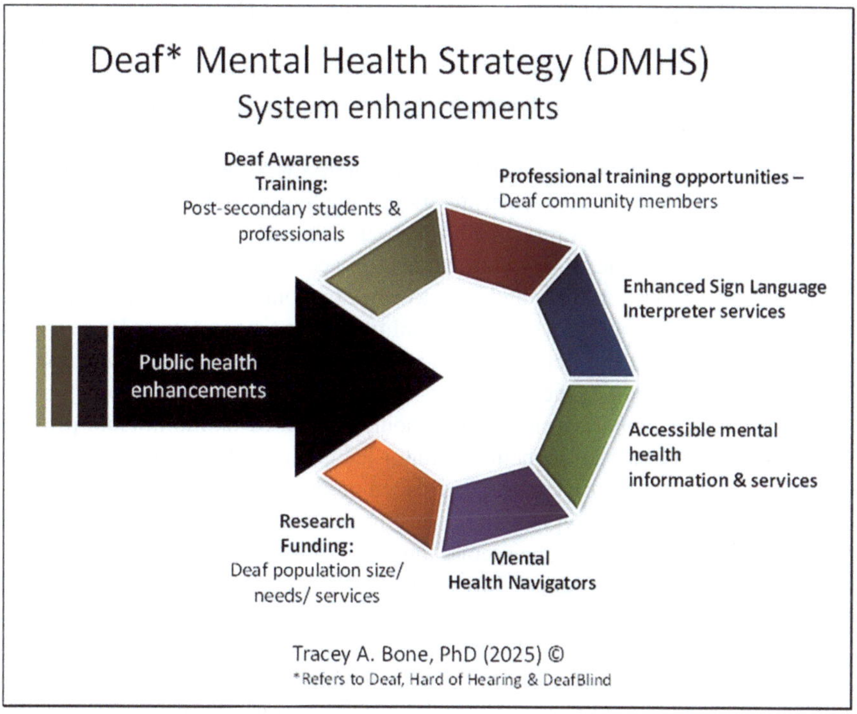

Fig. 14.1 Deaf* mental health strategy, Bone, 2025. Used with permission.

Interpreter or assistant is involved in the meeting, and ensuring the physical space is accommodating (i.e., avoiding visual noise, seating set-up, lighting, etc.) See Chap. 13 in this text for additional details regarding Deaf-centric design (see also Bone, 2019). Finally, any Deaf Awareness Training must include discussion on trauma experiences within the Deaf community, including the impact of Adverse Childhood Communication Experiences in the Deaf community (Kushalnagar et al., 2020). It is important that Deaf Awareness Training be provided by a member of the Deaf, Hard of Hearing, and/or Deafblind community, and those providing such training are adequately compensated for their training time out of respect for the specialized knowledge they bring to the cultural and educational experience.

2. **Professional Training Opportunities:** *Deaf Community Members*

   As is the case in other minority communities, many in the Deaf community would prefer to receive services from their own community, in this case native ASL users who understand Deaf culture and respect Deaf values. This DMHS strategy supports the development or enhancement of post-secondary educational opportunities to develop the professional workforce with individuals from the Deaf, Hard of Hearing, and Deafblind communities. Professional development opportunities would enhance the development of a workforce that has consistently been underrepresented in health care, academia, and social services in general. Professor Campbell from Saint Mary's University in Halifax reports that deaf students bring diversity in thinking and problem-solving in the post-secondary classroom, but feels academia is not making space for them (Vermes, 2024).

For Deaf students to feel welcome in academia will require additional funding to ensure ASL-English Interpreters are readily available through the students' academic in-class program, though also that access to a Sign Language Interpreter or other necessary communication access tool is provided for study time, class preparation time, and time to work on course-related group projects, factors often overlooked when accessibility is being considered. This support also applies for a Deaf person's attendance at other training webinars, conferences, or other events. One example is Mental Health First Aid, where current training requires completion of a two-hour, self-paced online module prior to attendance in the two subsequent facilitator-led modules. If ASL interpretation is not provided for the independent, self-paced module prior to the classroom content, ASL users may struggle with the on-line content as it is presented in written English, characteristically the second language of ASL first-language users.

3. **Enhanced Sign Language Interpreters Services:** *Number Trained and Certified*

The number of trained and certified Sign Language Interpreters in Canada is insufficient to meet the needs of the Deaf community, thereby limiting their access to essential services, professional development opportunities, and social opportunities. As reported by the National Deaf Center, interpreter scarcity is also reported in the United States, particularly in college settings (NDC, 2022). In Winnipeg, Manitoba, the ASL-English Interpretation Program (AEIP) was paused for several years. This reduced the number of new and qualified interpreters available to meet the needs of the Deaf community in Winnipeg, and various locations throughout Manitoba. A revised three-year AEIP program resumes in the Fall 2025 academic term in Winnipeg, which is intended to address that gap. It is important to note, however, that students in interpreter programs learn interpretation skills and general ASL proficiency, but not specialized terminology for specific fields (Vermes, 2024). New graduates will therefore require additional specialized training to work effectively in areas such as justice, STEM, academic settings, medical settings, mental health, and others. This DMHS recommends allocating additional government funding to increase the number of academic program spots available to train new ASL-English interpreters, and to support advanced skill development for new and existing interpreters to ensure interpreters have the ASL lexicon necessary for working effectively in specialized fields. Funding should also be made available to support the development of Deaf Interpreter (DI) training and certification, as well as funding to fully support their inclusion in services, programs and treatment resources when requested by members of the Deaf or Hard of Hearing community. The Deaf Interpreter is a Deaf person who provides an additional and specialized level of interpreting in American Sign Language, langues des signes quebecoise (LSQ) or other visual and tactual communication used by Deaf, Hard of Hearing or Deafblind individuals. As members of the Deaf community themselves, they bring cultural and life experiences to the communication interaction in a way a non-Deaf person could not.

4. **Accessible Mental Health Information and Services**

   Mental health information is available in various online portals; little of it is available in ASL, however, making it inaccessible for ASL or other Sign Language users. The Canadian Mental Health Association (CMHA) recently allocated a portion of its Manitoba Accessibility Funding toward the hiring of a Deaf Interpreter to translate selected mental health online content into ASL. This author co-coordinated the translation project alongside two members of the Deaf community in Winnipeg, J-L Irwin, and S. Montney. The translated content has now been posted on the Manitoba provincial CMHA website (CMHA Manitoba, 2025). Additional funding must continue to be be made available to support the translation of additional mental health educational materials to ensure that mental health educational content is equally available and accessible to Deaf, Hard of Hearing, and Deafblind Canadians. Funding must also be made available to support the training of existing mental health professionals under the Accessible Act Canada (SC 2019, c.10) which aims to identify, remove, and prevent barriers for persons with disabilities. The Act acknowledges ASL, LSQ, and ISL as the primary languages for communication in Deaf Canadians. It supports equal access to information and communication for Deaf Canadians in public spaces, employment, and government services, also requiring websites and media to be accessible through sign language and closed captioning by 2040 (Government of Canada, 2025).

5. **Mental Health Navigators**

   Limited availability of mental health content in ASL restricts the Deaf community's understanding of mental health, including protective and risk factors for mental health problems, appropriate intervention types, and awareness of appropriate programming. Mental Health (MH) Navigators with expertise in ASL, government, and community-based systems and services would assist the Deaf, Hard of Hearing, or Deafblind person to navigate through these complex systems. The MH Navigator would serve as a guide, advocate, and, with ASL fluency, conduit between the Deaf/Hard of Hearing or Deafblind individual seeking services, and the service provider/system. They would also serve an educator role and empower individuals to gain the skills necessary to navigate independently in the future. Navigators could assist to minimize service gaps while supporting recovery-oriented mental health care. This position is consistent with the Mental Health Commission of Canada's revised Quality Mental Health Care Framework, which focuses on equitable, integrated, and appropriate mental health care (MHCC, 2025).

6. **Research Funding: Deaf Population Size/Needs/Services**

   The government must allocate research funding targeted for examining the population prevalence of the Deaf, Hard of Hearing, and Deafblind communities in Canada, as past Canadian censuses have been unsuccessful in doing so (CAD, 2015). Funding would provide an opportunity to explore the size of the signing Deaf community, identify their mental health needs, and explore both what resources exist to meet the needs of this community, as well as gaps in service provision. The findings would be used to inform program development, human resource development, and mental health content development.

Research funding could also be used toward the development of technologies that better meet the communication needs of Deaf Sign Language users, including expanded telehealth practices, software avatars that sign, ASL translation of vital information in kiosks in train or bus stations, or airports, or other computer apps that support mental health through visual learning, such as mindfulness apps. This funding should also be used to expand the Video Relay Service in Canada (SVR Canada VRS, n.d.), a free service for Deaf, hard of hearing or speech-impaired Canadians who use Sign Language. This funding could also ensure that knowledge of the existing Canada VRS 9-8-8 suicide prevention services program is made available to all Canadians who use Sign Language, but may not have ready access to technology.

Lastly, research funding could be used to support the inclusion and development of Deaf, Hard of Hearing, or Deafblind post-secondary students first as Research Assistants in social science research, as well as research into the built environment and policy development, gaining necessary skills to move into professional programs. Students invited into the academy in this way could hopefully become the next generation of social researchers and professionals whose lived experiences could be used to expand the direction of the Deaf Mental Health Strategy in this chapter to more authentically meet the evolving needs of the Deaf, Hard of Hearing, and Deafblind communities.

Conclusion

This chapter proposes a Deaf-centric approach to mental health care in Canada. It is based on a compilation of knowledge gained from the authors' research with the Deaf, Hard of Hearing, and Deafblind communities, personal/professional experience in the area, as well as independent study in the area. It is grounded in my experiences as a sibling of a Deaf adult. I offer this strategy as a blueprint for discussion and change. It is intended to be organic and fluid, recognizing that the needs of Deaf Canadians vary, as do the needs of Deaf Canadians in various parts of Canada. It supports agency, resilience, and self-determination by centering the perspectives, language, culture, and identity of Deaf Canadians, with a focus on inclusive Deaf spaces, full language and communication access, and equitable educational opportunities. It is a strategy that I, a hearing academic and researcher, have proposed, though I believe my experiences as a family member of a Deaf adult, and work in and with the Deaf community positions me in a place to more emically offer this proposal. It is intended to spark interest in the Deaf, Hard of Hearing, and Deafblind community if unfamiliar to you, or to spark continued conversation within the community about what needs to change in Canada's mental health system to truly accommodate Deaf, Hard of Hearing, and Deafblind Canadians.

References

Bone, T. (2019). Deaf mental health: Enhancing linguistically and culturally appropriate clinical practice. In M. Zangeneh & A. Al-Krenawi (Eds.), *Culture, diversity, and mental health: enhancing clinical practice* (pp. 61–80). Springer Nature Switzerland.

Bone, T. A. (2018). No one is listening: the Deaf community shares their depression narratives. *Social Work in Mental Health, 17*(1), 1–22. https://doi.org/10.1080/15332985.2018.1498045

Canadian Association of the Deaf (CAD). (2015). *Statistics on Deaf Canadians*. https://cad-asc.ca/issuespositions/statistics-on-deaf-canadians/

Canadian Hearing Services (CHS). (2025). https://www.chs.ca/

Canadian Mental Health Association (CMHA). (2024). *The State of Mental Health in Canada 2024*. The State of Mental Health in Canada 2024. https://www.cmhaacrossmb.ca/news/the-state-of-mental-health-in-canada-2024/

Canadian Mental Health Association - Across Manitoba. (2025). *Accessibility & Support; ASL Wellness Resources*. https://www.cmhaacrossmb.ca/accessibility/

Crowe, T. (2017). You're Deaf? Breaking through myths for effective therapeutic practice. *Journal of social work in disability & rehabilitation, 16*(3-4), 230–246. https://doi.org/10.1080/1536710X.2017.1372239

Deaf Well-Being Program for Deaf, hard of hearing and Deaf-Blind. (2025). *Vancouver Coastal health*. https://deafwellbeing.vch.ca

Dixon, A. L. (2018). Mattering. In R. J. R. Levesque (Ed.), *Encyclopedia of adolescence*. Springer. https://doi.org/10.1007/978-3-319-33228-4_138

Flett, G. L. (2025). *Mattering as a core need in children and adolescents: Theoretical, clinical, and research perspectives*. American Psychological Association. E-Book.

Government of Canada. (2025 – July 8). *Accessible Canada Act S.C. 2019, c. 10*. Justice Laws Website. https://laws-lois.justice.gc.ca/eng/acts/a-0.6/page-1.html

Jonas, S. (2025 July 17). *Manitoba accessibility minister apologizing in ASL 'a step in the right direction' says deaf graduates*. APTNnews. https://www.aptnnews.ca/national-news/manitoba-accessibility-minister-apologizing-in-asl-a-step-in-the-right-direction-says-deaf-graduates/

Kushalnagar, P., Ryan, C., Paludneviciene, R., Spellun, A., & Gulati, S. (2020). Adverse childhood communication experiences associated with an increased risk of chronic diseases in adults who are deaf. *American Journal of Preventive Medicine, 59*(4), 548–554. https://doi.org/10.1016/j.amepre.2020.04.016

Mental Health Commission of Canada. (2025). *Revised Quality Mental Health Care Framework: Infographic* May 27, 2025. https://mentalhealthcommission.ca/resource/quality-mental-health-care-network-infographic/

National Deaf Center (NDC). (2022). *The ASL Interpreter Shortage and its Impact on Accessibility in College Settings. National Deaf Center on Postsecondary Outcomes* (December 2, 2022). https://nationaldeafcenter.org/news-items/he-asl-interpreter-shortage-and-its-impact-on-accessibility-in-college-settings/

North Carolina Department of Health and Human Services. *How to Communicate with your Deaf, Hard of Hearing, or Deafblind Patient*. Division of Services for the Deaf and Hard of Hearing. chrome-extension://efaidnbmnnnibpcajpcglclefindmkaj/https://www.ncdhhs.gov/how-communicate-your-deaf-hard-hearing-or-deafblind/download

Pertz, L., Plegue, M., Diehl, K., Zazove, P., & McKee, M. (2018). Addressing mental health needs for deaf patients through an integrated health care model. *Journal of deaf studies and deaf education, 23*(3), 240–248. https://doi.org/10.1093/deafed/eny002

SRV Canada VRS. (n.d.). *Using VRS*. https://srvcanadavrs.ca/en/911and988/

Vermes, J. (2024, April 4). *Deaf academics say a lack of ASL interpreters specialized in STEM is holding them back*. The Current, CBC radio. https://www.cbc.ca/radio/thecurrent/deaf-academics-stem-asl-interpretation-1.7162559

Correction to: Working in the field of Deaf Mental Health: What Clinicians Need to Know

Megan Kaluba, William Schmidt, Michal Morgan, Tim Likely, and Michael Dawthorne

Correction to: Chapter 13 in: T. Bone (ed.), *Deaf Mental Health*, Advances in Mental Health and Addiction, https://doi.org/10.1007/978-3-032-06274-1_13

The following corrections have been made to the chapter:

- On page 164, the term "*Polyvagal theory*" has been removed at the request of the corresponding author.
- On page 165, Figure 13.1 has been replaced with an updated version, including a revised ASL explanation.

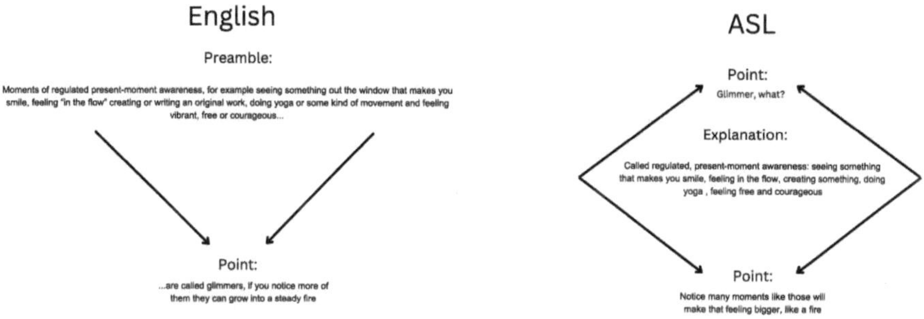

Fig. 13.1 Triangle (English) vs. Diamond (ASL): structure of speech

---

The updated version of this chapter can be found at
https://doi.org/10.1007/978-3-032-06274-1_13

T. Bone (ed.), *Deaf Mental Health*, Advances in Mental Health and Addiction,
https://doi.org/10.1007/978-3-032-06274-1_15

- On page 165, the term "*Polyvagal*" has been updated to "*somatic*."
- On page 165, the citation *(Dana, 2020)* in the footnote has been updated.
- On page 180, the term "*bilateral*" has been corrected to "*biolateral.*".

Index

T. Bone (ed.), *Deaf Mental Health*, Advances in Mental Health and Addiction,
https://doi.org/10.1007/978-3-032-06274-1

MIX
Papier aus verantwortungsvollen Quellen
Paper from responsible sources
FSC® C105338

If you have any concerns about our products,
you can contact us on
ProductSafety@springernature.com

In case Publisher is established outside the EU,
the EU authorized representative is:
Springer Nature Customer Service Center GmbH
Europaplatz 3, 69115 Heidelberg, Germany

Printed by Libri Plureos GmbH
in Hamburg, Germany